U.S. Department of Justice
Office of Justice Programs
Bureau of Justice Statistics

I0448305

Sexual Victimization in Prisons and Jails Reported by Inmates, 2011–12

National Inmate Survey, 2011–12

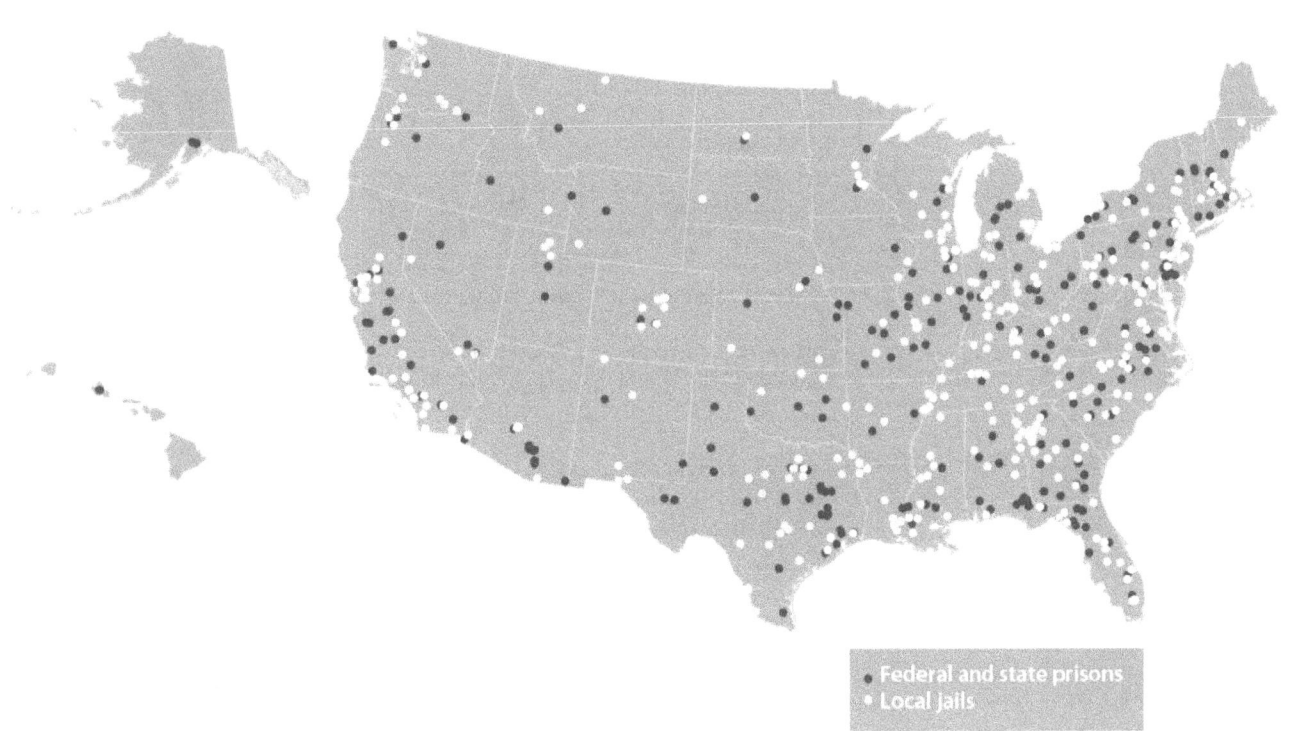

• Federal and state prisons
• Local Jails

Allen J. Beck, Ph.D.
BJS Statistician

Marcus Berzofsky, Dr.P.H., Rachel Caspar,
and Christopher Krebs, Ph.D., *RTI International*

May 2013, NCJ 241399

Bureau of Justice Statistics
William J. Sabol
Acting Director

BJS Website:
www.bjs.gov
askbjs@usdoj.gov

The Bureau of Justice Statistics is the statistics agency of the U.S. Department of Justice. William J. Sabol is the acting director.

This report was written by Allen J. Beck, Ph.D., BJS Statistician, and Marcus Berzofsky, Dr.P.H., Rachel Caspar, and Christopher Krebs, Ph.D., RTI International.

Paige M. Harrison (former BJS statistician) was the project manager for the NIS-3. RTI International staff, under a cooperative agreement and in collaboration with BJS, designed the survey, developed the questionnaires, and monitored the data collection and processing. The staff included Rachel Caspar, Principal Investigator/Instrumentation Task Leader; Christopher Krebs, Co-principal Investigator; Ellen Stutts, Co-principal Investigator and Data Collection Task Leader; Susan Brumbaugh, Logistics Task Leader; Jamia Bachrach, Human Subjects Task Leader; David Forvendel, Research Computing Task Leader; and Marcus Berzofsky, Statistics Task Leader. Ramona Rantala, BJS statistician, and RTI staff, including Heather Meier, Barbara Alexander, and Rodney Baxter, verified the report.

Morgan Young and Jill Thomas edited the report, and Barbara Quinn designed and produced the report under the supervision of Doris J. James.

May 2013, NCJ 241399

Sexual Victimization in Prisons and Jails Reported by Inmates, 2011–12

National Inmate Survey, 2011–12

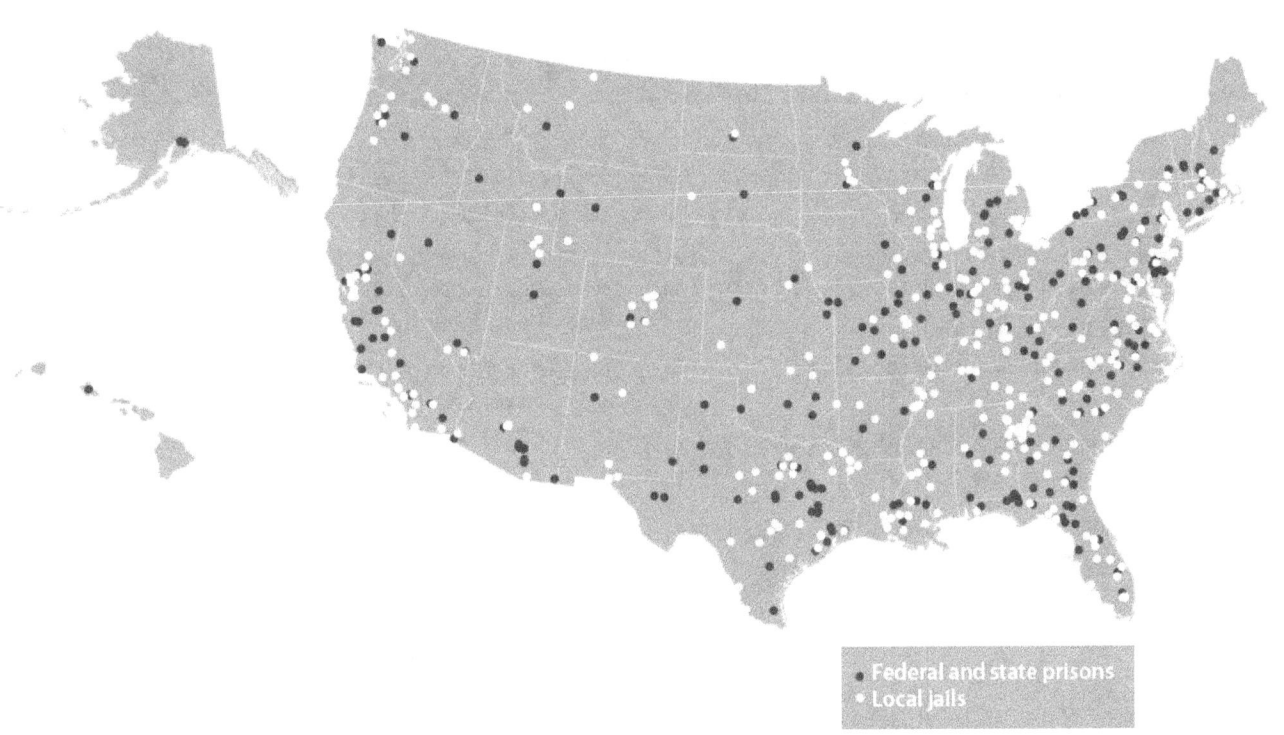

Federal and state prisons
Local jails

Allen J. Beck, Ph.D.
BJS Statistician

Marcus Berzofsky, Dr.P.H., Rachel Caspar,
and Christopher Krebs, Ph.D., *RTI International*

May 2013, NCJ 241399

Contents

List of tables

List of figures

List of appendix tables

Prevalence of sexual victimization

- In 2011-12, an estimated 4.0% of state and federal prison inmates and 3.2% of jail inmates reported experiencing one or more incidents of sexual victimization by another inmate or facility staff in the past 12 months or since admission to the facility, if less than 12 months.

- Using the same methodology since 2007, the rate of sexual victimization among state and federal prison inmates was 4.5% in 2007 and 4.0% in 2011-12; but, the difference was not statistically significant. Among jail inmates, the rate of sexual victimization remained unchanged—3.2% in 2007 and 3 2% in 2011-12.

- Among state and federal prison inmates, 2.0% (or an estimated 29,300 prisoners) reported an incident involving another inmate, 2.4% (34,100) reported an incident involving facility staff, and 0.4% (5,500) reported both an incident by another inmate and staff.

- About 1.6% of jail inmates (11,900) reported an incident with another inmate, 1.8% (13,200) reported an incident with staff, and 0 2% (2,400) reported both an incident by another inmate and staff.

- From 2007 to 2011-12, reports of "willing" sexual activity with staff (excluding touching) declined in prisons and jails, while reports of other types of sexual victimization remained stable.

Facility rankings

- Eleven male prisons, 1 female prison, and 9 jails were identified as high-rate facilities based on the prevalence of inmate-on-inmate sexual victimization in 2011-12. Eight male prisons, 4 female prisons, and 12 jails were identified as high rate based on the prevalence of staff sexual misconduct. Each of these facilities had a lower bound of the 95%-confidence interval that was at least 55% higher than the average rate among comparable facilities.

- Seven male prisons, 6 female prisons, and 4 jails were identified as low-rate facilities based on a small percentage of inmates reporting any sexual victimization by another inmate or staff and a low upper bound of the 95%-confidence interval around the rate.

- Among the 225 prisons and 358 jails in the survey, 13 prisons and 34 jails had no reported incidents of sexual victimization.

- Two military facilities and one Indian country jail had high rates of staff sexual misconduct in 2011-12. The Northwest Joint Regional Correctional Facility (Fort Lewis, Washington) (6.6%) and the Naval Consolidated Brig (Miramar, California) (4.9%) had high rates of staff sexual misconduct that were more than double the average of prisons (2.4%) and jails (1.8%) nationwide. The Oglala Sioux Tribal Offenders Facility (Pine Ridge, South Dakota) (10.8%) reported the highest rate of staff sexual misconduct among all tribal and nontribal jails in the survey.

Variations in victimization rates

- Patterns of inmate-on-inmate sexual victimization in 2011-12 were consistent with patterns in past surveys. Rates reported by prison and jail inmates were higher among females than males, higher among whites than blacks, and higher among inmates with a college degree than those who had not completed high school.

- Variations in staff sexual misconduct rates were also similar across surveys. Rates reported by inmates were higher among males in jails than females in jails, higher among black inmates in prisons and jails than white inmates in prisons and jails, and lower among inmates age 35 or older than inmates ages 20 to 24 in both prisons and jails.

- Inmates held for violent sexual offenses reported higher rates of inmate-on-inmate sexual victimization (3.7% in prison and 3.9% in jails) than inmates held for other offenses.

Special inmate populations

- In 2011-12, juveniles ages 16 to 17 held in adult prisons and jails did not have significantly higher rates of sexual victimization than adult inmates:

  - An estimated 1.8% of juveniles ages 16 to 17 held in prisons and jails reported being victimized by another inmate, compared to 2.0% of adults in prisons and 1.6% of adults in jails.

  - An estimated 3.2% of juveniles ages 16 to 17 held in prisons and jails reported experiencing staff sexual misconduct. Though higher, these rates were not statistically different from the 2.4% of adults in prisons and 1.8% of adults in jails.

  - Juveniles (ages 16 to 17) and young adults (ages 18 to 19 and 20 to 24) reported similar rates of sexual victimization for most of the key subgroups (sex, race or Hispanic origin, body mass index, sexual orientation, and offense).

- Inmates with serious psychological distress reported high rates of inmate-on-inmate and staff sexual victimization in 2011-12:

  - Among state and federal prison inmates, an estimated 6.3% of those identified with serious psychological distress reported that they were sexually victimized by another inmate. In comparison, among prisoners with no indication of mental illness, 0.7% reported being victimized by another inmate.

  - Similar differences were reported by jail inmates. An estimated 3.6% of those identified with serious psychological distress reported inmate-on-inmate sexual victimization, compared to 0.7% of inmates with no indication of mental illness.

  - Rates of serious psychological distress in prisons (14.7%) and jails (26.3%) were substantially higher than the rate (3.0%) in the U.S. noninstitutional population age 18 or older.

  - For each of the measured demographic subgroups, inmates with serious psychological distress reported higher rates of inmate-on-inmate sexual victimization than inmates without mental health problems.

- Inmates who reported their sexual orientation as gay, lesbian, bisexual, or other were among those with the highest rates of sexual victimization in 2011-12:

  - Among non-heterosexual inmates, 12.2% of prisoners and 8 5% of jail inmates reported being sexually victimized by another inmate; 5.4% of prisoners and 4.3% of jail inmates reported being victimized by staff.

  - In each demographic subgroup (sex, race or Hispanic origin, age, and education), non-heterosexual prison and jail inmates reported higher rates of inmate-on-inmate sexual victimization than heterosexual inmates.

  - Among inmates with serious psychological distress, non-heterosexual inmates reported the highest rates of inmate-on-inmate sexual victimization (21.0% of prison inmates and 14.7% of jail inmates).

Sexual Victimization in Prisons and Jails Reported by Inmates, 2011-12

National Inmate Survey-3

Between February 2011 and May 2012, BJS completed the third National Inmate Survey (NIS-3) in 233 state and federal prisons, 358 jails, and 15 special confinement facilities operated by Immigration and Customs Enforcement (ICE), the U.S. Military, and correctional authorities in Indian country. The survey, conducted by RTI International (Research Triangle Park, North Carolina), was administered to 92,449 inmates age 18 or older, including 38,251 inmates in state and federal prisons, 52,926 in jails, 573 in ICE facilities, 539 in military facilities, and 160 in Indian country jails. The survey was also administered to juveniles ages 16 to 17 held in adult prisons and jails. Based on 527 completed interviews of juveniles in state prisons and 1,211 interviews in local jails, the NIS-3 provides the first-ever national estimates of sexual victimization of juveniles held in adult facilities.

The NIS-3 is part of the National Prison Rape Statistics Program, which collects reported sexual violence from administrative records and allegations of sexual victimization directly from victims through surveys of inmates in prisons and jails and surveys of youth held in juvenile correctional facilities. Administrative records have been collected annually since 2004. Reports by victims of sexual victimization have been collected since 2007.

The NIS-3 survey consisted of an audio computer-assisted self-interview (ACASI) in which inmates used a touch-screen to interact with a computer-assisted questionnaire and followed audio instructions delivered via headphones. Some inmates (751) completed a short paper form instead of using the ACASI. Most of these inmates were housed in administrative or disciplinary segregation or were considered too violent to be interviewed.

> **The Prison Rape Elimination Act of 2003 (P.L. 108-79; PREA) requires the Bureau of Justice Statistics (BJS) to carry out a comprehensive statistical review and analysis of incidents and effects of prison rape for each calendar year. This report fulfills the requirement under Sec. 4c(2)(B)(ii) of the act to provide a list of prisons and jails according to the prevalence of sexual victimization.**

As in the NIS-1 (conducted 2007) and the NIS-2 (conducted 2008-09), the NIS-3 collected only allegations of sexual victimization. Since participation in the survey is anonymous and reports are confidential, the survey does not permit any follow-up investigation or substantiation of reported incidents through review. Some allegations in the NIS-3 may be untrue. At the same time, some inmates may not report sexual victimization experienced in the facility, despite efforts of survey staff to assure inmates that their responses would be kept confidential. Although the effects may be offsetting, the relative extent of under reporting and false reporting in the NIS-3 is unknown.

Incidents of sexual victimization

In 2011-12, 4.0% of prison inmates and 3.2% of jail inmates reported experiencing one or more incidents of sexual victimization

Among the 91,177 adult prison and jail inmates participating in the NIS-3 sexual victimization survey, 3,381 reported experiencing one or more incidents of sexual victimization in the past 12 months or since admission to the facility, if less than 12 months. Since the NIS-3 is a sample survey, weights were applied for sampled facilities and inmates within facilities to produce national-level and facility-level estimates. The estimated number of prison and jail inmates experiencing sexual victimization totaled 80,600 (or 4.0% of all prison inmates and 3.2% of jail inmates nationwide) (table 1).

Among all state and federal prison inmates, 2.0% (or an estimated 29,300 prisoners) reported an incident involving another inmate, and 2.4% (34,100) reported an incident involving facility staff. Some prisoners (0.4% or 5,500) reported sexual victimization by both another inmate and facility staff.

Among all jail inmates, about 1.6% (11,900) reported an incident with another inmate, and 1.8% (13,200) reported an incident with staff. Approximately 0.2% of jail inmates (2,400) reported being sexually victimized by both another inmate and staff.

TABLE 1

Adult inmates reporting sexual victimization, by type of facility and incident, National Inmate Survey, 2011–12

Type of incident[c]	Number of victims[a]		Percent of inmates		Standard errors[b]	
	Prisons	Jails	Prisons	Jails	Prisons	Jails
Total	57,900	22,700	4.0%	3.2%	0.2%	0.2%
Inmate-on-inmate	29,300	11,900	2.0%	1.6%	0.1%	0.1%
Nonconsensual sexual acts	15,400	5,100	1.1	0.7	0.1	0.1
Abusive sexual contacts only	13,900	6,800	1.0	0.9	0.1	0.1
Staff sexual misconduct	34,100	13,200	2.4%	1.8%	0.2%	0.1%
Unwilling activity	21,500	10,000	1.5	1.4	0.1	0.1
Excluding touching	15,400	7,400	1.1	1.0	0.1	0.1
Touching only	5,600	2,500	0.4	0.3	0.1	--
Willing activity	19,700	6,200	1.4	0.9	0.1	0.1
Excluding touching	17,000	5,200	1.2	0.7	0.1	0.1
Touching only	2,700	900	0.2	0.1	--	--

Note: Detail may not sum to total because inmates may report more than one type of victimization. They may also report victimization by both other inmates and staff.

--Less than 0.05%.

[a]Estimates of the number of victims nationwide are based on weighted data and rounded to the nearest 100.

[b]Standard errors may be used to construct confidence intervals around each estimate. See *Methodology* for calculations.

[c]See *Methodology* for terms and definitions.

Source: Bureau of Justice Statistics, National Inmate Survey, 2011–12.

The NIS-3 screened for specific sexual activities in which inmates may have been involved during the past 12 months or since admission to the facility, if less than 12 months. Inmates were then asked if they were forced or pressured to engage in these activities by another inmate or staff. (See appendices 1, 2, and 3 for specific survey questions.) Reports of inmate-on-inmate sexual victimization were classified as either nonconsensual sexual acts or abusive sexual contacts. (See text box for *Terms and definitions*.)

Approximately 1.1% of prisoners and 0.7% of jail inmates said they were forced or pressured to have nonconsensual sex with another inmate, including manual stimulation and oral, anal, or vaginal penetration. An additional 1.0% of prison inmates and 0.9% of jail inmates said they had experienced one or more abusive sexual contacts only or unwanted touching of specific body parts in a sexual way by another inmate.

An estimated 1.5% of prison inmates and 1.4% of jail inmates reported that they had sex or sexual contact unwillingly with staff as a result of physical force, pressure, or offers of special favors or privileges. An estimated 1.4% of all prison inmates and 0.9% of jail inmates reported they willingly had sex or sexual contact with staff. Any sexual contact between inmates and staff is illegal, regardless of whether an inmate reported being willing or unwilling, but this difference between willing and unwilling may be informative when addressing issues of staff training, prevention, and investigation.

Terms and definitions

Sexual victimization—all types of sexual activity, e.g., oral, anal, or vaginal penetration; hand jobs; touching of the inmate's buttocks, thighs, penis, breasts, or vagina in a sexual way; abusive sexual contacts; and both willing and unwilling sexual activity with staff.

Nonconsensual sexual acts—unwanted contacts with another inmate or any contacts with staff that involved oral, anal, vaginal penetration, hand jobs, and other sexual acts.

Abusive sexual contacts only—unwanted contacts with another inmate or any contacts with staff that involved touching of the inmate's buttocks, thigh, penis, breasts, or vagina in a sexual way.

Unwilling activity—incidents of unwanted sexual contacts with another inmate or staff.

Willing activity—incidents of willing sexual contacts with staff. These contacts are characterized by the reporting inmates as willing; however, all sexual contacts between inmates and staff are legally nonconsensual.

Staff sexual misconduct—includes all incidents of willing and unwilling sexual contact with facility staff and all incidents of sexual activity that involved oral, anal, vaginal penetration, hand jobs, blow jobs, and other sexual acts with facility staff.

The NIS-3 recorded slightly lower rates of sexual victimization in prisons compared to the NIS-1 and NIS-2, which was largely driven by a decline in the reported rates of staff sexual misconduct (table 2). Overall, the rate of sexual victimization was 4.5% in 2007 and 4.0% in 2011-12, but the difference was not statistically significant. (See *Methodology* for discussion of significance testing and standard errors.) Staff sexual misconduct considered "willing" by the victims was the only rate to show a decline, from 1.8% in 2008-09 to 1.4% in 2011-12. This drop was limited to willing sexual activity, excluding touching. In addition, willing sexual activity with staff (excluding touching only) in 2011-12 was significantly different from 2007 (dropping from 1.5% to 1.2%).

Among jail inmates, the overall rates of sexual victimization remained unchanged (3.2% in 2007, 3.1% in 2008-09, and 3.2% in 2011-12). The rates of staff sexual misconduct in jails were 2.0% in 2007, 2.0% in 2008-09, and 1.8% in 2011-12, but this decline was not statistically significant. Jail inmates in 2011-12 were less likely to report experiencing willing sexual activity with staff (0.9%) than jail inmates in 2007 (1.1%) and 2008-09 (1.1%). This decline was limited to willing sexual activity, excluding touching.

Facility-level rates

The NIS-3 provides a basis for identifying high rate and low rate facilities

As required under the Prison Rape Elimination Act, the NIS-3 provides facility-level estimates of inmate-on-inmate sexual victimization and staff sexual misconduct. Since these estimates are based on a sample of inmates rather than a complete enumeration, they are subject to sampling error. (See *Methodology* for description of sampling procedures.)

The precision of each of the facility-level estimates can be calculated based on the estimated standard error. Typically, a 95%-confidence interval around each survey estimate is calculated by multiplying the standard error by 1.96 and then adding and subtracting the result from the sample estimate to create an upper and lower bound. This interval expresses the range of values that could result among 95% of the different samples that could be drawn.

For small samples and estimates close to 0%, as is the case with facility-level estimates of sexual victimization by type of incident, the use of the standard error to construct the 95%-confidence interval may not be reliable. An alternative method developed by E. B. Wilson has been shown to perform better than the traditional method.[1,2]

[1]Brown, L.D., Cai, T., & DasGupta, A. (2001). "Interval Estimation for a Binomial Proportion." *Statistical Science*, 16(2), pp. 101–117.

[2]Wilson, E.B. (1927). "Probable Inference, the Law of Succession, and Statistical Inference." *Journal of the American Statistical Association*, 22(158), pp. 209–12.

TABLE 2
Prevalence of sexual victimization across inmate surveys, by type of incident, National Inmate Survey, 2007, 2008–09, and 2011–12

Type of incident	Percent of prison inmates			Percent of jail inmates		
	NIS-1 2007	NIS-2 2008–09	NIS-3 2011–12*	NIS-1 2007	NIS-2 2008–09	NIS-3 2011–12*
Total	4.5%	4.4%	4.0%	3.2%	3.1%	3.2%
Inmate-on-inmate	2.1%	2.1%	2.0%	1.6%	1.5%	1.6%
Nonconsensual sexual acts	1.3	1.0	1.1	0.7	0.8	0.7
Abusive sexual contacts only	0.8	1.0	1.0	0.9	0.7**	0.9
Staff sexual misconduct	2.9%	2.8%	2.4%	2.0%	2.0%	1.8%
Unwilling activity	1.7	1.7	1.5	1.3	1.5	1.4
Excluding touching	1.3	1.3	1.1	1.1	1.1	1.0
Touching only	0.4	0.4	0.4	0.3	0.4	0.3
Willing activity	1.7	1.8**	1.4	1.1**	1.1**	0.9
Excluding touching	1.5**	1.5**	1.2	0.9**	0.9**	0.7
Touching only	0.2	0.3	0.2	0.2	0.2	0.1

Note: Detail may not sum to total because inmates may report more than one type of victimization. They may also report victimization by both other inmates and staff. See appendix table 10 for standard errors.

*Comparison group.

**Difference with comparison group is significant at the 95%-confidence level. (See *Methodology* for tests of significance.)

Source: Bureau of Justice Statistics, National Inmate Survey, 2007, 2008–09, and 2011–12.

This method provides asymmetrical confidence intervals for facilities in which the lower bound is constrained to be no less than 0%. It also provides confidence intervals for facilities in which the survey estimates are 0% (but other similarly conducted samples could yield non-zero estimates).

Although the NIS-3 provides facility-level estimates and measures of precision, it cannot provide an exact ranking for all facilities as required under PREA. Rates of inmate-on-inmate sexual victimization and staff sexual misconduct differ across facilities, but the observed differences are not always statistically significant. To address PREA requirements, facilities have been categorized as having high rates or low rates based on criteria applied to the lower and upper bounds of the 95%-confidence interval for each facility (figure 1 and figure 2).

As with the NIS-2, the criterion that the lower bound of the confidence interval be at least 55% higher than the average rate for comparable facilities was used in the NIS-3 to identify high-rate male prisons, female prisons, and jails. The criterion that the upper bound of the confidence interval be lower than 65% of the average rate for comparable facilities was used to identify low-rate facilities.

To better identify variations among correctional facilities in rates of sexual victimization, prisons and jails are compared separately by type of sexual victimization. Though informative, an analysis of a single, overall prevalence rate of sexual victimization for each sampled facility would confound differing risk factors, circumstances, and underlying causes of victimization. For the same reasons, prisons are compared separately by the sex of inmates housed.

FIGURE 1
Confidence intervals at the 95% level for prisons with high rates of inmate-on-inmate sexual victimization, National Inmate Survey, 2011–12

Percent

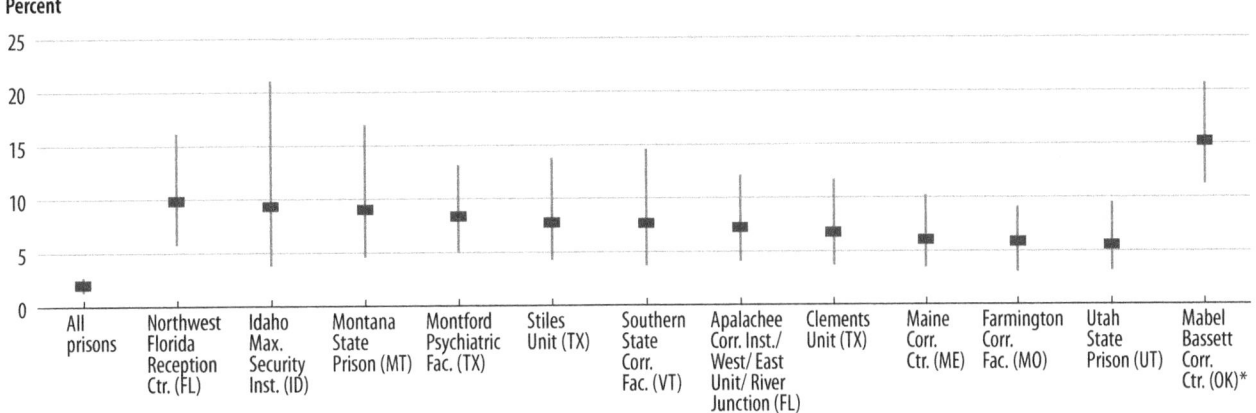

*Facility housed only female inmates.

Source: Bureau of Justice Statistics, National Inmate Survey, 2011–12.

FIGURE 2
Confidence intervals at the 95% level for jails with high rates of inmate-on-inmate sexual victimization, National Inmate Survey, 2011–12

Percent

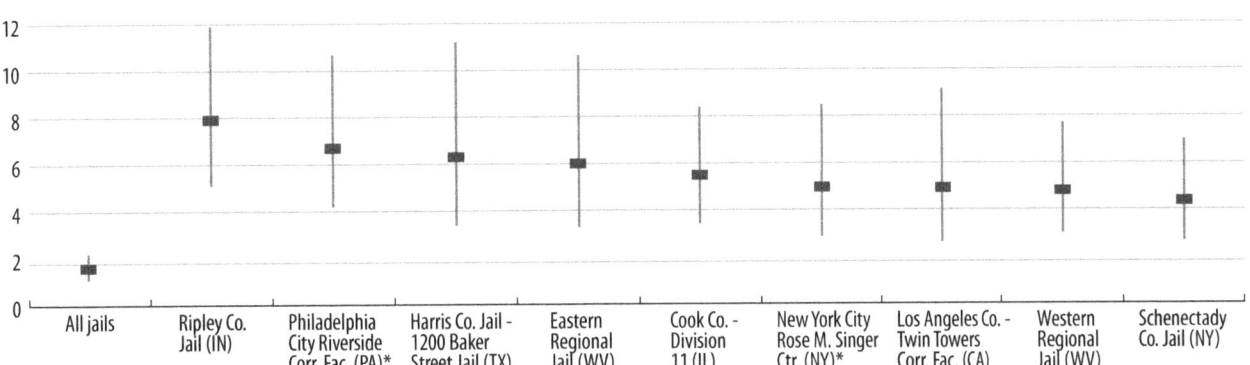

*Facility housed only female inmates.

Source: Bureau of Justice Statistics, National Inmate Survey, 2011–12.

The NIS-3 sample was designed to ensure a sufficient number of female-only prison facilities (44 facilities participated) and a sufficient number of female respondents (7,141 completed the survey) to allow for valid comparisons among female prisons. Four of the 358 jails that participated in the NIS-3 housed females only and one other jail was majority female. As a result, rates of sexual victimization in jails could not be compared separately by sex of inmates housed.

11 male prisons, 1 female prison, and 9 jails were identified as having high rates of inmate-on-inmate sexual victimization in 2011-12

Among the 233 prisons and 358 jails surveyed in the NIS-3, 11 male prisons, 1 female prison, and 9 jails were designated as high-rate facilities based on reports of inmate-on-inmate sexual

victimization (table 3). Each of these facilities had a rate of inmate-on-inmate sexual victimization that was at least twice the national rate of 1.7% for male prisons, 7.2% for female prisons, and 1.6% for jails. Each had a 95%-confidence interval with a lower bound that was at least 55% higher than the average rate among comparable facilities.

Among male prisons, Northwest Florida Reception Center (Florida), Idaho Maximum Security Institution, and Montana State Prison recorded inmate-on-inmate sexual victimization rates of 9.0% or greater. Mabel Bassett Correctional Center (Oklahoma), with a rate of 15.3%, was the only female prison that could be classified as high rate. Eleven other female-only prison facilities had rates of 10% or greater but did not meet the requirement of a lower bound that was 55% higher than the average rate for all female prisons. (See appendix table 2.)

TABLE 3
Facilities with high rates of inmate-on-inmate sexual victimization, by type of facility, National Inmate Survey, 2011–12

Facility name	Number of respondents[b]	Response rate	Any inmate-on-inmate incident[a]		
			Percent[c]	95%-confidence interval	
				Lower bound	Upper bound
All prisons	38,251	60.0%	2.0%	1.8%	2.3%
Male facilities	31,110	59.0%	1.7%	1.5%	2.0%
Northwest Florida Reception Ctr. (FL)	131	49.0	9.8	5.8	16.1
Idaho Max. Security Inst. (ID)	78	39.0	9.4	3.9	21.0
Montana State Prison (MT)	191	65.0	9.0	4.6	16.8
Montford Psychiatric Fac. (TX)	166	70.0	8.4	5.2	13.1
Stiles Unit (TX)	151	49.0	7.8	4.3	13.8
Southern State Corr. Fac. (VT)	109	55.0	7.7	3.9	14.6
Apalachee Corr. Inst./West/ East Unit/ River Junction (FL)	161	57.0	7.3	4.3	12.1
Clements Unit (TX)	141	44.0	6.8	3.8	11.7
Maine Corr. Ctr. (ME)	192	80.0	6.1	3.6	10.2
Farmington Corr. Fac. (MO)	240	84.0	5.8	3.6	9.3
Utah State Prison (UT)	233	73.0	5.6	3.2	9.5
Female facilities	7,141	69.0%	7.2%	5.9%	8.6%
Mabel Bassett Corr. Ctr. (OK)[d]	192	70.0	15.3	11.3	20.6
All jails	52,926	61.0%	1.6%	1.4%	1.9%
Ripley Co. Jail (IN)	51	89.0	7.9	5.1	11.9
Philadelphia City Riverside Corr. Fac. (PA)[d]	194	58.0	6.7	4.2	10.7
Harris Co. Jail - 1200 Baker Street Jail (TX)	238	58.0	6.3	3.4	11.2
Eastern Regional Jail (WV)	130	51.0	6.0	3.3	10.6
Cook Co. - Division 11 (IL)	272	76.0	5.5	3.5	8.4
New York City Rose M. Singer Ctr. (NY)[d]	202	63.0	5.0	2.9	8.4
Los Angeles Co. - Twin Towers Corr. Fac. (CA)	199	44.0	4.9	2.6	9.1
Western Regional Jail (WV)	215	68.0	4.8	3.0	7.7
Schenectady Co. Jail (NY)	162	68.0	4.4	2.7	7.0

Note: High-rate facilities are those in which the lower bound of the 95%-confidence interval is larger than 1.55 times the average among prisons by sex of inmates housed, and 1.55 times the average among all jail facilities.

[a]Weighted percent of inmates reporting one or more incidents of sexual victimization involving another inmate or facility staff in the past 12 months or since admission to the facility, if less than 12 months.

[b]Number of inmates who responded to the sexual victimization survey.

[c]Weights were applied so that inmates who responded accurately reflected the entire population of each facility on selected characteristics, including age, sex, race, sentence length, and time since admission.

[d]Facility housed only female inmates.

Source: Bureau of Justice Statistics, National Inmate Survey, 2011–12.

Ripley County Jail (Indiana) recorded an inmate-on-inmate sexual victimization rate of 7.9% and Philadelphia City Riverside Correctional Facility (Pennsylvania), a female-only jail facility, recorded a rate of 6.7%, both of which were more than four times the average rate among jails nationwide. Two other jails—Harris County Jail, Baker Street (Texas) and Eastern Regional Jail (Martinsburg, West Virginia)—each had rates of 6% or greater.

8 male prisons, 4 female prisons, and 12 jails were identified as having high rates of staff sexual misconduct

Twelve prisons were identified as high-rate facilities based on reports of staff sexual misconduct—eight male prisons and four female prisons (table 4). Twelve jails were also identified as high-rate facilities. Each had a confidence interval with a lower bound that was at least 55% higher than the national rate for male prisons (2.4%), female prisons (2.4%), and jails (1.8%) (figure 3 and figure 4).

In five state prisons, at least 9% of surveyed inmates reported being the victims of staff sexual misconduct, including 10.1% of inmates in Santa Rosa Correctional Institution (Florida), 9.9% in Montana State Prison, 9.6% in Walnut Grove Youth Correctional Facility (Mississippi), 9.5% in Clements Unit (Texas), and 10.7% in Denver Women's Correctional Facility (Colorado).

TABLE 4
Facilities with high rates of staff sexual misconduct, by type of facility, National Inmate Survey, 2011–12

Facility name	Number of respondents[b]	Response rate	Any staff sexual misconduct[a]		
				95%-confidence interval	
			Percent[c]	Lower bound	Upper bound
All prisons	38,251	60.0%	2.4%	2.0%	2.8%
Male facilities	31,110	59.0%	2.4%	2.0%	2.9%
Santa Rosa Corr. Inst. (FL)	185	60.0	10.1	6.5	15.5
Montana State Prison (MT)	191	65.0	9.9	5.3	17.7
Walnut Grove Youth Corr. Fac. (MS)	249	92.0	9.6	6.9	13.2
Clements Unit (TX)	141	44.0	9.5	5.7	15.3
Apalachee Corr. Inst./West/ East Unit/ River Junction (FL)	161	57.0	6.8	3.7	12.2
Coffield Unit (TX)	210	66.0	6.8	4.1	11.1
Wilkinson Co. Corr. Ctr. - CCA (MS)	173	67.0	6.4	3.8	10.6
Louisiana State Penitentiary (LA)	219	70.0	6.3	3.9	10.1
Female facilities	7,141	69.0%	2.4%	1.9%	3.0%
Denver Women's Corr. Fac. (CO)[d]	160	68.0	10.7	6.8	16.3
Broward Corr. Inst. (FL)[d]	154	64.0	7.3	3.9	13.3
Delores J. Baylor Women's Corr. Inst. (DE)[d]	165	83.0	7.0	4.6	10.3
Julia Tutwiler Prison (AL)[d]	181	68.0	6.8	4.1	10.9
All jails	52,926	61.0%	1.8%	1.7%	2.0%
Marion Co. Jail Intake Fac. (IN)	62	43.0	7.7	3.4	16.3
Baltimore City Det. Ctr. (MD)	261	66.0	6.7	4.3	10.2
St. Louis Med. Security Inst. (MO)	220	58.0	6.3	3.9	10.0
Philadelphia City Industrial Corr. Ctr. (PA)	207	69.0	6.3	3.9	10.0
Santa Clara Co. Main Jail (CA)	130	37.0	6.2	3.0	12.5
Ulster Co. Law Enforcement Ctr. (NY)	153	68.0	6.1	3.6	10.2
Houston Co. Jail (GA)	174	71.0	6.0	3.7	9.6
Contra Costa Co. Martinez Det. Fac. (CA)	143	42.0	5.9	3.2	10.4
Oakland Co. Law Enforcement Complex (MI)	148	49.0	5.9	3.0	11.1
New York City Rose M. Singer Ctr. (NY)[d]	202	63.0	5.9	3.7	9.4
New York City Otis Bantum Corr. Ctr. (NY)	170	44.0	5.6	2.9	10.5
Robeson Co. Jail (NC)	147	52.0	5.2	3.0	8.7

Note: High-rate facilities are those in which the lower bound of the 95%-confidence interval is larger than 1.55 times the average among prisons by sex of inmates housed, and 1.55 times the average among all jail facilities.

[a]Weighted percent of inmates reporting one or more incidents of sexual victimization involving another inmate or facility staff in the past 12 months or since admission to the facility, if less than 12 months.

[b]Number of inmates who responded to the sexual victimization survey.

[c]Weights were applied so that inmates who responded accurately reflected the entire population of each facility on selected characteristics, including age, sex, race, sentence length, and time since admission.

[d]Facility housed only female inmates.

Source: Bureau of Justice Statistics, National Inmate Survey, 2011–12.

Seven jails had staff sexual misconduct rates of at least 6%. Marion County Jail Intake Facility (Indiana) had the highest reported rate of staff sexual misconduct (7.7%), followed by Baltimore City Detention Center (Maryland) (6.7%), St. Louis Medium Security Institution (Missouri) (6.3%), and Philadelphia City Industrial Correctional Center (Pennsylvania) (6.3%).

The reported use or threat of physical force to engage in sexual activity with staff was generally low among all prison and jail inmates (0.8%); however, at least 5% of the inmates in three state prisons and one high-rate jail facility reported they had been physically forced or threatened with force. (See appendix tables 3 and 7.) The Clements Unit (Texas) had the highest percentage of inmates reporting sexual victimization involving physical force or threat of force by staff (8.1%), followed by Denver Women's Correctional Facility (Colorado) (7.3%), and Idaho Maximum Security

Institution (6.0%). Wilson County Jail (Kansas) led all surveyed jails, with 5.6% of inmates reporting that staff used physical force or threat of force to have sex or sexual contact.

While 0.8% of prison and jail inmates reported the use or threat of physical force, an estimated 1.4% of prison inmates and 1.2% of jail inmates reported being coerced by facility staff without any use or threat of force, including being pressured or made to feel they had to have sex or sexual contact. In 8 of the 24 facilities with high rates of staff sexual misconduct, at least 5% of the inmates reported such pressure by staff. Among state prisoners, the highest rates were reported by female inmates in the Denver Women's Correctional Facility (Colorado) (8.8%) and by male inmates in the Clements Unit (Texas) (8.7%). Among jail inmates, the highest rates were reported by inmates in the Rose M. Singer Center (New York) (5.6%) and the Contra Costa County Martinez Detention Facility (California) (5.2%).

FIGURE 3

Confidence intervals at the 95% level for prisons with high rates of staff sexual misconduct, National Inmate Survey, 2011–12

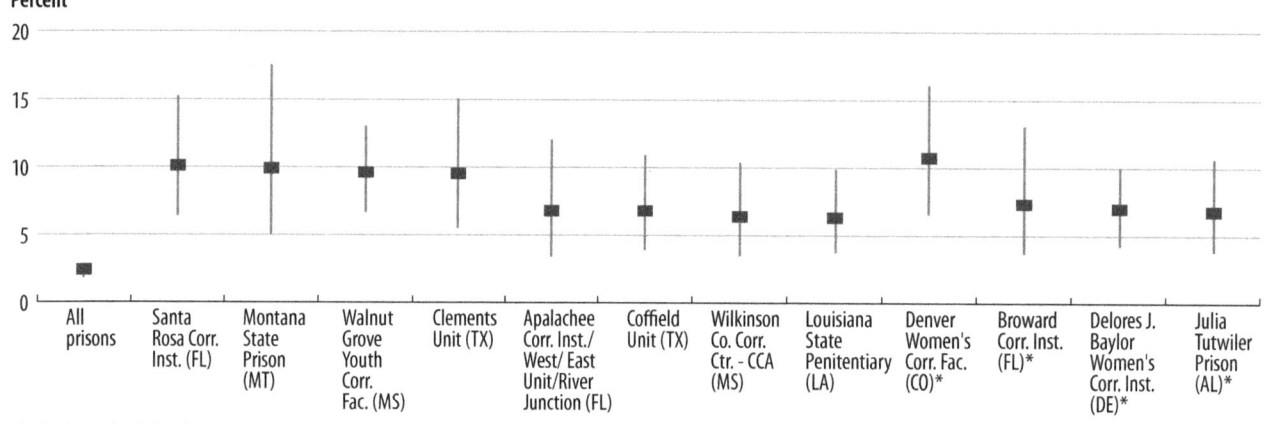

*Facility housed only female inmates.

Source: Bureau of Justice Statistics, National Inmate Survey, 2011–12.

FIGURE 4

Confidence intervals at the 95% level for jails with high rates of staff sexual misconduct, National Inmate Survey, 2011–12

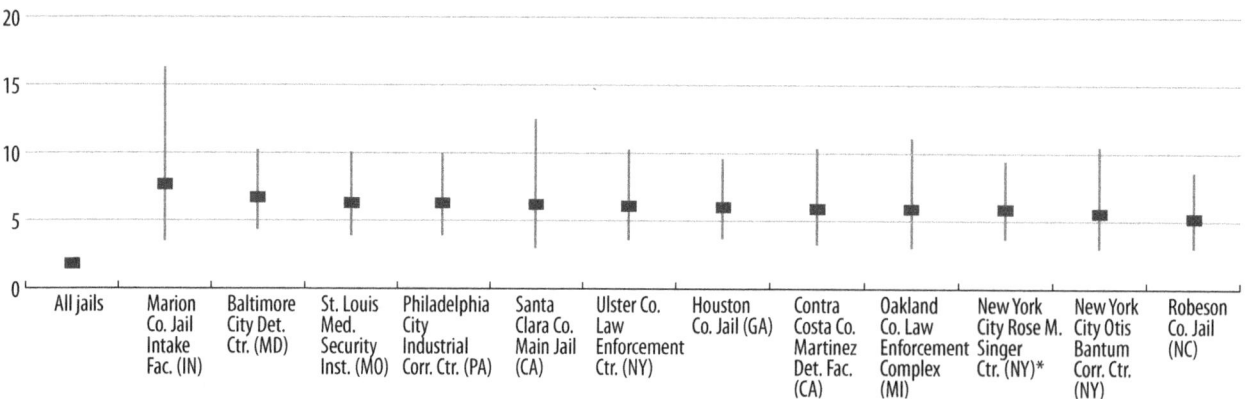

*Facility housed only female inmates.

Source: Bureau of Justice Statistics, National Inmate Survey, 2011–12.

7 male prisons, 6 female prisons, and 4 jails were identified as low-rate facilities for sexual victimization overall

Thirteen prisons and 34 jails had no reported incidents of sexual victimization of any kind. (See appendix tables 1 and 5.) Estimates of the number of inmates who experienced a sexual victimization in each of these facilities are also subject to sampling error and could vary if a different group of inmates had been interviewed. Although the lower bound of the 95%-confidence interval in each of these facilities is 0%, the upper bound varies depending on the number of completed interviews in each facility.

Combining reports of inmate-on-inmate sexual victimization and staff sexual misconduct, seven male prisons and six female prisons were designated as low-rate facilities. These designations were based on their low rate of sexual victimization overall and the upper bound of their 95%-confidence interval that was less than 65% of the average rate among male and female prisons (table 5). Six of these facilities had no reported incidents of sexual victimization, while seven facilities had at least one inmate who reported sexual victimization.

Danville Correctional Center (Illinois), with a reported sexual victimization rate of 0.5%, had a confidence interval with the lowest upper bound (1.8%) among male prisons. FCI Marianna Camp (operated in Florida by the Federal Bureau of Prisons), with a reported sexual victimization rate of 0.6%, had a confidence interval with the lowest upper bound (2.1%) among female prisons.

Four jails were designated as low-rate facilities based on the upper bound of the 95%-confidence interval that was less than 65% of the average for jails nationwide. Woodford County Detention Center (Kentucky), with a 0.1% overall sexual victimization rate, had a confidence interval with the lowest upper bound (0.6%).

TABLE 5
Facilities with low rates of sexual victimization, by type of facility, National Inmate Survey, 2011–12

| Facility name | Number of respondents[b] | Response rate | Inmates reporting any sexual victimization[a] | | |
| | | | Percent[c] | 95%-confidence interval | |
				Lower bound	Upper bound
All prisons	38,251	60.0%	4.0%	3.6%	4.5%
Male prisons	31,110	59.0%	3.7%	3.2%	4.3%
Danville Corr. Ctr. (IL)	205	70.0	0.5	0.2	1.8
Lawtey Corr. Inst. (FL)	198	80.0	0.0	0.0	1.9
CI Eden (TX)[d]	185	67.0	0.0	0.0	2.0
CI Reeves III (TX)[d]	188	69.0	0.4	0.1	2.0
CI Reeves I and II (TX)[d]	180	64.0	0.0	0.0	2.1
Jackie Brannon Corr. Ctr. (OK)	179	72.0	0.5	0.1	2.3
La Palma Corr. Ctr. (AZ)[d]	163	45.0	0.0	0.0	2.3
Female prisons	7,141	69.0%	8.5%	7.2%	10.0%
FCI Marianna Camp (FL)	172	88.0	0.6	0.2	2.1
FMC Lexington Camp (KY)	148	83.0	0.8	0.2	2.7
Decatur Corr. Ctr. (IL)	157	65.0	1.1	0.3	3.3
Brunswick Women's Reception and Pre-Release Ctr. (VA)	95	86.0	0.0	0.0	3.9
Woodman State Jail (TX)	139	57.0	1.3	0.4	4.3
Mary Frances Ctr. (NC)	68	85.0	0.0	0.0	5.3
All jails	52,926	61.0%	3.2%	2.9%	3.5%
Woodford Co. Det. Ctr. (KY)	34	51.0	0.1	0.0	0.6
Cameron Co. Carrizales-Rucker Det. Ctr. (TX)	262	72.0	0.3	0.1	1.6
Jefferson Co. Jail (CO)	205	62.0	0.0	0.0	1.8
Sarasota North Co. Jail (FL)	203	65.0	0.0	0.0	1.9

Note: Low-rate facilities are those in which the upper bound of the 95%-confidence interval is lower than 0.65 times the average among prisons by sex of inmates housed, and 0.65 times the average among all jail facilities.

[a]Percent of inmates reporting one or more incidents of sexual victimization involving another inmate or facility staff in the past 12 months or since admission to the facility, if less than 12 months.

[b]Number of inmates who responded to the sexual victimization survey.

[c]Weights were applied so that inmates who responded accurately reflected the entire population of each facility on selected characteristics, including age, sex, race, time since admission, and sentence length.

[d]Privately operated facility.

Source: Bureau of Justice Statistics, National Inmate Survey, 2011–12.

In 2011-12, two military facilities and one Indian country jail had high rates of staff sexual misconduct

The NIS-3 also surveyed 15 special confinement facilities, including 5 ICE facilities, 5 military facilities, and 5 Indian country jails. (See *Methodology* for sample description.) As a result of too few completed interviews, rates in two Indian country facilities—Hualapai Adult Detention Center (Arizona) and Standing Rock Law Enforcement and Adult Detention Center (North Dakota)—could not be provided.

Among ICE facilities, sexual victimization rates were highest in the Krome North Service Processing Center (Florida), in which 3.2% of detainees reported experiencing sexual victimization by another detainee and 3.0% reported experiencing staff sexual misconduct (table 6). Overall, an estimated 3.8% of detainees in this ICE facility reported experiencing one or more incidents of sexual victimization, which was somewhat lower than the 4.0% average in prisons nationwide and slightly higher than the 3.2% average in jails nationwide. (See appendix table 9.)

The Northwest Joint Regional Correctional Facility (Washington), which is operated by the U.S. Army Corrections Command and holds pretrial offenders

and short-term post-trial offenders, had a staff sexual misconduct rate (6.6%) that was more than double the average rate for prisons (2.4%) and jails (1.8%) nationwide. Inmates held at this military facility also reported a high rate of inmate-on-inmate sexual victimization (5.1%), which was also more than double the 2.0% average among prisons and 1.6% average among jails nationwide.

Inmates at the Naval Consolidated Brig Mirimar (California) reported high rates of staff sexual misconduct (4.9%) and inmate-on-inmate sexual victimization (3.0%). This facility, which is operated by the U.S. Navy, holds male inmates sentenced to terms of 10 years or less and female inmates regardless of sentence length from all military services.

Among all facilities sampled, staff sexual misconduct was highest in the Oglala Sioux Tribal Offenders Facility (South Dakota) (10.8%). Based on the 6.2% lower bound of the 95%-confidence interval, the rate of staff sexual misconduct in this Indian country facility was statistically higher than the rate reported for any jail nationwide. This facility, with a peak population of 147 in June 2011, was the most crowded facility among the 80 Indian jails in operation at midyear 2011. (See *Jails in Indian Country, 2011*, NCJ 238978.)

TABLE 6
Rates of sexual victimization in special correctional facilities, by type of incident and facility, National Inmate Survey, 2011–12

Facility name	Number of completed interviews	Any inmate-on-inmate incident			Any staff sexual misconduct		
			95%-confidence interval			95%-confidence interval	
		Percent[a]	Lower bound	Upper bound	Percent[a]	Lower bound	Upper bound
Immigration and Customs Enforcement facilities							
El Centro SPC (CA)	115	0.0%	0.0%	3.2%	0.8%	0.2%	3.4%
Jena/LaSalle Det. Fac. (LA)[b]	97	0.0	0.0	3.8	1.1	0.2	5.4
Krome North SPC (FL)	60	3.2	0.8	11.7	3.0	0.7	11.6
Otero Co. Processing Ctr. (NM)	140	1.7	0.6	4.4	0.5	0.1	2.4
Port Isabel Processing Ctr. (TX)	161	2.3	1.0	5.6	0.0	0.0	2.3
Military facilities							
Midwest Joint Regional Corr. Fac., Fort Leavenworth (KS)	82	1.0%	0.3%	3.6%	3.0%	1.3%	6.7%
Naval Consolidated Brig, Charleston (SC)	94	2.9	1.6	5.3	2.4	1.1	5.1
Naval Consolidated Brig, Miramar (CA)[c]	121	3.0	1.5	6.0	4.9	2.5	9.4
Northwest Joint Regional Corr. Fac. (WA)	85	5.1	1.9	13.0	6.6	2.9	14.1
United States Disciplinary Barracks, Fort Leavenworth (KS)	157	2.1	0.9	5.1	1.1	0.4	3.2
Indian country jails							
Hualapai Adult Det. Ctr. (AZ)[b]	7	^	^	^	^	^	^
Laguna Det. Ctr. (NM)[b]	26	0.0%	0.0%	12.9%	0.0%	0.0%	12.9%
Oglala Sioux Tribal Offenders Fac. (SD)[b]	56	1.8	0.5	6.4	10.8	6.2	17.9
San Carlos Dept. of Corr. and Rehabilitation - Adult and Juvenile Det. (AZ)[b]	64	0.0	0.0	5.7	1.6	0.6	4.2
Standing Rock Law Enforcement and Adult Det. Ctr. (ND)[b]	7	^	^	^	^	^	^

^Too few cases to provide reliable estimate.

[a]Weighted percent of inmates reporting one or more incidents of sexual victimization involving another inmate or facility staff in the past 12 months or since admission to the facility, if less than 12 months.

[b]Facility housed both males and females; both were sampled at this facility.

[c]Facility housed both males and females; only males were sampled at this facility.

Source: Bureau of Justice Statistics, National Inmate Survey, 2011–12.

Demographic and other characteristics

Overweight and obese prison inmates had lower rates of inmate-on-inmate sexual victimization and staff misconduct than inmates who were at or below a normal weight

Variations in reported sexual victimization rates across inmate demographic categories in the NIS-3 were consistent with past surveys:

- Rates of inmate-on-inmate sexual victimization among prison inmates were higher among females (6.9%) than males (1.7%), higher among whites (2.9%) or inmates of two or more races (4.0%) than among blacks (1.3%), higher among inmates with a college degree (2.7%) than among inmates who had not completed high school (1.9%), and lower among currently married inmates (1.4%) than among inmates who never married (2.1%) (table 7).

TABLE 7
Prevalence of sexual victimization, by type of incident and inmate characteristics, National Inmate Survey, 2011–12

Characteristic	Prison inmates reporting sexual victimization[a] Number of inmates[b]	Inmate-on-inmate	Staff sexual misconduct	Jail inmates reporting sexual victimization[a] Number of inmates[b]	Inmate-on-inmate	Staff sexual misconduct
Sex						
Male*	1,345,200	1.7%	2.4%	628,600	1.4%	1.9%
Female	96,600	6.9**	2.3	91,600	3.6**	1.4**
Race/Hispanic origin						
White[c]	430,000	2.9%**	1.6%**	240,500	2.0%**	1.4%**
Black[c]*	507,900	1.3	2.6	239,200	1.1	2.1
Hispanic	339,800	1.6	2.2	159,300	1.5	1.5**
Other[c,d]	38,200	1.7	2.6	18,900	1.2	1.8
Two or more races[c]	108,300	4.0**	3.9**	54,300	3.0**	3.2**
Age						
18–19	18,500	1.6%	2.4%	40,000	1.9%	2.6%
20–24*	162,500	2.2	3.5	145,800	2.0	2.4
25–34	457,100	2.3	2.9	250,700	1.9	2.2
35–44	398,200	2.0	2.3**	150,900	1.4**	1.5**
45–54	281,400	2.0	1.7**	102,800	1.1**	0.9**
55 or older	124,000	1.1**	0.8**	30,000	1.3	0.3**
Education						
Less than high school*	813,300	1.9%	2.4%	379,700	1.4%	1.8%
High school graduate	293,900	1.7	2.3	168,700	1.4	1.7
Some college[e]	231,100	2.7**	1.8	120,700	2.3**	1.9
College degree or more	98,700	2.7**	2.4	47,200	3.0**	2.7**
Marital status						
Married*	265,600	1.4%	1.9%	134,800	1.1%	1.8%
Widowed, divorced, or separated	390,500	1.9	1.6	165,800	1.9**	1.7
Never married	741,200	2.1**	2.5	410,800	1.7**	1.8
Body Mass Index						
Underweight	12,500	3.2%	3.6%	9,800	3.5%**	2.0%
Normal*	357,000	2.7	2.7	267,000	1.6	1.8
Overweight	632,200	1.4**	2.0**	272,200	1.5	1.7
Obese	348,700	1.8**	1.8**	133,000	1.7	1.9
Morbidly obese	32,700	2.7	3.7	14,400	3.0**	2.6

Note: See appendix table 11 for standard errors.

*Comparison group.

**Difference with comparison group is signficant at the 95%-confidence level.

[a]Percent of inmates reporting one or more incidents of sexual victimization involving another inmate or facility staff in the past 12 months or since admission to the facility, if less than 12 months.

[b]Estimated number of inmates at midyear 2011 and yearend 2011 in prisons and jails represented by NIS-3, excluding inmates under age 18. Estimates have been rounded to the nearest 100.

[c]Excludes persons of Hispanic or Latino origin.

[d]Includes American Indian, Alaska Native, Asian, Native Hawaiian, and other Pacific Islander.

[e]Includes persons with an associate degree.

Source: Bureau of Justice Statistics, National Inmate Survey, 2011–12.

- Similar patterns of inmate-on-inmate sexual victimization were reported by jail inmates. Female jail inmates (3.6%), whites (2.0%), and inmates with a college degree (3.0%) reported higher rates of victimization than males (1.4%), blacks (1.1%), and inmates who had not completed high school (1.4%).

- Rates of inmate-on-inmate sexual victimization were unrelated to age among state and federal prisoners, except for slightly lower rates among inmates age 55 or older.

- Rates were lower among jail inmates in the oldest age categories (ages 35 to 44, 45 to 54, and 55 or older) than among jail inmates ages 20 to 24.

- Patterns of staff sexual misconduct were different, with higher rates among males in jails (1.9%) than among females in jails (1.4%), and higher among black inmates in prisons (2.6%) and jails (2.1%) than among white inmates in prisons (1.6%) and jails (1.4%).

- In both prisons and jails, rates of reported staff sexual misconduct were lower among inmates in the oldest age categories (ages 35 to 44, 45 to 54, and 55 or older), compared to inmates in the 20 to 24 age category.

With a new survey question on the inmate's specific height in combination with a question on the inmate's weight, the NIS-3 provides the first opportunity to determine if rates of sexual victimization vary based on an inmate's Body Mass Index (BMI). Among state and federal prison inmates, obese inmates (with a BMI of 30 to 39) and overweight inmates (with a BMI of 25 to 30) had lower rates of inmate-on-inmate sexual victimization and staff sexual misconduct than inmates with a normal weight (with a BMI of 18.5 to 24) or who were underweight (a BMI of less than 18.5). (See *Methodology* for calculation of BMI.)

Among jail inmates, those underweight (3.5%) and those morbidly obese (BMI of 40 or greater) (3.0%) have nearly double the rate of inmate-on-inmate sexual victimization than inmates in other categories (1.6%, normal weight; 1.5%, overweight; and 1.7%, obese). There are no statistically significant variations in reported staff sexual misconduct among jail inmates across BMI categories.

Large differences in sexual victimization were found among inmates based on their sexual orientation and past sexual experiences

Inmates who identified their sexual orientation as gay, lesbian, bisexual, or other reported high rates of inmate-on-inmate sexual victimization and staff sexual misconduct:

- Among heterosexual state and federal prisoners, an estimated 1.2% reported being sexually victimized by another inmate, and 2.1% reported being victimized by staff. In comparison, among non-heterosexual prison inmates (including gay, lesbian, bisexual, and other sexual orientations), 12.2% reported being sexually victimized by another inmate, and 5.4% reported being sexually victimized by staff (table 8).

TABLE 8
Prevalence of sexual victimization, by type of incident and inmate sexual characteristics, National Inmate Survey, 2011–12

Sexual characteristic	Prison inmates reporting sexual victimization[a]			Jail inmates reporting sexual victimization[a]		
	Number of inmates[b]	Inmate-on-inmate	Staff sexual misconduct	Number of inmates[b]	Inmate-on-inmate	Staff sexual misconduct
Sexual orientation						
Heterosexual*	1,298,000	1.2%	2.1%	654,500	1.2%	1.7%
Non-heterosexual[c]	111,500	12.2%**	5.4%**	50,100	8.5%**	4.3%**
Number of sexual partners						
0–1*	227,500	1.1%	1.2%	106,900	1.5%	1.1%
2–4	173,300	2.3%**	1.6	99,900	1.7	1.4
5–10	242,200	2.1%**	1.5	127,800	1.6	1.2
11–20	218,500	2.5%**	2.9%**	117,100	1.8	1.6
21 or more	491,700	1.9%**	2.8%**	234,600	1.8	2.9%**
Prior sexual victimization						
Yes	178,800	12.0%**	6.7%**	94,200	8.3%**	5.1%**
No*	1,262,500	0.6	1.8	625,800	0.6	1.3

Note: See appendix table 12 for standard errors.

*Comparison group.

**Difference with comparison group is significant at the 95%-confidence level.

[a]Percent of inmates reporting one or more incidents of sexual victimization involving another inmate or facility staff in the past 12 months or since admission to the facility, if less than 12 months.

[b]Estimated number of inmates at midyear 2011 and yearend 2011 in prisons and jails represented by NIS-3, excluding inmates under age 18. Estimates have been rounded to the nearest 100.

[c]Includes gay, lesbian, bisexual, and other sexual orientations.

Source: Bureau of Justice Statistics, National Inmate Survey, 2011–12.

- Among jail inmates, heterosexual inmates reported lower rates of inmate-on-inmate sexual victimization (1.2%) and staff sexual misconduct (1.7%) than non-heterosexual inmates (8.5% for inmate-on-inmate and 4.3% for staff sexual misconduct).

- Inmates who experienced sexual victimization before coming to the facility were also more likely than inmates with no sexual victimization history to report incidents of sexual victimization involving other inmates and staff. Among inmates who experienced sexual victimization before coming to the facility, 12.0% of prisoners and 8.3% of jail inmates reported being sexually victimized

by another inmate at the current facility. An estimated 6.7% of prisoners and 5.1% of jail inmates who experienced sexual victimization before coming to the facility reported sexual victimization by staff.

In 2011-12, inmates held for a violent sexual offense reported higher rates of inmate-on-inmate sexual victimization than inmates held for other offenses

An estimated 3.7% of violent sex offenders in prison and 3.9% of violent sex offenders in jail reported being sexually victimized by another inmate in the last 12 months or since admission to the facility, if less than 12 months (table 9).

TABLE 9
Prevalence of sexual victimization, by type of incident and inmate criminal justice status and history, National Inmate Survey, 2011–12

Criminal justice status and history	Prison inmates reporting sexual victimization[a]			Jail inmates reporting sexual victimization[a]		
	Number of prison inmates[b]	Inmate-on-inmate	Staff sexual misconduct	Number of jail inmates[b]	Inmate-on-inmate	Staff sexual misconduct
Most serious offense						
Violent sexual offense*	211,300	3.7%	2.1%	34,300	3.9%	2.0%
Other violent	440,900	2.3**	3.4**	113,700	2.3**	3.3**
Property	244,100	2.4**	2.6	165,400	1.9**	1.7
Drug	310,300	0.7**	1.1**	153,900	1.1**	1.4
Other	162,900	1.7**	2.1	190,300	1.2**	1.6
Sentence length						
Less than 1 year	53,400	1.5%	1.6%	:	:	:
1–4 years*	350,400	1.8	1.3	:	:	:
5–9 years	311,100	1.6	2.2**	:	:	:
10–19 years	296,900	1.8	2.3**	:	:	:
20 years or more	239,300	2.2	2.5**	:	:	:
Life/death	139,600	2.7**	3.2**	:	:	:
Time in a correctional facility prior to current facility						
None	296,400	1.8%	1.5%	204,500	1.9%	1.5%
Less than 6 months	161,400	2.3	1.7	135,500	1.7	1.3
6–11 months	131,200	1.7	2.1	69,200	1.5	1.9
1–4 years	384,900	1.6	1.8	171,700	1.4**	2.1**
5 years or more	423,500	2.2	3.0**	129,700	1.6	2.5**
Number of times arrested						
1 time*	217,600	2.0%	1.7%	78,800	2.1%	1.3%
2–3	427,200	2.0	2.2	197,800	1.7	1.6
4–10	495,400	1.8	2.0	265,900	1.5	1.9**
11 or more	253,200	2.0	2.8**	164,400	1.5	2.3**
Time since admission						
Less than 1 month*	79,600	1.4%	0.8%	226,800	0.9%	1.2%
1–5 months	367,500	1.6	1.7**	341,100	1.7**	1.8**
6–11 months	263,200	2.2	2.6**	92,500	2.7**	2.5**
1–4 years	558,100	2.1	2.5**	58,000	2.6**	3.3**
5 years or more	172,400	2.9**	3.4**	1,600	2.1	3.2

Note: See appendix table 13 for standard errors.

: Not calculated.

*Comparison group.

**Difference with comparison group is significant at the 95%-confidence level.

[a]Percent of inmates reporting one or more incidents of sexual victimization involving another inmate or facility staff in the past 12 months or since admission to the facility, if less than 12 months.

[b]Estimated number of inmates at midyear 2011 and yearend 2011 in prisons and jails represented by NIS-3, excluding inmates under age 18. Estimates have been rounded to the nearest 100.

Source: Bureau of Justice Statistics, National Inmate Survey, 2011–12.

These rates were higher than those reported by inmates held for other offenses. Among state and federal prisoners, rates of inmate-on-inmate sexual victimization were—

- higher among prison inmates serving a sentence of life or death (2.7%) than among inmates serving a sentence of 1 to 4 years (1.8%).

- higher among prison inmates who had been at their current facility for 5 years or more (2.9%) than among inmates who had been admitted in the last month (1.4%).

Among jail inmates, the rate of inmate-on-inmate sexual victimization increased with the length of time served in the current facility, rising from 0.9% among inmates who had been at the facility for less than a month to 1.7% among inmates in jail for 1 to 5 months, 2.7% among inmates in jail for 6 to 11 months, and 2.6% among those in jail for 1 to 4 years.

Rates of staff sexual misconduct varied among inmates based on their criminal justice status and history

- Among state and federal prisoners, inmates with a long sentence, inmates who had served 5 years or more in prison prior to coming to the current facility, and inmates who had served 5 years or more at the current facility were more likely to report experiencing staff sexual misconduct than inmates with a sentence of 1 to 4 years, inmates who had not served any prior time, and inmates who had been admitted in the last month.

- Among jail inmates, the rate of reported staff sexual misconduct increased with time served in the current facility and was higher among inmates who had previously served time in a correctional facility for 1 year or more.

These variations in rates of sexual victimization among inmate subgroups based on demographic characteristics, sexual history and orientation, and criminal justice status are almost identical to those reported in the NIS-2. (See *Sexual Victimization in Prisons and Jails Reported by Inmates, 2008-09*, NCJ 231169, BJS Web, August 2010.)

Special inmate populations—Inmates ages 16 to 17

In 2011-12, juvenile inmates ages 16 to 17 held in adult facilities reported rates of sexual victimization similar to those of adult inmates

The NIS-3 was specially designed to provide estimates of sexual victimization for inmates ages 16 to 17 held in adult facilities. Previous NIS collections excluded inmates age 17 or younger due to special human subject issues (related to consent and assent, as well as risk of trauma in the survey process) and statistical issues (related to clustering of youth and the need to oversample to ensure a representative sample). To address issues of consent and risk, the NIS-3 juvenile sample was restricted to inmates ages 16 to 17 (who represented an estimated 95% of the 1,790 juveniles held in prisons at yearend 2011 and 97% of the 5,870 juveniles held in local jails at midyear 2011).

The NIS-3 was designed to oversample for facilities that house juveniles and to oversample juveniles within selected facilities. The resulting sample was structured to provide separate nationwide estimates for juveniles in prisons and jails, while providing national-level and facility-level estimates for adult inmates that were comparable to estimates in the NIS-1 and NIS-2. (See *Methodology* for the juvenile sample design.)

Juveniles ages 16 to 17 held in prisons and jails did not report significantly higher rates of sexual victimization than adult inmates. Although the overall rates for juveniles (4.5% in prisons and 4.7% in jails) were somewhat higher than those for adults (4.0% in prisons and 3.2% in jails), the differences were not statistically significant (table 10).

Rates of inmate-on-inmate sexual victimization are unrelated to age among state and federal prisoners (table 11). When compared to inmates in every other age category, inmate ages 16 to 17 reported experiencing inmate-on-inmate sexual victimization at similar rates. Among jail inmates, the rate of staff sexual misconduct was higher for inmates ages 16 to 17 than for older inmates; however, the differences were statistically significant only for inmates age 35 or older.

These data do not support the conclusion that juveniles held in adult prisons and jails are more likely to be sexually victimized than inmates in other age groups. Due to the relatively small number of juveniles held in state prisons (an estimated 1,700 inmates ages 16 to 17 at midyear 2011), BJS combined these data with reports from juveniles held in local jails (an estimated 5,700 inmates ages 16 to 17).

TABLE 10

Juvenile inmates reporting sexual victimization, by type of incident, National Inmate Survey, 2011–12

Type of incident[b]	Percent of inmates		
	All facilities	Prisons	Jails
Total	4.7%	4.5%	4.7%
Inmate-on-inmate	1.8%	1.8%	1.8%
Nonconsensual sexual acts	0.7	1.6	0.4
Abusive sexual contacts only	1.1	0.2	1.4
Staff sexual misconduct	3.2%	2.8%	3.3%
Unwilling activity	1.9	0.9	2.2
Excluding touching	1.6	0.9	1.9
Touching only	0.2	0.0	0.3
Willing activity	2.2	2.5	2.1
Excluding touching	2.2	2.5	2.1
Touching only	0.0	0.0	0.0
Number of inmates	7,400	1,700	5,700

Note: Detail may not sum to total because inmates may report more than one type of victimization. They may also report victimization by both other inmates and staff. See appendix table 14 for standard errors.

: Not calculated.

[a]Standard errors may be used to construct confidence intervals around each estimate. See *Methodology* for calculations.

[b]See *Methodology* for terms and definitions.

Source: Bureau of Justice Statistics, National Inmate Survey, 2011–12.

TABLE 11

Prevalence of sexual victimization, by type of incident and age of inmate, National Inmate Survey, 2011–12

	Prison inmates			Jail inmates		
Age	Number	Inmate-on-inmate	Staff sexual misconduct	Number	Inmate-on-inmate	Staff sexual misconduct
16–17*	1,700	1.8%	2.8%	5,700	1.8%	3.3%
18–19	18,550	1.6	2.4	40,000	1.9	2.6
20–24	162,520	2.2	3.5	145,770	2.0	2.4
25–34	457,060	2.3	2.9	250,690	1.9	2.2
35–44	398,230	2.0	2.3	150,890	1.4	1.5**
45–54	281,390	2.0	1.7	102,820	1.1	0.9**
55 or older	124,050	1.1	0.8	30,010	1.3	0.3**

Note: See appendix table 15 for standard errors.

*Comparison group.

**Difference with comparison group is significant at the 95%-confidence level.

Source: Bureau of Justice Statistics, National Inmate Survey, 2011–12.

Overall, the patterns of reported sexual victimization by juveniles were similar to those for adult inmates, including higher rates of staff sexual misconduct than rates of inmate-on-inmate sexual victimization:

- Of juveniles held in prisons and jails, 1.8% reported being victimized by another inmate in the past 12 months or since admission to the facility, if less than 12 months) (table 12). This rate was similar to the rate reported by adult prisoners (2.0%) and adult jail inmates (1.6%).

- Among juveniles held in prisons and jails nationwide, 3.2% reported experiencing staff sexual misconduct. Though higher, the rate was not statistically different from that of adults in prisons (2.4%) and adults in jails (1.8%).

Among juveniles and young adult inmates in 2011-12, patterns of sexual victimization across demographic subgroups showed little variation

Across subgroups defined by sex, race or Hispanic origin, BMI, sexual orientation, and most serious offense, juveniles and young adults reported experiencing similar rates of sexual victimization. Due to the small number of juveniles within each subgroup, few differences in sexual victimization rates across age groups were statistically significant. (Tests across age group not shown; see appendix table 14 for standard errors.)

TABLE 12

Prevalence of sexual victimization among juveniles ages 16–17 and inmates ages 18–19 and 20–24, by type of incident and inmate characteristics, National Inmate Survey, 2011–12

| | Prison and jail inmates reporting sexual victimization[a] | | | | | | | | |
| Characteristic | Number of inmates | | | Inmate-on-inmate | | | Staff sexual misconduct | | |
	Ages 16–17	18–19	20–24	Ages 16–17	18–19	20–24	Ages 16–17	18–19	20–24
All inmates	7,400	58,550	308,290	1.8%	1.8%	2.1%	3.2%	2.5%	2.9%
Sex									
Male*	6,930	54,220	280,670	1.6%	1.5%	1.8%	3.3%	2.6%	3.1%
Female	470	4,330	27,610	4.4	5.2**	5.7**	0.9**	0.8**	1.7**
Race/Hispanic origin									
White[c]	910	12,080	76,890	6.6%	3.8%**	3.6%**	3.4%	2.5	2.0%**
Black[c]*	3,760	24,770	115,000	1.1	1.0	1.2	3.3	2.5	3.0
Hispanic	1,820	14,730	78,470	1.1	1.6	1.5	3.5	2.0	3.0
Other[c,d]	100	1,120	8,200	0.0**	1.6	1.1	0.0**	1.8	4.7
Two or more races[c]	740	5,430	25,910	1.5	2.0	3.8**	1.9	3.8	3.6
Body Mass Index									
Underweight	340	1,260	3,670	5.9%	1.7%	2.5	6.6%	1.8%	4.1%
Normal*	4,410	33,850	139,140	1.1	1.8	2.0	2.9	2.6	2.4
Overweight	1,540	15,940	110,360	2.4	1.9	1.7	2.7	2.8	3.0
Obese	520	3,970	36,160	4.8	2.0	2.9	4.8	0.9**	3.2
Morbidly obese	70	310	3,740	0.0**	5.3	4.3	0.0**	7.3	5.0
Sexual orientation									
Heterosexual*	6,930	54,200	277,960	1.7%	1.1%	1.4%	3.0%	2.5%	2.6%
Non-heterosexual[e]	270	3,150	22,840	6.3	13.9**	11.3**	1.4	4.3	7.0**
Most serious offense									
Violent sexual offense*	160	2,200	18,830	7.5%	10.4%	6.9%	12.0%	3.0%	2.4%
Other violent	3,100	18,580	94,970	1.7	1.5	2.1**	4.3	3.6	4.1**
Property	2,170	18,480	70,730	1.0	1.5	2.4**	1.5**	2.4	2.5
Drug	480	6,980	53,990	4.8	1.3	1.4**	2.9	1.6	2.0
Other	870	8,230	50,900	2.3	1.8	1.2**	1.9**	1.3	2.1

Note: See appendix table 16 for standard errors.

*Comparison group.

**Difference with comparison group is significant at the 95%-confidence level.

[a]Percent of inmates reporting one or more incidents of sexual victimization involving another inmate or facility staff in the past 12 months or since admission to the facility, if less than 12 months.

[b]Estimated number of inmates at midyear 2011 in jails and yearend 2011 in prisons represented by NIS-3, excluding inmates under age 18. Estimates have been rounded to the nearest 100.

[c]Excludes persons of Hispanic or Latino origin.

[d]Includes American Indian, Alaska Native, Asian, Native Hawaiian, and other Pacific Islander.

[e]Includes gay, lesbian, bisexual, and other sexual orientations.

Source: Bureau of Justice Statistics, National Inmate Survey, 2011–12.

Among juvenile inmates ages 16 to 17 and young adult inmates ages 18 to 19 and 20 to 24—

- Young adult females reported higher rates of inmate-on-inmate sexual victimization than young adult males, while young adult males reported higher rates of staff sexual misconduct than young adult females.

- White non-Hispanic young adults (ages 18 to 19 and 20 to 24) reported higher rates of inmate-on-inmate sexual victimization than black non-Hispanic and Hispanic youth in the same age groups.

- Inmates ages 18 to 19 and 20 to 24 with a sexual orientation other than heterosexual experienced higher rates of sexual victimization by another inmate than heterosexual inmates in similar age groups.

- Male juvenile inmates reported higher rates of staff sexual misconduct (3.3%) than female juveniles (0.9%).

- Juvenile inmates held for violent sex offenses reported higher rates of staff sexual misconduct (12.0%) than those held for property offenses (1.5%).

Among juveniles victimized by other inmates in 2011-12, more than three-quarters experienced force or threat of force, and a quarter were injured

Juveniles ages 16 to 17 who reported sexual victimization by other inmates revealed that—

- Two-thirds were victimized more than once (65.5%) (table 13).

- An estimated 78.6% reported experiencing physical force or threat of force, and 39.8% were pressured by the perpetrator to engage in the sexual act or other sexual contact.

- More than a quarter (27.7%) were injured in at least one of the incidents.

- Fewer than 1 in 6 (15.4%) reported an incident to someone at the facility, a family member, or a friend.

Among juvenile inmates ages 16 to 17 who reported experiencing staff sexual misconduct—

- Three-quarters (75.8%) were victimized more than once.

- An estimated 43.7% said that staff used force or threat of force.

- An estimated 10.8% were injured in at least one of the incidents.

- Fewer than 1 in 10 (9.0%) reported the staff sexual misconduct to someone at the facility, a family member, or a friend.

TABLE 13
Circumstances surrounding incidents among juveniles ages 16–17 and inmates ages 18–19 and 20–24, by type of victimization, National Inmate Survey, 2011–12

| | Victims in prisons and jails | | | | | |
| | Inmate-on-inmate | | | Staff sexual misconduct | | |
Circumstance	Ages 16–17*	18–19	20–24	16–17*	18–19	20–24
Number of victims	130	1,070	6,490	230	1,470	9,070
Number of incidents[a]						
1	34.5%	26.2%	29.9%	24.2%	19.7%	27.9%
2 or more	65.5	73.8	70.1	75.8	80.3	72.1
Type of coercion or force[b]						
Without pressure or force	~	~	~	68.9%	59.9%	67.2%
Pressured	39.8%	62.6%	73.8%**	51.2	52.6	49.7
Force or threat of force	78.6	75.5	62.1	43.7	36.2	33.0
Ever injured	27.7%	33.2%	15.9%	10.8%	12.9%	13.5%
Ever report an incident	15.4%	29.9%	18.1%	9.0%	14.3%	16.9%

Note: See appendix table 17 for standard errors.

~Not applicable.

*Comparison group.

**Difference with comparison group is significant at the 95%-confidence level.

[a]Number of incidents by another inmate and number of reported willing and unwilling incidents of staff sexual misconduct.

[b]Detail sums to more than 100% because some inmates reported more than one victimization.

Source: Bureau of Justice Statistics, National Inmate Survey, 2011–12.

Special inmate populations— Inmates with mental health problems

The NIS-3 collected data on the mental health problems of inmates for the first time in 2011-12. Inmates were asked whether they had been told by a mental health professional that they had a mental disorder or if because of a mental health problem they had stayed overnight in a hospital or other facility, used prescription medicine, or they had received counseling or treatment from a trained professional. These items have been previously used by BJS to determine if inmates in prisons and jails had any history of mental health problems. (See *Mental Health Problems of Prison and Jail Inmates*, NCJ 213600, BJS Web, September 2006.)

A high percentage of inmates had a history of problems with their emotions, nerves, or mental health

An estimated 36.6% of prison inmates and 43.7% of jail inmates reported being told by a mental health professional that they had a mental health disorder, as specified in the *Diagnostic and Statistical Manual of Mental Disorders* (DSM-IV) (table 14). Inmates were asked specifically if they had ever been told they had manic depression, bipolar disorder, or other depressive disorder, schizophrenia or another psychotic disorder, post-traumatic stress disorder, or an anxiety or other personality disorder. (See *Methodology* for survey items and full list of disorders.)

More than a third of prison inmates (35.8%) and jail inmates (39.2%) said they had received some counseling or therapy from a trained professional for these problems. An estimated 8.9% of prisoners and 12.8% of jail inmates reported an overnight stay in a hospital or other facility before their current admission to prison or jail. Approximately 15.4% of prisoners and 19.7% of jail inmates reported taking prescription medication for these mental health and emotional problems at the time of the offense for which they were currently being held.

TABLE 14

Prevalence of victimization by current mental health status and history of mental health problems among inmates, by type of facility, National Inmate Survey, 2011–12

Mental health status	Adult prison inmates				Adult jail inmates			
	Number[b]	Percent	Inmate-on-inmate	Staff sexual misconduct	Number	Percent	Inmate-on-inmate	Staff sexual misconduct
Current mental health status[a]								
No mental illness*	926,800	67.1%	0.7%	1.1%	360,600	51.4%	0.7%	1.0%
Anxiety-mood disorder	251,700	18.2	2.8**	3.0**	155,800	22.2	1.3**	1.4**
Serious psychological distress	203,200	14.7	6.3**	5.6**	184,500	26.3	3.6**	3.6**
History of mental health problems[b]								
Ever told by mental health professional had disorder								
Yes	505,600	36.6%	3.8%**	3.4%**	305,400	43.7%	2.9%**	2.5%**
No*	875,500	63.4	0.8	1.3	393,500	56.3	0.6	1.2
Had overnight stay in hospital in year before current admission								
Yes	122,800	8.9	5.7%**	4.9%**	89,700	12.8%	4.4%**	3.4%**
No*	1,257,700	91.1	1.5	1.8	611,300	87.2	1.2	1.5
Used prescription medications at time of current offense								
Yes	211,800	15.4	4.5%**	3.3%**	137,700	19.7%	3.2%**	2.7%**
No*	1,165,000	84.6	1.4	1.8	561,400	80.3	1.2	1.5
Ever received professional mental health therapy								
Yes	492,000	35.8%	3.6%**	3.0%**	274,100	39.2%	2.8%**	2.3%**
No*	884,000	64.2	0.9	1.5	425,200	60.8	0.8	1.4

Note: See appendix table 18 for standard errors.

*Comparison group.

**Difference with comparison group is significant at the 95%-confidence level.

[a]Based on the K6 scale where a score of 1–7 indicates no mental illness, a score of 8–12 indicates anxiety mood-disorder, and a score of 13 or more indicates serious psychological distress. See *Methodology* for discussion of the K6 scale and past applications.

[b]See *Methodology* for survey items.

Source: Bureau of Justice Statistics, National Inmate Survey, 2011–12.

Inmates with a history of mental health problems had higher rates of sexual victimization than other inmates

Inmates who had been told by a mental health professional that they had a mental disorder were more likely than other inmates to report being sexually victimized while in prison or jail. Among inmates who had been told they had a specific DSM-IV disorder—

- During 2011-12, an estimated 3.8% of prison inmates and 2.9% of jail inmates reported that they were sexually victimized by another inmate.

- Approximately 3.4% of prison inmates and 2.5% of jail inmates reported that they were sexually victimized by staff during 2011-12.

Sexual victimization rates were also higher among inmates who had stayed overnight in a hospital or other treatment facility because of a mental health problem than among inmates who had no prior admission for mental health problems. Among those who had stayed overnight in a hospital for mental or emotional problems, 5.7% of prison inmates and 4.4% of jail inmates said they were victimized by another inmate, and 4.9% of prison inmates and 3.4% of jail inmates said they were victimized by facility staff.

Differences in sexual victimization rates among inmates were similar across other mental health measures. Rates of inmate-on-inmate sexual victimization were—

- Two to three times higher among inmates who were taking prescription medications for their mental health or emotional problems at the time of the current offense than among inmates who were not taking such medications.

- Three to four times higher among inmates who had received mental health counseling or treatment from a trained professional in the past than among inmates who had not received such counseling or treatment.

In 2011-12, nearly 15% of state and federal prisoners and 26% of jail inmates had symptoms of serious psychological distress

To determine whether inmates had a current mental health problem, BJS used the K6 screening scale in the NIS-3. The K6 was previously developed by Kessler and others for estimating the prevalence of serious mental illness in noninstitutional settings as a tool to identify cases of psychiatric disorder. It has been used widely in epidemiological surveys in the U.S. and internationally.[3,4]

The K6 consists of six questions that ask inmates to report how often during the past 30 days they had felt—

- nervous

- hopeless

- restless or fidgety

- so depressed that nothing could cheer them up

- everything was an effort

- worthless.

The response options were (1) all of the time, (2) most of the time, (3) some of the time, (4) a little of the time, and (5) none of the time. Following Kessler, the responses were coded from 4 to 0, with 4 assigned to "all of the time" and 0 assigned to "none of the time." A summary scale combining the responses from all six items was then produced with a range of 0 to 24. The summary score was then reduced to three categories: 0 to 7 indicated no mental illness, 8 to 12 indicated an anxiety-mood disorder, and 13 or higher indicated serious psychological distress (SPD).

Since 2008, the K6 scale has been used in federal epidemiological studies to measure symptoms of SPD rather than serious mental illness. Although the K6 has been demonstrated to be a good predictor of serious mental illness in prior studies, a technical advisory group, convened by the Center for Mental Health Services at the Substance Abuse and Mental Health Services Administration (SAMHSA), recommended that it should be supplemented with questions on functional impairment to improve statistical prediction and validity. (See *Methodology* for discussion of K6 scaling rules and current applications.)

Consistent with other measures of mental health or emotional problems, the K6 reveals that prison and jail inmates have high rates of SPD. An estimated 203,200 state and federal inmates and 185,500 jail inmates reported levels of psychological distress in the 30 days prior to the interview consistent with SPD. These estimates of current SPD represented nearly 15% of state and federal inmates and 26% of local jail inmates. These may be underestimates because some inmates with serious mental illness may have been unable to participate in the NIS-3 due to cognitive limitations that precluded them from fully understanding the informed consent procedures or the survey questions.

[3]Kessler, R.C., Barker, P.R., Colpe, L.J., Epstein, J.F., Gfroerer, J.C., Hiripi, E., Howes, M.J., Normand, S.L., Manderscheid, R.W., Walters, E.E., & Zaslavsky, A.M. (2003). "Screening for serious mental illness in the general population." *Archives of General Psychiatry*, 60, 184–189.

[4]Kessler, R.C., Green, J.G., Gruber, M.J., Sampson, N.A., Bromet, E., Cuitan, M., Furukawa, T.A., et al. (2010). "Screening for serious mental illness in the general population with the K6 screening scale: results from the WHO World Mental Health (WMH) survey initiative." *International Journal of Methods in Psychiatric Research*, 19 (Spp. 1) 4–22.

An additional 251,700 state and federal prisoners (18.2%) and 155,800 jail inmates (22.2%) reported lower levels of psychological distress, indicative of anxiety-mood disorders.

Rates of SPD in prisons and jails were substantially higher than the 3.0% rate of SPD observed in the 2012 National Health Interview Survey of the noninstitutional U.S. population age 18 or older, using the same K6 screener.[5] Although inmate populations are demographically different from the general U.S. population, these differences in the prevalence of SPD remain significant when comparisons are restricted to demographic subgroups most commonly held in prisons and jails (table 15):

- Among males, 3.0% of the general U.S. population was identified with SPD, compared to 14.7% of prisoners and 26.3% of jails inmates.

- Among persons ages 18 to 44, 2.7% of the general population, 14.8% of prisoners and 26.1% of jail inmates had SPD.

- Among black non-Hispanic adults, 2.6% of the general population was classified with SPD, compared to 13.0% of prisoners and 22.1% of jail inmates.

- Among white non-Hispanic adults, 2.9% of the general population, 17.5% of prisoners and 30.8% of jail inmates had SPD.

Inmates with SPD or anxiety-mood disorders reported high overall rates of sexual victimization in 2011-12

Inmates identified with SPD reported significantly higher rates of inmate-on-inmate sexual victimization and staff sexual misconduct than inmates without a mental health problem:

- Among state and federal inmates, an estimated 6.3% of those identified with SPD reported being sexually victimized by another inmate, and 5.6% reported being victimized by staff. In comparison, among prison inmates with no indication of mental illness or anxiety-mood disorders, 0.7% reported being sexually victimized by another inmate and 1.1% reported experiencing staff sexual misconduct.

- Similarly, jail inmates identified with SPD reported higher rates of inmate-on-inmate sexual victimization (3.6%) and staff sexual misconduct (3.6%) than inmates with no mental illness (0.7% for inmate-on-inmate and 1.0% for staff sexual misconduct).

TABLE 15

Prevalence of serious psychological distress among adults in prisons, jails, and the U.S. civilian noninstitutional population, 2011–12

Demographic characteristic	Percent with symptoms of serious psychological distress[a]		
	U.S. noninstitutional adult population[b]*	Inmates age 18 or older	
		Prison	Jail
Total	3.0%	14.7%**	26.3%**
Sex			
Male	2.8%	14.3%**	25.5%**
Female	3.7	20.8**	32.2**
Race/Hispanic origin			
White[c]	2.9%	17.5%**	30.8%**
Black[c]	2.6	13.0**	22.4**
Hispanic	3.6	11.6**	23.1**
Age			
18–44	2.7%	14.8%**	26.1%**
45–64	3.9	14.7**	27.7**
65 or older	1.9	9.5**	19.3**

Note: See appendix table 19 for standard errors.

*Comparison group.

**Difference with comparison group is significant at the 95%-confidence level.

[a]Based on a score of 13 or more on the K-6 scale.

[b]Based on household interviews of a national sample of the civilian noninstitutional population between January and September 2012.

[c]Excludes persons of Hispanic or Latino origin.

Sources: Bureau of Justice Statistics, National Inmate Survey, 2011–12; and Centers for Disease Control and Prevention, National Health Interview Survey, 2012.

---

[5]Centers for Disease Control and Prevention, *Early Release of Selected Estimates Based on Data from* Surveillance Among Adults in the United States, Morbidity and Mortality Weekly Report, 2011;60 (Suppl.) table 7.) January-September 2012, National Health Interview Survey. Figures 13.1-13.3, March 2013.

Inmates identified as having anxiety-mood disorders reported higher rates of sexual victimization than inmates who did not report a mental health problem. Inmates with anxiety-mood disorders reported lower victimization rates than inmates with SPD. Among inmates with anxiety-mood disorders—

- An estimated 2.8% of prison inmates and 1.3% of jail inmates reported that they were sexually victimized by another inmate.

- About 3.0% of prison inmates and 1.4% of jail inmates reported that they were sexually victimized by staff.

Inmates with mental illness reported higher rates of sexual victimization than inmates without mental health problems across subgroups

For each of the measured subgroups (i.e., sex, race or Hispanic origin, age, sexual orientation, and most serious offense), inmates with SPD reported higher rates of inmate-on-inmate sexual victimization than inmates without mental health problems (table 16). With the exception of jail inmates age 45 or older, the differences were large and statistically significant. Among inmates with SPD, non-heterosexual inmates reported the highest rates of inmate-on-inmate sexual victimization (an estimated 21.0% of prison inmates and 14.7% of jail inmates).

TABLE 16

Prevalence of inmate-on-inmate sexual victimization, by current mental health status and inmate characteristics, National Inmate Survey, 2011–12

Characteristic	Prison inmates reporting sexual victimization[a]			Jail inmates reporting sexual victimization[a]		
	No mental illness*	Anxiety-mood disorder	Serious psychological distress	No mental illness*	Anxiety-mood disorder	Serious psychological distress
Sex						
Male	0.5%	2.2%**	5.6%**	0.5%	1.1%**	3.2%**
Female	3.4	8.9**	12.9**	2.3	2.8	5.8**
Race/Hispanic origin[c]						
White[d]	1.1%	3.9%**	7.0%**	0.8%	1.4%**	4.0%**
Black[d]	0.3	1.5**	5.3**	0.5	0.9	2.7**
Hispanic	0.6	2.2**	5.3**	0.6	1.3**	3.8**
Age						
18–24	0.4%	3.4%**	7.4%**	0.5%	1.8%**	4.8%**
25–34	0.9	3.2**	6.1**	1.0	1.6**	3.6**
35–44	0.5	2.4**	6.9**	0.5	0.7	3.4**
45 or older	0.7	2.4**	5.4**	0.6	0.8	2.2
Sexual orientation						
Heterosexual	0.4%	1.6%**	4.0%**	0.5%	1.0%**	2.6%**
Non-heterosexual[e]	5.9	13.4**	21.0**	5.0	5.1	14.7**
Most serious offense						
Violent sexual offense	1.5%	4.8%**	9.5%**	1.4%	4.1%	6.7%**
Other violent	0.9	3.1**	6.1**	1.2	1.8	3.9**
Property	0.5	3.1**	8.1**	0.8	1.6**	4.1**
Drug	0.3	1.2**	2.8**	0.3	0.6	2.9**
Other	0.6	1.3	4.2**	0.5	0.8	2.9**

Note: See appendix table 20 for standard errors.

*Comparison group.

**Difference with comparison group is signficant at the 95%-confidence level.

[a]Percent of inmates reporting one or more incidents of sexual victimization involving another inmate or facility staff in the past 12 months or since admission to the facility, if less than 12 months.

[b]Estimated number of inmates at midyear 2011 in jails and yearend 2011 in prisons represented by NIS-3, excluding inmates under age 18. Estimates have been rounded to the nearest 100.

[c]Due to small sample size, estimates for other races, including American Indian, Alaska Native, Asian, Native Hawaiian, and other Pacific Islander, and two or more races, are not shown.

[d]Excludes persons of Hispanic or Latino origin.

[e]Includes gay, lesbian, bisexual, and other sexual orientations.

Source: Bureau of Justice Statistics, National Inmate Survey, 2011–12.

Patterns of staff sexual misconduct were similar to those of inmate-on-inmate victimization. Staff sexual misconduct was also higher among inmates with SPD than those without mental health problems (table 17). With the exception of female jail inmates, the differences within each demographic subgroup were statistically significant. Among inmates with SPD, non-heterosexual prison inmates recorded the highest rate (10.5%) of sexual victimization by staff.

TABLE 17
Prevalence of staff sexual misconduct, by current mental health status and inmate characteristics, National Inmate Survey, 2011–12

Characteristic	Prison inmates reporting sexual victimization[a]			Jail inmates reporting sexual victimization[a]		
	No mental illness*	Anxiety-mood disorder	Serious psychological distress	No mental illness*	Anxiety-mood disorder	Serious psychological distress
Sex						
Male	1.1%	3.0%**	5.7%**	1.0%	1.4%**	4.0%**
Female	1.0	2.4**	5.2**	1.1	1.0	1.7
Race/Hispanic origin[c]						
White[d]	0.6%	2.0%**	3.6%**	0.8%	0.7%	2.5%**
Black[d]	1.2	4.1**	6.1**	1.1	1.7	4.7**
Hispanic	1.1	1.7	6.8**	0.5	1.2**	3.9**
Age						
18–24	1.8%	3.1%	7.4%**	1.2%	1.8%**	5.1%**
25–34	1.6	3.4**	6.1**	1.3	1.6	3.9**
35–44	0.9	3.3**	5.6**	0.7	0.9	3.3**
45 or older	0.6	2.0**	4.3**	0.4	0.7	1.4**
Sexual orientation						
Heterosexual	1.0%	2.9%**	4.8%**	0.9%	1.3%**	3.4%**
Non-heterosexual[e]	3.4	3.6	10.5**	3.0	2.4	6.2**
Most serious offense						
Violent sexual offense	1.4%	2.3%	4.1%**	1.2%	1.2%	3.3%
Other violent offense	1.7	3.8**	7.2**	2.2	2.2	5.7**
Property	1.1	3.1**	6.7**	0.8	1.6**	3.3**
Drug	0.4	2.9	2.3**	0.7	1.0	2.8**
Other	0.8	1.7	5.9**	0.8	1.0	3.5**

Note: See appendix table 21 for standard errors.

*Comparison group.

**Difference with comparison group is significant at the 95%-confidence level.

[a]Percent of inmates reporting one or more incidents of sexual victimization involving another inmate or facility staff in the past 12 months or since admission to the facility, if less than 12 months.

[b]Estimated number of inmates at midyear 2011 in jails and yearend 2011 in prisons represented by NIS-3, excluding inmates under age 18. Estimates have been rounded to the nearest 100.

[c]Due to small sample size, estimates for other races, including American Indian, Alaska Native, Asian, Native Hawaiian, and other Pacific Islander, and two or more races, are not shown.

[d]Excludes persons of Hispanic or Latino origin.

[e]Includes gay, lesbian, bisexual, and other sexual orientations.

Source: Bureau of Justice Statistics, National Inmate Survey, 2011–12.

Reports of sexual victimization differed among inmates with SPD and other inmates

Among prison and jail inmates who reported inmate-on-inmate sexual victimization, those with SPD were more likely than those without mental health problems to be—

- victimized more than once (80.4% compared to 62.6%)
- forced or threatened with force by the perpetrator (71.2% compared to 57.7%)
- injured (26.4% compared to 12.3%) (table 18).

Among victims of staff sexual misconduct, inmates with SPD were more likely than those without mental health problems to—

- report being pressured by staff (73.4% compared to 50.2%) or forced or threatened with force (47.2% compared to 33.8%)
- be injured by staff (19.8% compared to 6.3%)
- report at least one victimization to someone at the facility, a family member, or a friend (24.9% compared to 14.1%).

TABLE 18
Circumstances surrounding incidents among adult inmates, by current mental health status and type of victimization, National Inmate Survey, 2011–12

| | Victims in prisons and jails | | | | | |
| | Inmate-on-inmate | | | Staff sexual misconduct | | |
Circumstance	No mental illness*	Anxiety-mood disorder	Serious psychological distress	No mental illness*	Anxiety-mood disorder	Serious psychological distress
Number of victims	8,880	9,040	19,490	13,910	9,580	18,130
Number of incidents[a]						
1	37.4%	33.5%	19.6%**	23.4%	25.5%	23.6%
2 or more	62.6	66.5	80.4**	76.6	74.5	76.4
Type of coercion or force[b]						
Without pressure or force	~	~	~	64.1%	57.2%	43.6%**
Pressured	72.7%	79.4%	73.7%	50.2	54.8	73.4**
Force or threat of force	57.7	61.9	71.2**	33.8	29.8	47.2**
Ever injured	12.3%	14.1%	26.4%**	6.3%	6.1%	19.8%**
Ever report an incident	21.2%	15.4%	23.1%	14.1%	18.4%	24.9%**

Note: See appendix table 22 for standard errors.

~Not applicable.

*Comparison group.

**Difference with comparison group is significant at the 95%-confidence level.

[a]Number of sexual acts by another inmate and number of reported willing and unwilling incidents of staff sexual misconduct.

[b]Detail sums to more than 100% because some inmates reported more than one victimization.

Source: Bureau of Justice Statistics, National Inmate Survey, 2011–12.

Special inmate populations—Inmates with a non-heterosexual sexual orientation

To date, all of the BJS victim self-report surveys conducted under PREA have found that inmates with the highest rates of sexual victimization are those who reported their sexual orientation as gay, lesbian, bisexual, or other. For example, among non-heterosexual inmates interviewed in the NIS-2, 11.2% of prison inmates and 7.2% of jail inmates reported being victimized by another inmate in the past 12 months or since admission to the facility, if less than 12 months. Among former state prison inmates interviewed in the National Former Prisoner Survey (NFPS, conducted in 2008), more than a third of non-heterosexual males (33% of bisexuals and 39% of gays and lesbians) reported being sexually victimized by another inmate during their most recent period of incarceration. Combined with the higher rates among non-heterosexual inmates in the NIS-3 (12.2% in prisons and 8.5% in jails), the surveys clearly identify a high-risk population. Although the NIS-2 and NFPS provide detailed multivariate models that control for other risk factors, NIS-3 provides additional detail on this population.

Across subgroups, inmate-on-inmate victimization rates were higher for non-heterosexual inmates than heterosexual inmates

In every measured subgroup (i.e., sex, race or Hispanic origin, age, education, and mental health problems), non-heterosexual prison and jail inmates reported higher rates of inmate-on-inmate sexual victimization than heterosexual inmates (table 19). Rates of sexual victimization by other inmates against non-heterosexual inmates were at least 10 times greater than that of heterosexual inmates when the victim was also male, black, Hispanic, or had less than a high school education. These differences were smaller, but still large, among non-heterosexual female inmates (2.5 times larger), whites (more than 6 times larger), and high school graduates (8 times larger).

Within each of the other demographic subgroups, staff-on-inmate victimization rates were at least double for non-heterosexual inmates compared to heterosexual inmates. Among non-heterosexual prison and jail inmates, rates of staff sexual misconduct were the highest for inmates ages 18 to 24 (6.7%), blacks (6.2%), and males (6.1%).

TABLE 19

Prevalence of sexual victimization, by type of incident and inmate sexual orientation, National Inmate Survey, 2011–12

Characteristic	Inmate-on-inmate		Staff sexual misconduct	
	Heterosexual*	Non-heterosexual[a]	Heterosexual*	Non-heterosexual[a]
Sex				
Male	1.0%	11.9%**	2.0%	6.1%**
Female	3.6	9.4**	1.4	3.0**
Race/Hispanic origin[b]				
White[c]	1.7%	11.4%**	1.3%	3.2%**
Black[c]	0.6	10.6**	2.2	6.2**
Hispanic	1.0	10.1**	1.8	5.9**
Age				
18–24	1.3%	11.6%**	2.5%	6.7%**
25–44	1.2	11.9**	2.2	5.0**
45 or older	0.9	8.9**	1.1	4.2**
Education				
Less than high school	1.0%	11.0%**	2.0%	5.1%**
High school graduate	1.1	9.0**	2.0	4.9
Some college or more	1.7	12.6**	1.8	4.8**
Current mental health status				
No mental illness	0.4%	5.7%**	1.0%	3.2%**
Anxiety-mood disorder	1.3	10.7**	2.3	3.2
Serious psychological distress	3.3	18.6**	4.1	8.8**

Note: Prison and jail inmates have been combined to obtain a sufficient number of non-heterosexual inmates. See appendix table 23 for standard errors.

*Comparison group.

**Difference with comparison group is significant at the 95%-confidence level.

[a]Includes gay, lesbian, bisexual, and other sexual orientations.

[b]Due to small sample size, estimates for other races, including American Indian, Alaska Native, Asian, Native Hawaiian, and other Pacific Islander, and persons of two or more races, are not shown.

[c]Excludes persons of Hispanic or Latino origin.

Source: Bureau of Justice Statistics, National Inmate Survey, 2011–12.

Non-heterosexual victims (82.9%) were more likely than heterosexual victims (68.0%) to report that the victimization by another inmate involved pressure, but less likely to report that it involved force or threat of force (62.0% for non-heterosexual compared to 69.7% for heterosexual victims) (table 20). In addition, non-heterosexual victims (84.2%) of staff sexual misconduct were more likely than heterosexual victims (71.4%) to report more than one incident.

TABLE 20

Circumstances surrounding incidents of sexual victimization among heterosexual and non-heterosexual inmates, National Inmate Survey, 2011–12

| Circumstance | Victims in prisons and jails | | | |
| | Inmate-on-inmate | | Staff sexual misconduct | |
	Heterosexual*	Non-heterosexual[a]	Heterosexual*	Non-heterosexual[a]
Number of victims	22,960	17,910	38,320	8,130
Number of incidents[b]				
1	32.5%	25.9%	28.6%	15.8%**
2 or more	67.5	74.1	71.4	84.2**
Type of coercion or force[c]				
Without pressure or force	~	~	53.0%	60.6%
Pressured	68.0%	82.9%**	60.1	63.8
Force or threat of force	69.7	62.0**	37.8	41.7
Ever injured	22.5%	20.9%	11.0%	15.6%
Ever report an incident	27.5%	19.4%**	19.5%	26.7%

Note: Prison and jail inmates have been combined to obtain a sufficient number of non-heterosexual inmates. See appendix table 24 for standard errors.

~Not applicable.

*Comparison group.

**Difference with comparison group is significant at the 95%-confidence level.

[a]Includes gay, lesbian, bisexual, and other sexual orientations.

[b]Number of incidents by another inmate and number of reported willing and unwilling incidents of staff sexual misconduct.

[c]Based only on victims reporting incidents involving force, threat of force, or pressure.

Source: Bureau of Justice Statistics, National Inmate Survey, 2011–12.

The National Inmate Survey, 2011-12 (NIS-3) was conducted in 233 state and federal prisons, 358 jails, and 15 special facilities (military, Indian country, and Immigration and Customs Enforcement (ICE)) between February 2011 and May 2012. The data were collected by RTI International under a cooperative agreement with the Bureau of Justice Statistics (BJS).

The NIS-3 comprised two questionnaires—a survey of sexual victimization and a survey of mental and physical health, past drug and alcohol use, and treatment for substance abuse. Inmates were randomly assigned to receive one of the questionnaires so that at the time of the interview the content of the survey remained unknown to facility staff and the interviewers.

A total of 106,532 inmates participated in NIS-3, including the sexual victimization survey or the randomly assigned companion survey. Combined, the surveys included 43,721 inmates in state and federal prisons, 61,351 inmates in jails, 605 inmates in military facilities, 192 inmates in Indian country jails, and 663 inmates in facilities operated by ICE.

The interviews, which averaged 35 minutes in length, used computer-assisted personal interviewing (CAPI) and audio computer-assisted self-interviewing (ACASI) data collection methods. For approximately the first two minutes, survey interviewers conducted a personal interview using CAPI to obtain background information and date of admission to the facility. For the remainder of the interview, respondents interacted with a computer-administered questionnaire using a touchscreen and synchronized audio instructions delivered via headphones. Respondents completed the ACASI portion of the interview in private, with the interviewer either leaving the room or moving away from the computer.

A shorter paper questionnaire was made available for inmates who were unable to come to the private interviewing room or interact with the computer. The paper form was completed by 751 prison inmates (or 1.9% of all prison interviews)—733 were completed by adult prison inmates (1.9% of adult prison inmate interviews) and 18 were completed by prisoners ages 16 to 17 (3.4% of all prison inmate interviews of inmates ages 16 to 17). The paper questionnaire was also completed by 264 jail inmates (0.5% of all jail inmate interviews)—255 were completed by adults (0.5% of adult jail inmate interviews) and 9 were completed by jail inmates ages 16 to 17 (0.7% of jail inmate interviews of inmates ages 16 to 17). In addition, five paper questionnaires were completed by military inmates (0.9%

of all military inmate interviews). Most of these inmates were housed in administrative or disciplinary segregation or were considered too violent to be interviewed.

Before the interview, inmates were informed verbally and in writing that participation was voluntary and that all information provided would be held in confidence. Interviews were conducted in either English (96% in prisons, 95% in jails, 35% in ICE facilities, and 100% in military and Indian country facilities) or Spanish (4% in prisons, 5% in jails, and 65% in ICE facilities).

Selection of state and federal prisons

A sample of 241 state and federal prisons was drawn to produce a sample representing the 1,158 state and 194 federal adult confinement facilities identified in the 2005 Census of State and Federal Adult Correctional Facilities, supplemented with updated information from websites maintained by each state's department of corrections (DOC) and the Federal Bureau of Prisons (BOP). The 2005 census was a complete enumeration of adult state prisons, including all publicly operated and privately operated facilities under contract to state correctional authorities.

The NIS-3 was restricted to confinement facilities— institutions in which fewer than 50% of the inmates were regularly permitted to leave, unaccompanied by staff, for work, study, or treatment. Such facilities included prisons, penitentiaries, prison hospitals, prison farms, boot camps, and centers for reception, classification, or alcohol and drug treatment. The NIS-3 excluded community-based facilities, such as halfway houses, group homes, and work release centers.

Based on BJS's 2011 National Prisoner Statistics and 2005 Census of State and Federal Adult Correctional Facilities, the prisons in the study universe held an estimated 1,238,000 state and 203,800 federal inmates age 18 or older and 1,700 state inmates ages 16 to 17 at yearend 2011. Facilities that had been closed and new facilities that had opened since the 2005 census were identified via review of DOC and BOP websites. Facilities determined to be closed were removed from the NIS-3 frame and new facilities were added.

State and federal confinement facilities were sequentially sampled with probabilities of selection proportionate to size (as measured by the number of inmates held in state prisons on December 30, 2005, and in federal prisons on September 9, 2010).

Facilities on the sampling frame were stratified by sex of inmates housed, whether the facility had a mental health function, and whether the facility held five or more juveniles:

- Among facilities that housed males, the measure of size for facilities that held male inmates and participated in the NIS-1 in 2007 or NIS-2 in 2008-09 were adjusted to lower their probability of selection in the NIS-3.

- Among facilities with an inmate population that was at least 50% female, the measure of size for facilities that participated in the NIS-2 was reduced to lower their probability of selection in the NIS-3.

- The measures of size were further adjusted to increase the probability of selection of facilities with large juvenile populations.

Within each stratum, facilities in the sampling frame were first sorted by region, state, and public or private operation:

- The sample measures of size for facilities housing only female inmates were increased by a factor of 5 to ensure a sufficient number of women and allow for meaningful analyses of sexual victimization by sex. This led to an allocation of 51 female facilities (out of 233) in the sample.

- An additional 25 facilities were allocated to the stratum with facilities that have a mental health function, and another 20 facilities were allocated to the strata that housed juveniles.

- This led to the allocation of 66 facilities known to have a mental health function—49 male facilities and 17 female facilities—and 38 facilities that housed juveniles (36 facilities that housed males and 2 facilities that housed females).

Facilities were sampled ensuring that at least one facility in every state was selected. Federal facilities were grouped together and treated like a state for sampling purposes. The remaining facilities were selected from each region with probabilities proportionate to size.

Of the 241 selected prison facilities, 7 had closed prior to the start of data collection: Metro State Prison (Georgia), Hillsborough Corr. Inst. (Florida), Gates Corr. Inst. (Connecticut), Brush Corr. Fac. (Colorado), Burnet Co. Intermediate Sanction Fac. (Texas), and Diamondback Corr. Fac. (Oklahoma). One facility—Chittenden Regional Corr. Fac. (Vermont)—had transitioned from holding males to females during the data collection period and was considered a closed facility. All other selected prison facilities participated fully in NIS-3.

Selection of inmates within prisons

A roster of inmates was obtained just prior to the start of data collection at each facility. Inmates age 15 or younger and inmates who were released prior to data collection were deleted from the roster. Eligible inmates within a facility were placed into one of two strata based on their ages. Inmates who were ages 16 to 17 (juveniles) were placed in one stratum and inmates age 18 or older (adults) were placed in the other. Inmates age 15 or younger were considered ineligible for the NIS-3.

Selection of adult inmates within prisons

The number of adult inmates sampled in each facility varied based on six criteria—

- an expected sexual victimization prevalence rate of 4%

- a desired level of precision based on a standard error of 1.75%

- a projected 70% response rate among selected inmates

- a 10% chance among participating inmates of not receiving the sexual victimization questionnaire

- an adjustment factor of 1.9 to account for the complex survey design

- the size of the facility.

Each eligible adult inmate was assigned a random number and sorted in ascending order. Inmates were selected from the list up to the expected number of inmates determined by the sampling criteria.

Selection of inmates ages 16 to 17 within prisons

The number of inmates ages 16 to 17 sampled in each facility varied based on the number who appeared on the roster:

- If fewer than 50 were on the roster, all inmates ages 16 to 17 were selected.

- If between 50 and 149 were on the roster, 75% were sampled (with a minimum of 50).

- If 150 or more were on the roster, 75% were sampled (with a minimum of 150).

In cases in which not all inmates ages 16 to 17 were selected, each eligible inmate ages 16 to 17 was assigned a random number and sorted in ascending order. Inmates were selected from the list up to the expected number of inmates determined by the sampling criteria.

A total of 74,655 prison inmates were selected. After selection, 2,233 ineligible inmates were excluded—1,441 (1.9%) were released or transferred to another facility before interviewing began, 657 (0.9%) were mentally or physically unable to be interviewed, 10 (0.01%) were age 15 or younger or their age could not be obtained during the interview process, 56 (0.5%) were selected in error (i.e., an inmate was incorrectly listed on the facility roster), 21 (0.03%) were only in the facility on weekends, and 47 (0.06%) were on unsupervised work release or only served time on weekends.

Of all selected eligible prison inmates, 32% refused to participate in the survey, 0.5% were not available to be interviewed (e.g., in court, in medical segregation, determined by the facility to be too violent to be interviewed, or restricted from participation by another legal jurisdiction), and 0.5% were not interviewed due to survey logistics (e.g., language barriers, releases, or transfers to another facility after interviewing began).

Overall, 43,721 prison inmates participated in the survey, yielding a response rate of 60%. Approximately 90% of the participating inmates (38,778) received the sexual assault survey. (See appendix table 1 for the number of participating inmates in each prison facility.)

Selection of jail facilities

A sample of 393 jails was drawn to represent the 2,957 jail facilities identified in the Census of Jail Inmates, 2005, and the sample was supplemented with information obtained during the NIS-1 and NIS-2. The 2005 census was a complete enumeration of all jail jurisdictions, including all publicly operated and privately operated facilities under contract to jail authorities. The NIS-3 was restricted to jails that had six or more inmates on June 30, 2005. Jails identified as closed or ineligible during the NIS-1 and NIS-2 were removed from the NIS-3 frame. Based on estimates from the Annual Survey of Jails, 2011, the jails in the NIS-3 held an estimated 720,171 inmates age 18 or older and 5,700 inmates ages 16 to 17 on June 30, 2011.

Jail facilities were sequentially sampled with probabilities of selection proportionate to size (as measured by the number of inmates held on June 30, 2005).

- Two facilities that were unable to participate in the NIS-2 were selected with certainty in the NIS-3.

- The measures of size for facilities that participated in the NIS-1 or NIS-2 were adjusted to give them a lower probability of selection.

- Facilities with juveniles had their measures of size adjusted to increase their probability of selection.

- Facilities were stratified such that facilities in each of the 10 largest jail jurisdictions were placed into a stratum. Within the large jurisdiction stratum, three facilities were selected from the five largest jurisdictions with probabilities proportionate to size, and two facilities were selected from the next five largest jurisdictions with probabilities proportionate to size.

- All other facilities were placed in a single stratum and then sorted by region, state, and public or private operation. Facilities were sampled to ensure that at least one jail facility in every state was selected. The remaining jail facilities were selected from each region with probabilities proportionate to size.

Of the 393 selected jails in the NIS-3, 20 facilities refused to participate:

- Covington Co. Jail (Alabama)
- Mobile Co. Metro Jail (Alabama)
- Delaware Co. George W. Hill Corr. Fac. (Pennsylvania)
- Montcalm Co. Jail (Michigan)
- Will Co. Adult Det. Fac. (Illinois)
- Northumberland Co. Prison (Pennsylvania)
- Kenosha Co. Pre-Trial Det. Fac. (Wisconsin)
- Carroll Co. Jail (Tennessee)
- Brevard Co. Jail (Florida)
- Pinellas Co. North Division (Florida)
- Hillsborough Co. Falkenburg Road Jail (Florida)
- Paulding Co. Det. Ctr. (Georgia)
- Whitfield Co. Jail (Georgia)
- Marion Co. Jail (Tennessee)
- Sandoval Co. Det. Ctr. (New Mexico)
- Williamson Co. Jail (Texas)
- Montgomery Co. Jail (North Carolina)
- Catahoula Parish Corr. Ctr. (Louisiana)
- Escambia Co. Det. Ctr. (Alabama)
- Orleans Parish House of Det. (Louisiana).

Williamsburg Co. Jail (South Carolina), was excused due to construction at the facility. In Nassau Co. Corr. Ctr. (New York), data were collected only among inmates ages 16 to 17 due to lack of space to interview both adults and juveniles ages 16 to 17.

Fourteen facilities were determined to be ineligible: six had closed, two were considered part of another facility on the sampling frame, three had fewer than six eligible inmates, two were facilities containing only unsupervised work release inmates, and one had active litigation related to sexual victimization. All other selected jail facilities participated fully in NIS-3.

Selection of inmates within jails

A roster of inmates was obtained just prior to the start of data collection at each facility. Inmates age 15 or younger and inmates who had not been arraigned were removed from the roster. Eligible inmates within a facility were placed into one of two stratum based on their age. Inmates who were ages 16 to 17 (juveniles) were placed in one stratum and inmates age 18 or older (adults) were placed in the other. Inmates age 15 or younger were considered ineligible for the NIS-3.

Selection of adult inmates within jails

The number of adult inmates sampled in each facility varied based on six criteria:

- an expected prevalence rate of sexual victimization of 3%
- a desired level of precision based on a standard error of 1.4%
- a projected 65% response rate among selected inmates
- a 10% chance among participating inmates of not receiving the sexual victimization questionnaire
- an adjustment factor of 1.9 to account for the complex survey design
- a pre-arraignment adjustment factor equal to 1 in facilities where the status was known for all inmates and less than 1 in facilities where only the overall proportion of inmates who were pre-arraigned was known.

Each eligible adult inmate was assigned a random number and sorted in ascending order. Inmates were selected from the list up to the expected number of inmates determined by the sampling criteria.

Due to the dynamic nature of jail populations, a second roster of inmates was obtained on the first day of data collection. Eligible adult inmates who appeared on the second roster but who had not appeared on the initial roster were identified. These inmates had been arraigned since the initial roster was created or were newly admitted to the facility and arraigned. A random sample of these new inmates was chosen using the same probability of selection used to sample from the first roster.

Selection of inmates ages 16 to 17 within jails

The number of inmates ages 16 to 17 sampled in each facility varied based on the number who appeared on the roster:

- If fewer than 50 were on the roster, all inmates ages 16 to 17 were selected.
- If between 50 and 149 were on the roster, 75% were sampled (with a minimum of 50).
- If 150 or more were on the roster, 75% were sampled (with a minimum of 150).

In facilities in which not all inmates ages 16 to 17 were selected, each eligible inmate ages 16 to 17 was assigned a random number and sorted in ascending order. Inmates were selected from the list up to the expected number of inmates determined by the sampling criteria.

As with adult jail inmates, a second roster obtained on the first day of data collection was used to identify inmates that had been arraigned since the initial roster was created or newly admitted. A random sample of these new inmates was chosen using the same probability of selection used to sample from the first roster.

A total of 112,594 jail inmates was selected. After selection, 11,342 ineligible inmates were excluded—9,479 (8.4%) were released or transferred to another facility before interviewing began, 1,036 (0.8%) were mentally or physically unable to be interviewed, 25 (0.02%) were age 15 or younger or their age could not be obtained during the interview process, 296 (0.3%) were selected in error (i.e., an inmate was incorrectly listed on the facility roster), and 484 (0.4%) were on unsupervised work release or only served time on weekends.

Of all selected inmates, 22% refused to participate in the survey, 1.1% were not available to be interviewed (e.g., in court, in medical segregation, determined by the facility to be too violent to be interviewed, or restricted from participation by another legal jurisdiction), and 8% were not interviewed due to survey logistics (e.g., language barriers, releases, and transfers to another facility after interviewing began).

Overall, 61,351 jail inmates participated in the survey, yielding a response rate of 61%. Approximately 90% of the participating inmates (54,137) received the sexual victimization survey. (See appendix table 5 for the number of participating inmates in each jail facility.)

Selection of special confinement facilities

A sample of 16 special facilities was drawn to represent the inmate populations in military, Indian country, and ICE facilities. Five military, six Indian country, and five ICE facilities were included.

The military frame came from the military correctional facilities population report on April 1, 2011. The Indian country frame came from the BJS report, *Jails in Indian Country, 2009*, NCJ 232223, BJS Web, February 2011. The ICE frame came from the ICE integrated decision support system on March 21, 2011.

Military, Indian country, and ICE facilities were sequentially selected with probability proportionate to the adjusted number of inmates in the facility. The measures of size (population) were adjusted to reduce the probability of selection among facilities included in the NIS-2.

Tohono O'odham Adult Detention Facility (Arizona) refused to participate in the NIS-3. All other selected special confinement facilities participated fully in the survey.

Selection of inmates in special confinement facilities

For purposes of inmate selection, military facilities were treated as prisons, and Indian country and ICE facilities were treated like jails. The assumptions used to determine the sample size within a prison or jail and the corresponding selection procedures were used. However, in ICE facilities, a second sample of newly admitted inmates was not drawn due to an inability to identify new inmates on the ICE rosters. In addition, inmates in ICE facilities who did not speak English or Spanish were defined as ineligible for the study.

Overall, 2,874 inmates were selected, including 910 in military facilities, 300 in Indian country facilities, and 1,664 in ICE facilities. After selection, 163 ineligible inmates were excluded—28 (1.0%) were released or transferred to another facility before interviewing began, 46 (1.1%) were mentally or physically unable to be interviewed, 3 (0.1%) were sampled in error, 2 (0.1%) were inmates in custody only on the weekend, and 84 (3.0%) in ICE facilities did not speak English or Spanish.

Overall, 1,272 inmates participated in the survey (605 in military, 192 in Indian country, and 663 in ICE facilities), yielding a response rate of 68% in military, 68% in Indian country, and 43% in ICE facilities. Approximately 90% of the participating inmates (1,379) received the sexual victimization survey (539 in military, 160 in Indian country, and 573 in ICE facilities). (See appendix table 9 for the number of participating inmates in each special confinement facility.)

Weighting and nonresponse adjustments

Responses from interviewed inmates were weighted to provide national-level and facility-level estimates. Each interviewed inmate was assigned an initial weight corresponding to the inverse of the probability of selection within each sampled facility. A series of adjustment factors was applied to the initial weight to minimize potential bias due to nonresponse and to provide national estimates.

Bias occurs when the estimated prevalence is different from the actual prevalence for a given facility. In each facility, bias could result if the random sample of inmates did not accurately represent the facility population. Bias could also result if the nonrespondents were different from the respondents. Post-stratification and nonresponse adjustments were made to the data to compensate for these two possibilities. These adjustments included—

- calibration of the weights of the responding inmates within each facility so that the estimates accurately reflected the facility's entire population in terms of known demographic characteristics. These characteristics included distributions by inmate age, sex, race, sentence length, and time since admission. This adjustment ensured that the estimates better reflected the entire population of the facility and not just the inmates who were randomly sampled.

- calibration of the weights so that the weight from a non-responding inmate was assigned to a responding inmate with similar demographic characteristics. This adjustment ensured that the estimates accurately reflected the full sample, rather than only the inmates who responded.

For each inmate, these adjustments were based on a generalized exponential model, developed by Folsom and Singh, and applied to the sexual victimization survey respondents.[6]

A final ratio adjustment to each inmate weight was made to provide national-level estimates for the total number of inmates age 18 or older and the total number of inmates ages 16 to 17 who were held in jails at midyear 2011 or in prison at yearend 2011. These ratios represented the estimated number of inmates by sex (from BJS's 2011 Annual Survey of Jails and 2011 National Prisoner Statistics) divided by the number of inmates by sex for adults and overall for juvenile inmates ages 16 to 17 in the NIS-3, after calibration for sampling and nonresponse. The national estimates for state prisons were 1,154,600

---

[6]Folsom, Jr., R.E., & Singh, A.C. (2002). "The Generalized Exponential Model for Sampling Weight Calibration for Extreme Values, Nonresponse, and Poststratification." *Proceedings of the American Statistical Association, Survey Research Methods Section*, pp. 598–603.

adult males, 83,400 adult females, and 1,700 juveniles ages 16 to 17; for federal prisons, 190,600 adult males and 13,200 adult females (there were no juveniles ages 16 to 17 in federal custody); and for jails (with an average daily population of six or more inmates), 628,620 adult males, 91,551 adult females, and 5,700 juveniles ages 16 to 17.

Final ratio adjustments were not applied to inmate weights in military, Indian country, and ICE facilities. Estimates for special confinement facilities were made at the facility level only.

Standard errors and tests of significance

The NIS-3 is statistically unable to provide an exact ranking for all facilities as required under PREA. As with any survey, the NIS estimates are subject to error arising from the fact that they are based on a sample rather than a complete enumeration. Within each facility, the estimated sampling error varies by the size of the estimate, the number of completed interviews, and the size of the facility.

A common way to express this sampling variability is to construct a 95%-confidence interval around each survey estimate. Typically, multiplying the standard error by 1.96 and then adding or subtracting the result from the estimate produces the confidence interval. This interval expresses the range of values that could result among 95% of the different samples that could be drawn.

For small samples and estimates close to 0%, as is the case with sexual victimization in most prisons and jails, the use of the standard error to construct the 95%-confidence interval may not be reliable. An alternative developed by Wilson has been shown to perform better than the traditional method when constructing a confidence interval. (See footnote 1 on page 10.) This method produces an asymmetrical confidence interval around the facility estimates in which the lower bound is constrained to be greater than or equal to 0%. It also provides confidence intervals for facilities in which the survey estimates are zero (but other similarly conducted surveys could yield non-zero estimates). (See tables 3, 4, 5, and 6 and appendix tables 1, 2, 4, 5, 6, 8, and 9.)

When applied to large samples, the traditional and the Wilson confidence intervals are nearly identical. As a result, the tables that show national estimates display traditional standard errors. (See tables 1 and 2.) The traditional standard errors have also been used to compare estimates of sexual victimization among selected groups of inmates that have been defined by type of incident, demographic subgroup, sexual history, and criminal justice status. (See tables 7 through 9 and 11 through 20.) To facilitate the

analysis, rather than provide the detailed estimates for every standard error, differences in the estimates of sexual victimization for subgroups in these tables have been tested and notated for significance at the 95%-level of confidence.

For example, the difference in the rate of inmate-on-inmate sexual victimization among female prison inmates (6.9%) compared to male prison inmates (1.7%) is statistically significant at the 95%-level of confidence (table 7). In all tables providing detailed comparisons, statistically significant differences at the 95%-level of confidence or greater have been designated with two asterisks (**).

Exposure period

To calculate comparative rates of sexual victimization, respondents were asked to provide the most recent date of admission to the current facility. If the date of admission was at least 12 months prior to the date of the interview, inmates were asked questions related to their experiences during the past 12 months. If the admission date was less than 12 months prior to the interview, inmates were asked about their experiences since they had arrived at the facility.

The average exposure period of inmates participating in the sexual victimization survey was—

- 8.8 months for federal prisoners
- 8.1 months for adult state prisoners
- 5.5 months for juveniles ages 16 to 17 in state prisons
- 3.7 months for jail inmates
- 7.6 months for inmates in military facilities
- 2.8 months for inmates in ICE facilities
- 2.0 months for inmates in Indian country facilities.

Measurement of sexual victimization

The survey of sexual victimization relied on inmates reporting their direct experiences, rather than inmates reporting on the experiences of other inmates. Questions related to inmate-on-inmate sexual activity were asked separately from questions related to staff sexual misconduct. (For specific survey questions, see appendices 1 and 2.)

The ACASI survey began with a series of questions that screened for specific sexual activities without restriction, including both wanted and unwanted sex and sexual contacts with other inmates. To fully measure all sexual activities, questions related to the touching of body parts in a sexual way were followed by questions related to manual stimulation and questions related to acts involving oral, anal, and vaginal sex. The nature of coercion (including use of physical force, pressure, and other forms of coercion) was measured for each type of reported sexual activity.

ACASI survey items related to staff sexual misconduct were asked in a different order. Inmates were first asked about being pressured or being made to feel they had to have sex or sexual contact with the staff and then asked about being physically forced. In addition, inmates were asked if any facility staff had offered favors or special privileges in exchange for sex. Finally, inmates were asked if they willingly had sex or sexual contact with staff. All reports of sex or sexual contact between an inmate and facility staff, regardless of the level of coercion, were classified as staff sexual misconduct.

The ACASI survey included additional questions related to both inmate-on-inmate sexual victimization and staff sexual misconduct. These questions, known as latent class measures, were included to assess the reliability of the survey questionnaire. After being asked detailed questions, all inmates were asked a series of general questions to determine if they had experienced any type of unwanted sex or sexual contact with another inmate or had any sex or sexual contact with staff. (See appendix 3.)

The entire ACASI questionnaire (listed as the National Inmate Survey-3) and the shorter paper and pencil survey form (PAPI) are available on the BJS website at www.bjs.gov.

Interviews checked for inconsistent response patterns

Once data collection was completed, individual response patterns were assessed to identify interviewer error, interviews that had been completed in too short of time, and incomplete interviews. In 141 interviews, the interviewers administered sex-specific survey items inconsistent with the sex of the inmate. In 693 interviews, the inmate failed to complete enough questions to be considered a completed interview. These interviews were excluded from the calculations of sexual victimization.

Interviews were also examined for inconsistent response patterns. A list of 31 indicators were developed based on inmate characteristics (e.g., education, age, marital status, and time since admission) and items related to victimization (e.g., number of times, injuries, willing contact with staff, sex of staff perpetrator, and reporting of victimization). Indicators compared responses to initial questions with responses to detailed follow-up questions. The indicators were identified as unlikely, highly unlikely, or extremely unlikely.

Of the 31 indicators, 21 were deemed unlikely, 7 were deemed highly unlikely, and 3 were deemed extremely unlikely. An example of an unlikely indicator is when a respondent indicated victimization occurred, but responded no to all types of victimization. An example of a highly unlikely indicator is when a responded indicated that the first time a victimization occurred was before the inmate was admitted to the facility. An example of an extremely unlikely indicator is if the inmate responded yes to 12 or more of the sex-specific victimization items and indicated being victimized 11 or more times to both staff sexual misconduct and inmate-on-inmate victimization. If any of the extremely unlikely indicators were triggered and at least one highly unlikely indicator or four or more unlikely indicators were triggered, the inmate's data were removed.

The amount of time the interview took was also reviewed. Inmates whose average time for the sexual victimization items was less than 2 seconds per item and inmates whose total time was less than 10 minutes for English respondents and less than 12 minutes for Spanish respondents had their data removed.

Overall, the results revealed very high levels of consistency in survey responses. Of the 92,689 respondents to the sexual victimization survey, 87 triggered one extremely highly unlikely flag. Of these, 20 met the additional criteria for removal. In addition, data for 12 respondents were removed because their interviews did not meet the length of interview criteria. Among the 32 cases that were removed, 1 respondent was in a federal facility, 13 respondents were in state prisons (2 were juveniles ages 16 to 17), and 18 respondents were in jails. These 32 inmates came from separate facilities (i.e., only one inmate from each of these facilities was removed) and were excluded from the calculation of sexual victimization.

Calculation of Body Mass Index (BMI)

BMI is a measurement of body fat, based on height and weight, that applies to both men and women ages 18 to 65. BMI can be used to determine if a person is underweight (18.5 or less), normal (18.5 to 24.9), overweight (25 to 29.9), obese (30 to 39.9), or morbidly obese (40 or greater). The calculation in the NIS-3 was based on the following formula provided by the Centers for Disease Control and Prevention:

$$BMI = weight\ (pounds)\ /\ [height\ (inches)]^2\ x\ 703.$$

Screening for serious psychological distress (SPD) and history of mental health problems

The NIS-3 included four items to measure the prevalence of any problems with emotions, nerves, or mental health an inmate may have had in the past:

R24. Have you ever been told by a mental health professional, such as a psychiatrist or psychologist, that you had…

   a. manic depression, a bipolar disorder or mania?

   b. a depressive disorder?

   c. schizophrenia or another psychotic disorder?

   d. post-traumatic stress disorder (PTSD)?

   e. another anxiety disorder, such as panic disorder or obsessive compulsive disorder (OCD)?

   f. a personality disorder, such as antisocial or borderline personality?

   g. a mental or emotional condition other than those listed above?

R27. During the 12 months before you were admitted to [this facility / any facility to serve time on your current sentence], did you stay overnight or longer in any type of hospital or other facility to receive treatment or counseling for problems you were having with your emotions, nerves, or mental health?

R30. At the time of the offense for which you are currently [being held / serving time], were you taking prescription medicine for any problem you were having with your emotions, nerves, or mental health?

R33. Have you ever received counseling or therapy from a trained professional, such as a psychiatrist, psychologist, social worker, or nurse, for any problem you were having with your emotions, nerves, or mental health?

Development of the K6

The K6 is a six-item scale designed to provide rapid assessment of the prevalence of serious psychological distress (SPD) in population surveys. (See page 25 for the six items and response categories.) Developed by Kessler and colleagues, the K6 has become widely used in epidemiological surveys throughout the world. It is included in three general population surveys in the U.S.—the Behavioral Risk Factor Surveillance System and the National Health Interview Survey (conducted by the Centers for Disease Control and Prevention) and the National Survey on Drug Use and Health (conducted by the U.S. Substance Abuse and Mental Health Services Administration).

The K6 has been recognized as a broad screener rather than a specific screener for any one mental disorder. Kessler and others have shown that the K6 outcomes are consistent with blinded clinical diagnoses of SPD in general population samples. Moreover, their statistical analyses of alternative scoring rules for the sex items have shown the unweighted sum (based on codes 0 to 4, with a total sum ranging from 0 to 24) to be virtually identical to sums using other weighting schemes. Although its use under PREA is to determine risk related to SPD and the incidence of sexual victimization, more specific screening scales could have been used to determine if sexual victimization was associated with particular kinds of mental disorder.

Prior to 2004, the K6 was used in the National Survey on Drug Use and Health (NSDUH) to estimate the prevalence of serious mental illness. In 2008, following the recommendation of a technical advisory group, convened by the Center for Mental Health Services at the SAMHSA, NSDUH supplemented the K6 scale with questions on functional impairment. Functional impairment is defined as difficulties that substantially interfere with or limit role functioning in one or more major life activities, including basic living skills; instrumental living skills; and functioning in social, family, and vocational or educational contexts.[7] However, the NIS-3 did not include any items related to functional impairment, since past measures and scales are not appropriate for inmates held in prisons or jails.

The use of K6 for predicting serious mental illness has never been validated in a correctional setting. It may be expected that some inmates feel nervous, hopeless, restless or fidgety, sad or depressed, or worthless due to their confinement rather than due to an underlying mental health disorder. Consequently, the exact cut point for serious psychological distress may be higher than 13 among inmates than among persons in the general population.

However, the link between SPD and sexual victimization rates remains strong, regardless of the exact cut point in the K6 scale. For example, had the cut point for serious psychological distress in the NIS been raised to 17 (from 13), inmate-on-inmate sexual victimization rates would have increased to 7.6% among prison inmates and 4.4%

---

[7]Gfroerer, J., Hedden, S., Barker, P., Bose, J., & Aldworth, J. (2012). "Estimating Mental Illness in an Ongoing National Survey," Federal Committee on Statistical Methodology, available at www.fcsm. gov/12papers/Gfroerer_2012FCSM_VII-A.pdf

among jail inmates, and staff sexual misconduct rates would have increased to 7.2% among prison inmates and 4.4% among jail inmates.

Imputation of missing data

SPD status was determined by the sum of the responses to the K6 items. Since some inmates did not respond to all six items, inclusion and imputation criteria were developed. Only respondents who answered at least four of the K6 items were included in the estimates of SPD status.

A missing K6 item was imputed in a nearest neighbor approach (i.e., the donor value for the imputed value was the nearest previous nonmissing K6 response). If the nearest K6 item was missing, then the value from the first nonmissing response preceding the missing item was used as the donor. For example, if item 2 was not answered, but item 1 was answered, then the value from the first K6 item was used as the value for the selected K6 item. If the first K6 item was missing, then the first nonmissing value that followed was used as the donor. Since only respondents who answered at least four of the K6 items were included in the analysis, the donor response was never more than two items away from the item with the missing response.

In prisons, among the 38,251 adult respondents, 555 (1.5%) answered fewer than four items and thus were not included in the estimates of SPD. Of the adult prison inmates who responded to four or more items, 931 (2.4%) had one or two items imputed.

In jails, among the 52,926 adult respondents, 1,106 (2.1%) answered fewer than four items and therefore were not included in the estimates of SPD status. Of the adult jail inmates who responded to four or more items, 1,840 (3.5%) had one or two items imputed.

Terms and definitions

Sexual victimization—all types of sexual activity, e.g., oral, anal, or vaginal penetration; hand jobs; touching of the inmate's buttocks, thighs, penis, breasts, or vagina in a sexual way; abusive sexual contacts; and both willing and unwilling sexual activity with staff.

Nonconsensual sexual acts—unwanted contacts with another inmate or any contacts with staff that involved oral, anal, vaginal penetration, hand jobs, and other sexual acts.

Abusive sexual contacts only—unwanted contacts with another inmate or any contacts with staff that involved touching of the inmate's buttocks, thigh, penis, breasts, or vagina in a sexual way.

Unwilling activity—incidents of unwanted sexual contacts with another inmate or staff.

Willing activity—incidents of willing sexual contacts with staff. These contacts are characterized as willing by the reporting inmates; however, all sexual contacts between inmates and staff are legally nonconsensual.

Staff sexual misconduct—includes all incidents of willing and unwilling sexual contact with facility staff and all incidents of sexual activity that involved oral, anal, vaginal penetration, hand jobs, blow jobs, and other sexual acts with facility staff.

Related prior publications

Eight BJS reports on sexual victimization in prisons and jails:

Sexual Violence Reported by Correctional Authorities, 2004 (NCJ 210333)

Sexual Violence Reported by Correctional Authorities, 2005 (NCJ 214646)

Sexual Violence Reported by Correctional Authorities, 2006 (NCJ 218914)

Sexual Victimization Reported by Adult Correctional Authorities, 2007-2008 (NCJ 231172)

Sexual Victimization in State and Federal Prisons Reported by Inmates, 2007 (NCJ 219414)

Sexual Victimization in Local Jails Reported by Inmates, 2007 (NCJ 221946)

Sexual Victimization in Prisons and Jails Reported by Inmates, 2008-09 (NCJ 231169)

Sexual Victimization Reported by Former State Prisoners, 2008 (NCJ 237363).

An overview of all of the BJS prison rape collections: *PREA Data Collection Activities, 2012* (NCJ 238640)

These reports are available on the BJS website at www.bjs.gov.

Males

E16. During the last 12 months, did another inmate use physical force to touch your butt, thighs, or penis in a sexual way?

E17. During the last 12 months, did another inmate, without using physical force, pressure you or make you feel that you had to let them touch your butt, thighs, or penis in a sexual way?

E22. During the last 12 months, did another inmate use physical force to make you give or receive a hand job?

E23. During the last 12 months, did another inmate, without using physical force, pressure you or make you feel that you had to give or receive a hand job?

E26. During the last 12 months, did another inmate use physical force to make you give or receive oral sex or a blow job?

E27. During the last 12 months, did another inmate, without using physical force, pressure you or make you feel that you had to give or receive oral sex or a blow job?

E32. During the last 12 months, did another inmate use physical force to make you have anal sex?

E33. During the last 12 months, did another inmate, without using physical force, pressure you or make you feel that you had to have anal sex?

E34. During the last 12 months, did another inmate use physical force to make you have any type of sex or sexual contact other than sexual touching, hand jobs, oral sex or blow jobs, or anal sex?

E35. During the last 12 months, did another inmate, without using physical force, pressure you or make you feel that you had to have any type of sex or sexual contact other than sexual touching, hand jobs, oral sex or blow jobs, or anal sex?

Females

E18. During the last 12 months, did another inmate use physical force to touch your butt, thighs, breasts, or vagina in a sexual way?

E19. During the last 12 months, did another inmate, without using physical force, pressure you or make you feel that you had to let them touch your butt, thighs, breasts, or vagina in a sexual way?

E24. During the last 12 months, did another inmate use physical force to make you give or receive oral sex?

E25. During the last 12 months, did another inmate, without using physical force, pressure you or make you feel that you had to give or receive oral sex?

E28. During the last 12 months, did another inmate use physical force to make you have vaginal sex?

E29. During the last 12 months, did another inmate, without using physical force, pressure you or make you feel that you had to have vaginal sex?

E32. During the last 12 months, did another inmate use physical force to make you have anal sex?

E33. During the last 12 months, did another inmate, without using physical force, pressure you or make you feel that you had to have anal sex?

E34. During the last 12 months, did another inmate use physical force to make you have any type of sex or sexual contact other than sexual touching, oral sex, vaginal sex, or anal sex?

E35. During the last 12 months, did another inmate, without using physical force, pressure you or make you feel that you had to have any type of sex or sexual contact other than sexual touching, oral sex, vaginal sex, or anal sex?

Appendix 2. Survey items related to staff sexual misconduct, National Inmate Survey, 2011–12

These next questions are about the behavior of staff at this facility during the last 12 months. By staff we mean the employees of this facility and anybody who works as a volunteer in this facility.

G4. During the last 12 months, have any facility staff pressured you or made you feel that you had to let them have sex or sexual contact with you?

G5. During the last 12 months, have you been physically forced by any facility staff to have sex or sexual contact?

G7. During the last 12 months, have any facility staff offered you favors or special privileges in exchange for sex or sexual contact?

G2. During the last 12 months, have you willingly had sex or sexual contact with any facility staff?

G11. [IF G2 OR G4 OR G5 OR G7 = Yes] During the last 12 months, which of the following types of sex or sexual contact did you have with a facility staff person?

G11a. You touched a facility staff person's body or had your body touched in a sexual way.

G11b. You gave or received a hand job.

G11c. You gave or received oral sex or a blow job.

G11d. You had vaginal sex.

G11e. You had anal sex.

Appendix 3. Follow-up questions for inmates reporting no sexual activity, National Inmate Survey, 2011–12

Follow-up questions for inmates reporting no sexual activity in the screener questions for sexual activity with inmates:

LCM1. During the last 12 months, did another inmate use physical force, pressure you, or make you feel that you had to have any type of sex or sexual contact?

LCM2. How long has it been since another inmate in this facility used physical force, pressured you, or made you feel that you had to have any type of sex or sexual contact?

1. Within the past 7 days
2. More than 7 days ago but within the past 30 days
3. More than 30 days ago but within the past 12 months
4. More than 12 months ago
5. This has not happened to me at this facility

Follow-up questions for inmates reporting no sexual activity in the screener questions for sexual activity with staff:

LCM5. During the last 12 months, have you had any sex or sexual contact with staff in this facility whether you wanted to have it or not?

LCM6. How long has it been since you had any sex or sexual contact with staff in this facility whether you wanted to or not?

1. Within the past 7 days
2. More than 7 days ago but within the past 30 days
3. More than 30 days ago but within the past 12 months
4. More than 12 months ago
5. This has not happened to me at this facility

APPENDIX TABLE 1
Characteristics of state and federal prisons and prevalence of sexual victimization, by facility, National Inmate Survey, 2011–12

Facility name	Number of inmates in custody[c]	Respondents to sexual victimization survey[d]	Response rate[e]	Inmates reporting sexual victimization[a]		
					95%-confidence interval[b]	
				Percent[f]	Lower bound	Upper bound
Total	386,307	38,778	60.4%	4.0%	3.6%	4.5%
Alabama						
Bibb Corr. Fac.	1,928	219	72.9%	5.8%	3.6%	9.4%
G.K. Fountain Corr. Fac./J.O. Davis Corr. Fac.	1,233	194	66.7	5.7	3.3	9.6
Julia Tutwiler Prison[g]	964	181	68.2	14.1	10.1	19.3
St. Clair Corr. Fac.	1,331	178	64.4	5.5	2.8	10.7
Alaska						
Anchorage Corr. Complex West	472	119	57.0%	5.9%	3.1%	10.7%
Hiland Mountain Corr. Ctr.[g]	412	139	76.0	12.9	8.5	19.1
Arizona						
ASPC - Douglas	2,512	163	55.6%	1.2%	0.3%	4.5%
ASPC - Eyman	4,919	200	41.2	4.1	2.0	8.2
ASPC - Perryville[g]	3,417	208	66.9	9.1	5.9	13.9
ASPC - Tuscon[h]	5,092	273	72.7	3.7	1.9	7.2
ASPC - Yuma	4,190	158	50.6	1.9	0.6	5.6
Florence Corr. Ctr.[h,j]	2,809	188	67.4	1.0	0.3	3.5
La Palma Corr. Ctr.[i]	3,023	163	45.1	0.0	0.0	2.3
Red Rock Corr. Ctr.[i]	1,525	62	18.8	2.9	0.8	10.0
Arkansas						
Ouachita River Corr. Unit	2,558	136	80.2%	4.2%	2.1%	8.5%
California						
Avenal State Prison	5,619	183	61.3%	1.2%	0.3%	4.4%
California Corr. Ctr.	3,527	120	39.0	2.1	0.7	6.0
California Corr. Inst.	4,939	161	38.7	5.4	2.4	11.5
California Inst. for Women[g]	1,952	146	51.6	6.7	3.8	11.3
California Men's Colony	6,273	168	51.8	1.5	0.6	4.2
California Rehabilitation Ctr.	4,173	137	45.2	2.5	0.8	7.3
Calipatria State Prison	4,408	92	30.8	2.3	0.8	6.4
Central California Women's Fac.[g]	3,745	196	67.6	10.1	6.5	15.3
Chuckawalla Valley State Prison	3,169	158	52.7	2.7	1.1	6.7
Corcoran State Prison	4,812	155	35.7	6.4	3.0	12.9
Corr. Training Fac.	6,635	214	66.4	3.2	1.6	6.3
Sacramento State Prison	2,827	93	29.7	3.3	1.2	8.7
Salinas Valley State Prison	3,589	143	45.8	3.8	1.8	7.6
San Quentin State Prison	3,495	156	50.3	3.8	1.6	8.6
Sierra Conservation Ctr.	3,451	187	59.8	1.4	0.5	3.9
Solano State Prison	4,649	202	64.8	2.0	0.8	5.0
Valley State Prison for Women[g]	3,513	178	56.3	11.5	7.5	17.2
Colorado						
Buena Vista Corr. Ctr.	929	128	55.3%	3.3%	1.5%	7.1%
Denver Women's Corr. Fac.[g]	777	160	68.2	19.3	13.8	26.3
Skyline Corr. Ctr.	248	95	54.9	3.7	1.4	8.9
Connecticut						
Manson Youth Inst.	446	242	84.3%	5.2%	3.4%	7.9%
York Corr. Inst.[g]	1,087	206	76.3	12.0	8.3	17.2
Delaware						
Central Violation of Probation Ctr.	216	138	88.3%	3.0%	1.7%	5.3%
Delores J. Baylor Women's Corr. Inst.[g]	360	165	82.9	13.6	10.0	18.3
James T. Vaughn Corr. Ctr.	2,538	167	57.4	5.3	2.7	10.0

Characteristics of state and federal prisons and prevalence of sexual victimization, by facility, National Inmate Survey, 2011–12

Facility name	Number of inmates in custody[c]	Respondents to sexual victimization survey[d]	Response rate[e]	Inmates reporting sexual victimization[a]		
					95%-confidence interval[b]	
				Percent[f]	Lower bound	Upper bound
Florida						
Apalachee Corr. Inst./West/East Unit/River Junction	2,230	161	56.9%	12.2%	8.0%	18.3%
Broward Corr. Inst.[g]	699	154	64.4	12.0	7.6	18.6
Calhoun Corr. Inst. and Work Camp	1,615	185	64.2	4.1	2.2	7.7
Central Florida Reception Ctr. East and South	2,057	115	48.0	0.0	0.0	3.4
Florida State Prison and Work Camp	2,082	133	44.2	5.2	2.6	10.2
Jackson Corr. Inst. and Work Camp	1,522	129	46.1	4.0	1.7	9.1
Lancaster Corr. Inst. and Work Camp	908	184	69.0	5.5	3.2	9.3
Lawtey Corr. Inst.	806	198	79.7	0.0	0.0	1.9
Levy Forestry Camp[g]	159	91	66.0	6.1	3.1	11.9
Marion Corr. Inst. and Work Camp	1,455	238	83.2	2.2	1.1	4.6
Martin Corr. Inst. and Work Camp	1,489	189	66.4	5.8	3.4	9.7
Northwest Florida Reception Ctr.	2,073	135	48.9	13.7	8.8	20.7
Santa Rosa Corr. Inst.	2,686	185	60.0	14.0	9.5	20.3
Taylor Corr. Inst. and Annex	2,996	206	67.1	2.7	1.1	6.0
Zephyrhills Corr. Inst.	656	156	62.5	7.9	4.7	13.0
Georgia						
Autry State Prison	1,662	132	46.2%	6.1%	3.3%	11.1%
Burruss Corr. Training Ctr.	763	228	79.7	0.6	0.1	2.6
D. Ray James Prison[i]	2,066	195	66.0	0.5	0.1	2.7
Lee Arrendale State Prison[g]	1,664	211	78.9	5.9	3.5	9.7
Macon State Prison	1,706	215	74.1	5.8	3.5	9.5
Rogers State Prison	1,479	235	80.2	2.2	1.0	4.8
Valdosta State Prison	1,457	139	50.6	10.5	6.5	16.7
Ware State Prison	1,521	231	78.0	4.6	2.7	7.8
Washington State Prison	1,537	216	82.3	2.2	1.0	4.7
Hawaii						
Waiawa Corr. Fac.	280	155	92.0%	6.2%	4.2%	8.8%
Idaho						
Idaho Max. Security Inst.	388	78	39.3%	14.0%	7.0%	25.9%
St. Anthony Work Camp	230	72	43.2	2.3	0.5	9.4
Illinois						
Danville Corr. Ctr.	1,833	206	69.7%	0.5%	0.2%	1.8%
Decatur Corr. Ctr.[g]	683	157	65.0	1.1	0.3	3.3
Dwight Corr. Ctr.[g]	1,029	203	81.0	10.7	7.1	15.6
Hill Corr. Ctr.	1,843	248	84.1	4.9	2.7	8.7
Menard Corr. Ctr.	3,660	162	51.4	2.6	1.1	6.0
Pittsfield Work Camp	401	79	35.7	0.0	0.0	4.6
Stateville Corr. Ctr.	3,670	229	74.2	1.0	0.4	3.0
Western Illinois Corr. Ctr.	1,932	156	55.0	3.7	1.6	8.1
Indiana						
Miami Corr. Fac.	3,168	203	65.5%	3.2%	1.5%	7.0%
Reception-Diagnostic Ctr.	645	148	63.2	2.4	1.1	5.5
Rockville Corr. Fac.[g]	1,140	224	83.1	7.6	4.3	12.9
Wabash Valley Corr. Fac.	2,080	169	49.1	3.2	1.3	7.7
Iowa						
Anamosa State Penitentiary	1,166	166	59.0%	4.5%	2.3%	8.7%
Kansas						
Lansing Corr. Fac.	2,241	191	66.3%	6.7%	4.0%	11.0%
Norton Corr. Fac.	808	128	61.6	5.1	2.6	9.9

Characteristics of state and federal prisons and prevalence of sexual victimization, by facility, National Inmate Survey, 2011–12

Facility name	Number of inmates in custody[c]	Respondents to sexual victimization survey[d]	Response rate[e]	Inmates reporting sexual victimization[a]		
					95%-confidence interval[b]	
				Percent[f]	Lower bound	Upper bound
Kentucky						
Eastern Kentucky Corr. Complex	1,704	154	50.3%	6.3%	3.6%	10.9%
Kentucky State Reformatory	2,039	156	53.3	6.4	3.6	11.3
Otter Creek Corr. Complex[i]	640	117	47.3	7.0	3.8	12.3
Louisiana						
B.B. Rayburn Corr. Ctr.	1,157	187	70.1%	4.1%	2.1%	8.0%
Elayn Hunt Corr. Ctr.	2,158	184	68.9	6.5	3.7	11.0
Louisiana State Penitentiary	5,351	220	69.5	8.5	5.5	12.8
Maine						
Maine Corr. Ctr.[h]	617	192	80.5%	6.1%	3.6%	10.2%
Maryland						
Maryland Corr. Inst. - Hagerstown	2,021	180	61.4%	3.1%	1.5%	6.4%
Maryland Corr. Inst. for Women[g]	827	151	54.8	12.7	8.5	18.4
Maryland Corr. Training Ctr.	2,653	203	64.7	3.4	1.7	6.8
Metropolitan Transition Ctr.	635	106	43.9	3.2	1.4	7.6
Massachusetts						
Old Colony Corr. Ctr.	856	181	69.3%	5.6%	3.4%	9.3%
Michigan						
Bellamy Creek Corr. Fac.	1,822	186	58.1%	4.4%	2.2%	8.6%
Central Michigan Corr. Fac.	2,455	226	76.0	2.7	1.2	6.0
Lakeland Corr. Fac.	1,368	222	78.0	5.6	3.4	9.3
Saginaw Corr. Fac.	1,459	215	78.0	2.9	1.4	6.0
Thumb Corr. Fac.	955	181	58.3	3.2	1.3	7.4
Minnesota						
MCF - Moose Lake	1,019	191	70.0%	4.4%	2.5%	7.8%
MCF - Shakopee[g]	564	156	67.8	13.0	8.4	19.6
Mississippi						
Pike Co. Community Work Ctr.	46	29	79.5%	0.0%	0.0%	11.7%
Walnut Grove Youth Corr. Fac.[i]	976	281	92.0	9.9	7.2	13.6
Wilkinson Co. Corr. Fac.[i]	881	173	66.8	7.5	4.6	11.8
Missouri						
Algoa Corr. Ctr.	1,485	152	53.3%	0.0%	0.0%	2.5%
Farmington Corr. Fac.	2,602	240	83.9	7.9	5.2	11.8
South Central Corr. Fac.	1,576	182	62.6	7.2	4.2	12.1
Tipton Corr. Ctr.	1,155	152	51.0	1.3	0.4	4.5
Western Missouri Corr. Ctr.	1,910	161	54.0	3.4	1.7	6.9
Western Reception, Diagnostic and Corr. Ctr.	1,876	187	67.1	1.5	0.5	4.1
Women's Eastern Reception, Diagnostic and Corr. Ctr.[g]	1,535	198	68.9	8.7	5.3	13.7
Montana						
Montana State Prison	1,443	191	65.3%	13.9%	8.8%	21.4%
Nebraska						
Lincoln Corr. Ctr.	491	141	64.2%	4.5%	2.4%	8.1%
Nevada						
Florence McClure Women's Corr. Ctr.[g]	705	142	61.0%	16.3%	10.8%	23.7%
High Desert State Prison	2,713	192	59.4	2.5	1.0	6.4
Lovelock Corr. Ctr.	1,609	191	61.9	3.8	1.8	7.6
New Hampshire						
New Hampshire State Prison for Men	1,370	193	69.2%	5.5%	2.9%	10.3%
New Hampshire State Prison for Women[g]	111	78	84.0	8.2	5.5	12.1
New Jersey						
Bayside State Prison	2,241	119	39.6%	3.4%	1.3%	8.6%
Mountainview Youth Corr. Fac.	1,060	151	53.2	3.1	1.4	6.7
South Woods State Prison	3,398	131	44.1	5.2	2.3	11.3

Characteristics of state and federal prisons and prevalence of sexual victimization, by facility, National Inmate Survey, 2011–12

Facility name	Number of inmates in custody[c]	Respondents to sexual victimization survey[d]	Response rate[e]	Inmates reporting sexual victimization[a]	95%-confidence interval[b]	
				Percent[f]	Lower bound	Upper bound
New Mexico						
Lea Co. Corr. Fac.[i]	1,137	135	51.4%	4.5%	2.2%	9.2%
New Mexico Women's Corr. Fac.[g,i]	599	157	65.2	14.3	10.1	19.9
New York						
Auburn Corr. Fac.	1,710	195	67.4%	9.8%	6.3%	14.7%
Cayuga Corr. Fac.	979	165	60.9	2.7	1.2	5.7
Gowanda Corr. Fac.	1,503	239	85.6	3.4	1.8	6.1
Lakeview Shock Incarceration Corr. Fac.[h]	950	233	85.4	1.9	0.8	4.3
Otisville Corr. Fac.	407	128	61.1	8.3	4.9	13.7
Washington Corr. Fac.	705	180	69.0	3.9	2.0	7.3
Wyoming Corr. Fac.	1,576	217	73.5	3.1	1.6	6.0
North Carolina						
Harnett Corr. Inst.	987	160	58.9%	3.6%	1.8%	7.0%
Lanesboro Corr. Inst.	982	161	37.0	3.3	1.5	7.1
Mary Frances Ctr.[g,i]	93	68	84.6	0.0	0.0	5.3
Maury Corr. Inst.	961	102	29.0	5.6	2.7	11.3
North Carolina Corr. Inst. for Women[g]	1,138	150	57.8	13.0	8.3	19.6
Odom Corr. Inst.	531	129	59.0	3.3	1.5	7.4
Western Youth Inst.	668	227	70.6	1.1	0.4	3.2
North Dakota						
North Dakota State Penitentiary	517	146	61.5%	5.3%	2.9%	9.3%
Ohio						
Allen Corr. Inst.	1,340	116	41.2%	3.2%	1.1%	9.0%
Belmont Corr. Inst.	2,648	167	55.0	2.4	0.9	5.8
Chillicothe Corr. Inst.	2,944	197	59.4	5.1	2.8	9.0
Franklin Medical Ctr.[h]	577	129	55.9	0.0	0.0	2.9
Madison Corr. Inst.	2,333	172	47.0	7.2	3.5	14.3
Noble Corr. Inst.	2,561	186	62.1	4.5	2.4	8.1
Northeast Pre-Release Ctr.[g]	553	157	65.5	7.6	4.5	12.3
Pickaway Corr. Fac.	2,185	188	65.4	5.3	2.9	9.5
Oklahoma						
Dr. Eddie Warrior Corr. Ctr.[g]	717	187	75.3%	9.4%	6.3%	13.8%
Jackie Brannon Corr. Ctr.	709	179	72.1	0.5	0.1	2.3
Mabel Bassett Corr. Ctr.[g]	1,054	193	70.1	17.5	13.1	22.9
North Fork Corr. Fac.[i]	2,326	46	17.2	1.7	0.3	8.7
Oregon						
Coffee Creek Corr. Fac.[g]	1,107	207	69.1%	10.8%	7.5%	15.3%
Deer Ridge Corr. Inst.	754	165	65.7	3.2	1.5	6.6
Oregon State Penitentiary	1,989	203	62.3	2.9	1.4	6.1
Pennsylvania						
Cambridge Springs State Corr. Inst.[g]	856	199	76.6%	4.1%	2.3%	7.3%
Chester State Corr. Inst.	1,237	195	70.0	1.5	0.5	4.1
Houtzdale State Corr. Inst.	2,268	175	55.7	1.8	0.6	5.4
Mahanoy State Corr. Inst.	2,323	202	68.6	0.9	0.3	3.2
Muncy State Corr. Inst.[g]	1,443	216	75.6	11.4	8.2	15.8
Pine Grove State Corr. Inst.	798	196	68.2	7.1	4.0	12.2
Somerset State Corr. Inst.	2,237	183	61.0	4.5	2.2	9.1
Waymart State Corr. Inst.	1,426	189	66.1	1.4	0.4	5.1
Rhode Island						
Donald Price Med. Security Fac.	290	151	81.9%	2.6%	1.4%	4.8%

Characteristics of state and federal prisons and prevalence of sexual victimization, by facility, National Inmate Survey, 2011–12

Facility name	Number of inmates in custody[c]	Respondents to sexual victimization survey[d]	Response rate[e]	Inmates reporting sexual victimization[a]		
					95%-confidence interval[b]	
				Percent[f]	Lower bound	Upper bound
South Carolina						
Camille Griffin Graham Corr. Inst.[g]	495	129	67.5%	8.7%	5.2%	14.1%
Kershaw Corr. Inst.	1,473	232	78.9	5.6	3.2	9.7
Kirkland Reception and Evaluation Ctr.	1,672	233	85.3	2.8	1.4	5.8
Turbeville Corr. Inst.	1,163	214	74.6	3.2	1.6	6.2
Tyger River Corr. Inst.	1,287	206	63.7	1.9	0.7	4.8
South Dakota						
South Dakota Women's Prison[g]	220	118	74.7%	13.2%	9.5%	18.1%
Tennessee						
Riverbend Max. Security Inst.	698	87	16.5%	1.2%	0.3%	4.1%
Texas						
Byrd Unit	1,095	183	60.9%	1.8%	0.8%	4.4%
Carole Young Medical Fac. Complex[g]	402	162	79.5	1.7	0.8	3.6
Clemens Unit	1,168	173	55.8	6.4	3.1	12.7
Clements Unit	3,631	141	43.6	11.9	7.6	18.0
Coffield Unit	4,113	210	66.1	7.9	4.9	12.4
Dawson State Jail[h,i]	2,202	188	63.7	2.4	1.1	5.1
Eastham Unit	2,439	207	68.1	4.7	2.7	8.2
Gist State Jail	1,997	213	72.2	1.5	0.5	4.1
Gurney Transfer Fac.	1,834	179	62.3	1.5	0.5	4.2
Henley State Jail[g]	423	138	69.0	2.4	1.0	5.8
Hodge Unit	928	154	21.9	2.1	0.8	5.3
Holliday Transfer Fac.	2,077	161	52.9	2.8	1.1	7.1
Huntsville Unit	1,530	171	67.1	0.9	0.2	2.9
McConnell Unit	2,905	172	54.2	5.3	2.8	10.0
Michael Unit	3,257	179	57.1	6.0	3.4	10.3
Montford Psychiatric Fac.	819	166	70.2	10.2	6.7	15.2
Murray Unit[g]	1,315	168	63.7	15.3	10.7	21.4
Plane State Jail[g]	2,175	175	63.0	4.4	2.2	8.9
Powledge Unit	1,119	170	61.3	2.9	1.0	8.0
Stiles Unit	2,935	151	49.4	11.9	7.5	18.6
Willacy Co. State Jail[i]	1,069	151	55.6	1.1	0.3	3.8
Woodman State Jail[g]	796	140	56.8	1.3	0.4	4.3
Utah						
Central Utah Corr. Fac.	1,105	193	69.9%	5.5%	3.2%	9.2%
Utah State Prison[h]	3,746	233	73.1	6.4	3.8	10.5
Vermont						
Southeast State Corr. Fac.	92	58	71.1%	5.1%	2.3%	10.9%
Southern State Corr. Fac.	359	109	55.3	9.9	5.6	16.9
Virginia						
Brunswick Women's Reception and Pre-Release Ctr.[g]	131	95	85.8%	0.0%	0.0%	3.9%
Dillwyn Corr. Ctr.	1,061	163	60.3	4.5	2.2	9.0
Sussex II State Prison	1,276	204	74.1	5.4	3.0	9.5
Washington						
Clallam Bay Corr. Ctr.	894	146	53.2%	5.1%	2.6%	9.6%
Monroe Corr. Complex	2,229	183	60.2	2.9	1.2	7.0
Washington State Penitentiary	2,017	119	41.2	5.2	2.2	11.9
West Virginia						
Huttonsville Corr. Ctr.	1,147	128	46.6%	8.1%	4.4%	14.6%
Wisconsin						
Green Bay Corr. Inst.	1,076	208	72.2%	4.8%	2.8%	7.9%
Oshkosh Corr. Ctr.	2,020	223	74.3	4.7	2.7	8.1

Characteristics of state and federal prisons and prevalence of sexual victimization, by facility, National Inmate Survey, 2011–12

Facility name	Number of inmates in custody[c]	Respondents to sexual victimization survey[d]	Response rate[e]	Inmates reporting sexual victimization[a]		
					95%-confidence interval[b]	
				Percent[f]	Lower bound	Upper bound
Wyoming						
Wyoming Honor Farm	153	97	69.9%	2.9%	1.5%	5.5%
Federal Facilities (Bureau of Prisons)						
CI Eden[i]	1,556	185	67.5%	0.0%	0.0%	2.0%
CI Reeves I and II[i]	2,395	180	63.7	0.0	0.0	2.1
CI Reeves III[i]	1,345	188	69.2	0.4	0.1	2.0
CI Rivers[i]	1,416	159	58.3	0.9	0.2	4.7
FCI Allenwood Low	1,398	149	52.4	1.9	0.7	5.2
FCI Big Spring Camp	209	70	45.7	1.2	0.3	5.0
FCI Butner Med. I Camp	328	99	49.1	0.0	0.0	3.7
FCI Butner Med. II	1,722	180	61.0	2.2	0.7	7.1
FCI Forrest City Med.	1,725	152	51.4	0.6	0.1	2.9
FCI Greenville Camp[g]	353	130	65.8	4.1	2.1	8.0
FCI Jesup	1,127	132	46.5	0.0	0.0	2.8
FCI Lompoc	1,413	164	57.5	0.6	0.1	2.8
FCI Manchester Camp	495	110	49.0	0.9	0.2	4.1
FCI Marianna Camp[g]	296	172	88.5	0.6	0.2	2.1
FCI Milan	1,525	163	58.6	2.4	1.0	6.0
FCI Seagoville	1,562	194	67.4	1.1	0.4	3.1
FCI Tallahassee[g]	1,250	157	60.2	5.8	3.2	10.3
FCI Terre Haute	1,182	92	34.6	2.2	0.5	8.2
FDC Philadelphia[h]	1,093	162	59.1	1.8	0.7	4.8
FMC Carswell[g]	1,413	193	64.6	4.2	2.3	7.5
FMC Devens	1,027	155	57.2	2.6	1.2	5.8
FMC Lexington Camp[g]	285	148	83.2	0.8	0.2	2.7
FPC Alderson[g]	1,130	237	83.6	2.7	1.2	5.9
Limestone Co. Det. Ctr.[i]	1,021	157	60.1	0.6	0.1	3.1
MCFP Springfield	1,163	80	33.5	1.8	0.6	5.2
USP Hazelton - Female[g]	487	111	49.0	5.2	2.6	10.2
USP Lee	1,479	101	32.3	1.7	0.5	5.7
USP Tucson	1,521	140	42.2	7.3	3.9	13.4

[a]Includes all types of sexual victimization, including oral, anal, or vaginal penetration, hand jobs, touching of the inmate's butt, thighs, penis, breasts, or vagina in a sexual way, and other sexual acts occurring in the past 12 months or since admission to the facility, if shorter.

[b]Indicates that different samples in the same facility would yield prevalence rates falling between the lower and upper bound estimates 95 out of 100 times.

[c]Number of inmates in custody on day when the facility provided the sample roster.

[d]Number of respondents completing the sexual victimization survey. (See *Methodology.*)

[e]Response rate is equal to the number of respondents divided by the number of eligible sampled inmates times 100 percent.

[f]Weights were applied so that inmates who responded accurately reflected the entire population of each facility on select characteristics, including age, sex, race, sentence length, and time served. (See *Methodology.*)

[g]Female facility.

[h]Facility housed both males and females; both were sampled at this facility.

[i]Privately operated facility.

Source: Bureau of Justice Statistics, National Inmate Survey, 2011–12.

Percent of prison inmates reporting sexual victimization, by type of incident and facility, National Inmate Survey, 2011–12

	Inmate-on-inmate[a]			Staff sexual misconduct[a]		
	Percent victimized[c]	95%-confidence interval[b]		Percent victimized[c]	95%-confidence interval[b]	
Facility name		Lower bound	Upper bound		Lower bound	Upper bound
Total	2.0%	1.8%	2.3%	2.4%	2.0%	2.8%
Alabama						
Bibb Corr. Fac.	3.1%	1.5%	6.0%	3.6%	2.0%	6.5%
G.K. Fountain Corr. Fac./J.O. Davis Corr. Fac.	4.4	2.3	8.2	2.3	1.0	5.2
Julia Tutwiler Prison[d]	10.0	6.8	14.6	6.8	4.1	10.9
St. Clair Corr. Fac.	3.2	1.3	7.6	3.5	1.4	8.4
Alaska						
Anchorage Corr. Complex West	3.7%	1.8%	7.5%	2.2%	0.7%	6.5%
Hiland Mountain Corr. Ctr.[d]	9.9	6.2	15.5	3.0	1.2	7.4
Arizona						
ASPC - Douglas	0.0%	0.0%	2.3%	1.2%	0.3%	4.5%
ASPC - Eyman	1.8	0.7	4.4	3.2	1.4	7.2
ASPC - Perryville[d]	7.5	4.6	11.9	2.1	0.8	5.4
ASPC - Tuscon[e]	1.3	0.5	3.9	2.4	1.0	5.4
ASPC - Yuma	0.5	0.1	3.0	1.4	0.4	5.0
Florence Corr. Ctr.[e,f]	0.5	0.1	2.7	0.5	0.1	2.7
La Palma Corr. Ctr.[f]	0.0	0.0	2.3	0.0	0.0	2.3
Red Rock Corr. Ctr.[f]	0.0	0.0	5.8	2.9	0.8	10.0
Arkansas						
Ouachita River Corr. Unit	3.0%	1.2%	7.2%	1.3%	0.5%	3.6%
California						
Avenal State Prison	1.2%	0.3%	4.4%	0.0%	0.0%	2.1%
California Corr. Ctr.	1.4	0.4	5.0	0.7	0.1	3.9
California Corr. Inst.	3.3	1.1	9.4	2.0	0.7	6.0
California Inst. for Women[d]	3.6	1.7	7.4	4.2	2.1	8.3
California Men's Colony	1.5	0.6	4.2	0.0	0.0	2.2
California Rehabilitation Ctr.	1.4	0.3	5.2	1.1	0.2	5.9
Calipatria State Prison	0.7	0.1	3.8	1.6	0.4	5.5
Central California Women's Fac.[d]	9.5	6.1	14.7	2.1	0.8	5.1
Chuckawalla Valley State Prison	2.7	1.1	6.7	0.0	0.0	2.4
Corcoran State Prison	2.4	0.9	5.9	4.3	1.6	11.0
Corr. Training Fac.	1.6	0.6	3.9	2.8	1.3	5.7
Sacramento State Prison	2.4	0.8	7.6	2.2	0.6	7.9
Salinas Valley State Prison	2.2	0.8	5.6	3.0	1.4	6.3
San Quentin State Prison	1.7	0.4	5.9	2.7	1.1	6.8
Sierra Conservation Ctr.	0.4	0.1	2.3	1.0	0.3	3.4
Solano State Prison	0.5	0.1	2.5	2.0	0.8	5.0
Valley State Prison for Women[d]	11.5	7.5	17.2	3.9	1.8	8.0
Colorado						
Buena Vista Corr. Ctr.	1.5%	0.5%	4.9%	3.3%	1.5%	7.1%
Denver Women's Corr. Fac.[d]	13.4	8.8	19.9	10.7	6.8	16.3
Skyline Corr. Inst.	0.0	0.0	3.9	3.6	1.4	8.9
Connecticut						
Manson Youth Inst.	1.3%	0.5%	3.1%	4.0%	2.5%	6.3%
York Corr. Fac.[d]	11.0	7.4	16.0	2.5	1.0	6.3
Delaware						
Central Violation of Probation Ctr.	0.7%	0.2%	2.0%	2.4%	1.2%	4.5%
Delores J. Baylor Women's Corr. Inst.[d]	10.7	7.4	15.3	7.0	4.6	10.3
James T. Vaughn Corr. Ctr.	3.6	1.7	7.6	1.7	0.5	5.7

Percent of prison inmates reporting sexual victimization, by type of incident and facility, National Inmate Survey, 2011–12

	Inmate-on-inmate[a]			Staff sexual misconduct[a]		
	Percent victimized[c]	95%-confidence interval[b]		Percent victimized[c]	95%-confidence interval[b]	
Facility name		Lower bound	Upper bound		Lower bound	Upper bound
Florida						
Apalachee Corr. Inst./West/East Unit/River Junction	7.3%	4.3%	12.1%	6.8%	3.7%	12.2%
Broward Corr. Inst.[d]	5.4	2.9	9.9	7.3	3.9	13.3
Calhoun Corr. Inst. and Work Camp	1.7	0.7	4.3	2.4	1.0	5.5
Central Florida Reception Ctr. East and South	0.0	0.0	3.4	0.0	0.0	3.4
Florida State Prison and Work Camp	2.8	1.0	7.2	3.3	1.5	7.1
Jackson Corr. Inst. and Work Camp	1.8	0.5	6.1	3.0	1.2	7.6
Lancaster Corr. Inst. and Work Camp	2.7	1.2	5.7	3.4	1.7	6.7
Lawtey Corr. Inst.	0.0	0.0	1.9	0.0	0.0	1.9
Levy Forestry Camp[d]	4.7	2.1	10.4	1.4	0.4	4.3
Marion Corr. Inst. and Work Camp	1.0	0.4	2.6	1.6	0.7	3.8
Martin Corr. Inst. and Work Camp	4.3	2.3	7.8	2.5	1.1	5.5
Northwest Florida Reception Ctr.	9.8	5.8	16.1	4.9	2.3	10.2
Santa Rosa Corr. Inst.	4.6	2.1	9.4	10.1	6.5	15.5
Taylor Corr. Inst. and Annex	0.4	0.1	2.2	2.2	0.9	5.5
Zephyrhills Corr. Inst.	2.9	1.3	6.1	5.5	2.9	10.3
Georgia						
Autry State Prison	1.9%	0.7%	5.2%	4.2%	2.0%	8.8%
Burruss Corr. Training Ctr.	0.0	0.0	1.9	0.6	0.1	2.6
D. Ray James Prison[f]	0.5	0.1	2.7	0.0	0.0	1.9
Lee Arrendale State Prison[d]	5.9	3.5	9.7	0.0	0.0	1.8
Macon State Prison	1.3	0.5	3.6	5.3	3.1	8.9
Rogers State Prison	0.0	0.0	1.6	2.2	1.0	4.8
Valdosta State Prison	5.0	2.5	9.8	6.5	3.4	11.9
Ware State Prison	0.4	0.1	1.8	4.6	2.7	7.8
Washington State Prison	0.0	0.0	1.7	2.1	1.0	4.7
Hawaii						
Waiawa Corr. Fac.	4.1%	2.6%	6.4%	2.1%	1.1%	3.9%
Idaho						
Idaho Max. Security Inst.	9.4%	3.9%	21.0%	8.2%	3.1%	19.7%
St. Anthony Work Camp	0.0	0.0	5.1	2.3	0.5	9.4
Illinois						
Danville Corr. Ctr.	0.5%	0.2%	1.8%	0.3%	0.1%	1.4%
Decatur Corr. Ctr.[d]	1.1	0.3	3.3	0.0	0.0	2.4
Dwight Corr. Ctr.[d]	9.2	6.0	14.0	4.2	2.2	7.9
Hill Corr. Ctr.	0.8	0.2	2.5	4.1	2.1	7.9
Menard Corr. Ctr.	0.4	0.1	2.4	2.6	1.1	6.0
Pittsfield Work Camp	0.0	0.0	4.6	0.0	0.0	4.6
Stateville Corr. Ctr.	0.0	0.0	1.7	1.0	0.4	3.0
Western Illinois Corr. Ctr.	2.2	0.8	6.1	3.0	1.2	7.4
Indiana						
Miami Corr. Fac.	1.6%	0.5%	4.9%	2.7%	1.1%	6.4%
Reception-Diagnostic Ctr.	1.3	0.4	3.9	1.2	0.4	3.6
Rockville Corr. Fac.[d]	5.8	3.2	10.4	1.8	0.5	6.5
Wabash Valley Corr. Fac.	1.7	0.5	5.7	2.3	0.8	6.3
Iowa						
Anamosa State Penitentiary	4.0%	2.0%	8.2%	0.5%	0.1%	2.4%
Kansas						
Lansing Corr. Fac.	2.9%	1.4%	6.2%	5.1%	2.8%	9.1%
Norton Corr. Fac.	1.6	0.5	5.2	4.5	2.2	9.1
Kentucky						
Eastern Kentucky Corr. Complex	2.0%	0.7%	5.6%	5.7%	3.2%	10.1%
Kentucky State Reformatory	3.4	1.5	7.7	4.5	2.2	8.9
Otter Creek Corr. Complex[f]	4.7	2.3	9.6	2.9	1.2	6.7

Percent of prison inmates reporting sexual victimization, by type of incident and facility, National Inmate Survey, 2011–12

Facility name	Inmate-on-inmate[a]			Staff sexual misconduct[a]		
	Percent victimized[c]	95%-confidence interval[b]		Percent victimized[c]	95%-confidence interval[b]	
		Lower bound	Upper bound		Lower bound	Upper bound
Louisiana						
B.B. Rayburn Corr. Ctr.	2.7%	1.1%	6.3%	2.1%	0.9%	5.0%
Elayn Hunt Corr. Ctr.	3.5	1.6	7.5	4.6	2.5	8.4
Louisiana State Penitentiary	3.5	1.7	7.0	6.3	3.9	10.1
Maine						
Maine Corr. Ctr.[e]	6.1%	3.6%	10.2%	1.8%	0.6%	5.1%
Maryland						
Maryland Corr. Inst. - Hagerstown	1.5%	0.5%	4.1%	1.6%	0.6%	4.4%
Maryland Corr. Inst. for Women[d]	8.4	5.2	13.2	5.6	3.0	10.3
Maryland Corr. Training Ctr.	1.6	0.6	4.5	2.4	1.0	5.3
Metropolitan Transition Ctr.	0.8	0.2	3.8	3.2	1.4	7.6
Massachusetts						
Old Colony Corr. Ctr.	3.1%	1.5%	6.1%	2.6%	1.2%	5.4%
Michigan						
Bellamy Creek Corr. Fac.	0.7%	0.1%	3.4%	4.3%	2.2%	8.6%
Central Michigan Corr. Fac.	1.3	0.5	3.5	1.8	0.6	5.1
Lakeland Corr. Fac.	1.7	0.7	3.9	4.0	2.1	7.4
Saginaw Corr. Fac.	0.4	0.1	2.1	2.9	1.4	6.0
Thumb Corr. Fac.	1.4	0.4	4.4	2.5	0.9	6.5
Minnesota						
MCF - Moose Lake	2.8%	1.4%	5.6%	2.6%	1.2%	5.5%
MCF - Shakopee[d]	12.8	8.2	19.4	0.5	0.2	1.5
Mississippi						
Pike Co. Community Work Ctr.	0.0%	0.0%	11.7%	0.0%	0.0%	11.7%
Walnut Grove Youth Corr. Fac.[f]	0.4	0.1	1.6	9.6	6.9	13.2
Wilkinson Co. Corr. Fac.[f]	1.1	0.3	3.4	6.4	3.8	10.6
Missouri						
Algoa Corr. Ctr.	0.0%	0.0%	2.5%	0.0%	0.0%	2.5%
Farmington Corr. Fac.	5.8	3.6	9.3	3.7	2.0	6.7
South Central Corr. Fac.	1.0	0.3	3.6	6.1	3.4	10.9
Tipton Corr. Ctr.	0.0	0.0	2.5	1.3	0.4	4.5
Western Missouri Corr. Ctr.	1.1	0.3	3.9	2.3	1.0	5.3
Western Reception, Diagnostic and Corr. Ctr.	0.0	0.0	2.0	1.5	0.5	4.1
Women's Eastern Reception, Diagnostic and Corr. Ctr.[d]	7.8	4.6	12.8	1.3	0.5	3.6
Montana						
Montana State Prison	9.0%	4.6%	16.8%	9.9%	5.3%	17.7%
Nebraska						
Lincoln Corr. Ctr.	0.5%	0.1%	2.1%	4.0%	2.1%	7.6%
Nevada						
Florence McClure Women's Corr. Ctr.[d]	16.3%	10.8%	23.7%	2.1%	0.8%	5.3%
High Desert State Prison	1.3	0.4	4.7	1.2	0.3	4.5
Lovelock Corr. Ctr.	2.3	0.9	5.7	1.5	0.5	4.4
New Hampshire						
New Hampshire State Prison for Men	2.2%	0.9%	5.3%	3.3%	1.3%	7.9%
New Hampshire State Prison for Women[d]	5.8	3.5	9.3	2.4	1.2	4.8
New Jersey						
Bayside State Prison	2.0%	0.6%	7.1%	1.4%	0.4%	4.9%
Mountainview Youth Corr. Fac.	0.8	0.2	4.2	3.1	1.4	6.7
South Woods State Prison	3.5	1.3	8.8	4.0	1.5	10.2
New Mexico						
Lea Co. Corr. Fac.[f]	1.3%	0.4%	4.4%	3.2%	1.3%	7.7%
New Mexico Women's Corr. Fac. [d,f]	12.2	8.3	17.5	6.0	3.4	10.5

Percent of prison inmates reporting sexual victimization, by type of incident and facility, National Inmate Survey, 2011–12

Facility name	Inmate-on-inmate[a]			Staff sexual misconduct[a]		
	Percent victimized[c]	95%-confidence interval[b]		Percent victimized[c]	95%-confidence interval[b]	
		Lower bound	Upper bound		Lower bound	Upper bound
New York						
Auburn Corr. Fac.	3.7%	1.9%	7.3%	6.0%	3.4%	10.4%
Cayuga Corr. Fac.	0.0	0.0	2.3	2.7	1.2	5.7
Gowanda Corr. Fac.	1.1	0.4	3.2	2.6	1.3	5.1
Lakeview Shock Incarceration Corr. Fac.[e]	0.5	0.1	2.4	1.9	0.8	4.3
Otisville Corr. Fac.	3.7	1.7	8.1	5.9	3.2	10.6
Washington Corr. Fac.	1.0	0.3	3.1	2.9	1.4	6.1
Wyoming Corr. Fac.	1.4	0.5	3.8	1.7	0.7	4.0
North Carolina						
Harnett Corr. Inst.	1.9%	0.8%	4.7%	1.9%	0.8%	4.7%
Lanesboro Corr. Inst.	0.0	0.0	2.3	3.3	1.5	7.1
Mary Frances Ctr.[d,f]	0.0	0.0	5.3	0.0	0.0	5.3
Maury Corr. Inst.	1.9	0.7	5.0	3.7	1.4	9.4
North Carolina Corr. Inst. for Women[d]	11.4	7.1	17.8	4.9	2.3	10.1
Odom Corr. Inst.	0.9	0.2	3.9	3.3	1.5	7.4
Western Youth Inst.	0.6	0.1	2.5	0.5	0.1	2.3
North Dakota						
North Dakota State Penitentiary	2.5%	1.1%	5.6%	3.3%	1.6%	6.9%
Ohio						
Allen Corr. Inst.	1.5%	0.3%	7.7%	1.7%	0.5%	5.7%
Belmont Corr. Inst.	1.6	0.6	4.6	0.7	0.1	3.8
Chillicothe Corr. Inst.	4.5	2.4	8.1	0.8	0.2	3.3
Franklin Medical Ctr.[e]	0.0	0.0	2.9	0.0	0.0	2.9
Madison Corr. Inst.	3.0	1.2	7.3	4.2	1.5	11.4
Noble Corr. Inst.	0.8	0.3	2.3	3.7	1.8	7.3
Northeast Pre-Release Ctr.[d]	5.2	3.0	8.8	2.4	0.8	7.0
Pickaway Corr. Fac.	3.2	1.5	6.7	2.1	0.8	5.3
Oklahoma						
Dr. Eddie Warrior Corr. Ctr.[d]	8.1%	5.3%	12.3%	2.4%	1.0%	5.5%
Jackie Brannon Corr. Ctr.	0.5	0.1	2.3	0.0	0.0	2.1
Mabel Bassett Corr. Ctr.[d]	15.3	11.3	20.6	3.4	1.8	6.6
North Fork Corr. Fac.[f]	0.0	0.0	7.7	1.6	0.3	8.7
Oregon						
Coffee Creek Corr. Fac.[d]	8.0%	5.2%	12.0%	4.7%	2.7%	8.1%
Deer Ridge Corr. Inst.	2.3	1.1	5.0	0.9	0.2	4.1
Oregon State Penitentiary	2.1	0.8	5.0	0.9	0.3	3.1
Pennsylvania						
Cambridge Springs State Corr. Inst.[d]	3.7%	1.9%	6.7%	0.9%	0.3%	2.7%
Chester State Corr. Inst.	0.5	0.1	2.3	1.0	0.3	3.6
Houtzdale State Corr. Inst.	0.0	0.0	2.1	1.8	0.6	5.4
Mahanoy State Corr. Inst.	0.0	0.0	1.9	0.9	0.3	3.2
Muncy State Corr. Inst.[d]	8.9	6.0	12.9	3.6	2.0	6.4
Pine Grove State Corr. Inst.	2.0	0.8	4.6	6.3	3.4	11.4
Somerset State Corr. Inst.	2.9	1.1	7.4	3.1	1.3	7.1
Waymart State Corr. Inst.	1.0	0.2	5.0	0.4	0.1	2.1
Rhode Island						
Donald Price Med. Security Fac.	0.9%	0.4%	2.4%	1.7%	0.8%	3.6%
South Carolina						
Camille Griffin Graham Corr. Inst.[d]	6.5%	3.6%	11.4%	3.0%	1.3%	6.7%
Kershaw Corr. Inst.	3.0	1.3	6.8	2.6	1.3	5.3
Kirkland Reception and Evaluation Ctr.	1.5	0.5	3.9	1.4	0.5	3.7
Turbeville Corr. Inst.	1.5	0.5	3.9	2.3	1.0	5.0
Tyger River Corr. Inst.	0.9	0.3	2.9	1.0	0.3	3.8

Percent of prison inmates reporting sexual victimization, by type of incident and facility, National Inmate Survey, 2011–12

Facility name	Inmate-on-inmate[a]			Staff sexual misconduct[a]		
	Percent victimized[c]	95%-confidence interval[b]		Percent victimized[c]	95%-confidence interval[b]	
		Lower bound	Upper bound		Lower bound	Upper bound
South Dakota						
South Dakota Women's Prison[d]	12.4%	8.8%	17.3%	2.6%	1.2%	5.4%
Tennessee						
Riverbend Max. Security Inst.	0.4%	0.1%	2.0%	1.2%	0.3%	4.1%
Texas						
Byrd Unit	0.9%	0.3%	2.8%	1.0%	0.3%	3.3%
Carole Young Medical Fac. Complex[d]	1.2	0.5	3.0	1.3	0.5	3.1
Clemens Unit	2.9	0.9	8.8	3.5	1.5	8.2
Clements Unit	6.8	3.8	11.7	9.5	5.7	15.3
Coffield Unit	1.1	0.3	3.8	6.8	4.1	11.1
Dawson State Jail[e,f]	1.4	0.5	3.9	1.6	0.6	4.1
Eastham Unit	2.3	1.0	5.1	2.9	1.4	5.9
Gist State Jail	0.6	0.1	2.9	0.9	0.2	3.1
Gurney Transfer Fac.	1.5	0.5	4.2	0.6	0.1	2.9
Henley State Jail[d]	1.7	0.6	4.9	0.8	0.2	3.2
Hodge Unit	1.9	0.7	5.2	0.7	0.2	2.6
Holliday Transfer Fac.	1.0	0.3	3.7	1.8	0.5	6.1
Huntsville Unit	0.5	0.1	2.6	0.3	0.1	1.7
McConnell Unit	3.4	1.4	8.0	2.3	1.1	4.9
Michael Unit	4.4	2.3	8.4	2.1	0.8	5.2
Montford Psychiatric Fac.	8.4	5.2	13.1	5.0	2.7	9.2
Murray Unit[d]	11.3	7.3	17.0	4.4	2.3	8.2
Plane State Jail[d]	2.1	0.9	5.2	2.3	0.8	6.5
Powledge Unit	1.8	0.5	6.5	1.1	0.2	5.2
Stiles Unit	7.8	4.3	13.8	6.2	3.2	11.4
Willacy Co. State Jail[f]	1.1	0.3	3.8	0.6	0.1	2.8
Woodman State Jail[d]	1.3	0.4	4.3	0.0	0.0	2.7
Utah						
Central Utah Corr. Fac.	3.7%	2.0%	6.9%	2.7%	1.2%	5.7%
Utah State Prison[e]	5.6	3.2	9.5	1.2	0.4	3.6
Vermont						
Southeast State Corr. Fac.	2.2%	0.7%	6.5%	5.1%	2.3%	10.9%
Southern State Corr. Fac.	7.7	3.9	14.6	4.8	2.2	10.3
Virginia						
Brunswick Women's Reception and Pre-Release Ctr.[d]	0.0%	0.0%	3.9%	0.0%	0.0%	3.9%
Dillwyn Corr. Ctr.	0.8	0.2	3.9	3.7	1.7	8.0
Sussex II State Prison	1.3	0.4	4.6	4.1	2.2	7.7
Washington						
Clallam Bay Corr. Ctr.	1.6%	0.5%	5.1%	3.5%	1.6%	7.5%
Monroe Corr. Complex	0.3	0.1	1.6	2.6	1.0	6.8
Washington State Penitentiary	3.3	1.1	9.4	1.9	0.5	6.9
West Virginia						
Huttonsville Corr. Ctr.	2.8%	1.0%	7.5%	6.5%	3.2%	12.8%
Wisconsin						
Green Bay Corr. Inst.	2.4%	1.2%	4.7%	2.4%	1.1%	5.1%
Oshkosh Corr. Ctr.	3.9	2.1	7.2	1.1	0.4	3.1
Wyoming						
Wyoming Honor Farm	1.0%	0.3%	3.0%	2.9%	1.5%	5.5%

Percent of prison inmates reporting sexual victimization, by type of incident and facility, National Inmate Survey, 2011–12

Facility name	Inmate-on-inmate[a]			Staff sexual misconduct[a]		
	Percent victimized[c]	95%-confidence interval[b]		Percent victimized[c]	95%-confidence interval[b]	
		Lower bound	Upper bound		Lower bound	Upper bound
Federal Facilities (Bureau of Prisons)						
CI Eden[f]	0.0%	0.0%	2.0%	0.0%	0.0%	2.0%
CI Reeves I and II[f]	0.0	0.0	2.1	0.0	0.0	2.1
CI Reeves III[f]	0.0	0.0	2.0	0.4	0.1	2.0
CI Rivers[f]	0.9	0.2	4.7	0.0	0.0	2.4
FCI Allenwood Low	0.5	0.1	2.8	1.4	0.4	4.5
FCI Big Spring Camp	0.0	0.0	5.2	1.2	0.3	5.0
FCI Butner Med. I Camp	0.0	0.0	3.7	0.0	0.0	3.7
FCI Butner Med. II	1.4	0.3	7.0	0.8	0.2	2.7
FCI Forrest City Med.	0.0	0.0	2.5	0.6	0.1	2.9
FCI Greenville Camp[d]	3.3	1.5	7.0	0.8	0.2	3.2
FCI Jesup	0.0	0.0	2.8	0.0	0.0	2.8
FCI Lompoc	0.0	0.0	2.3	0.6	0.1	2.8
FCI Manchester Camp	0.9	0.2	4.1	0.0	0.0	3.4
FCI Marianna Camp[d]	0.6	0.2	2.1	0.0	0.0	2.2
FCI Milan	1.2	0.3	4.0	1.3	0.4	4.4
FCI Seagoville	1.1	0.4	3.1	0.0	0.0	1.9
FCI Tallahassee[d]	4.0	2.1	7.8	2.3	0.8	6.1
FCI Terre Haute	0.5	0.1	2.7	1.6	0.3	8.3
FDC Philadelphia[e]	1.2	0.4	4.0	0.6	0.1	3.0
FMC Carswell[d]	4.2	2.3	7.5	0.4	0.1	2.2
FMC Devens	1.3	0.4	4.1	1.4	0.5	3.8
FMC Lexington Camp[d]	0.8	0.2	2.7	0.0	0.0	2.5
FPC Alderson[d]	2.3	1.0	5.5	0.4	0.1	1.8
Limestone Co. Det. Ctr.[f]	0.6	0.1	3.1	0.0	0.0	2.4
MCFP Springfield	1.2	0.3	4.2	0.6	0.1	3.4
USP Hazelton - Female[d]	4.4	2.0	9.2	0.8	0.2	3.7
USP Lee	0.9	0.2	4.8	0.7	0.1	3.9
USP Tucson	4.1	1.7	9.5	3.2	1.3	7.9

Note: Detail may sum to more than total victimization rate because victims may have reported both inmate-on-inmate and staff-on-inmate sexual victimization.

[a]Includes all types of sexual victimization, including oral, anal, or vaginal penetration, hand jobs, touching of the inmate's butt, thighs, penis, breasts, or vagina in a sexual way, and other sexual acts occurring in the past 12 months, or since admission to the facility, if shorter.

[b]Indicates that different samples in the same facility would yield prevalence rates falling between the lower and upper bound estimates 95 out of 100 times.

[c]Weights were applied so that inmates who responded accurately reflected the entire population of each facility on select characteristics, including age, sex, race, time served, and sentence length. (See *Methodology*.)

[d]Female facility.

[e]Facility housed both males and females; both were sampled at this facility.

[f]Privately operated facility.

Source: Bureau of Justice Statistics, National Inmate Survey, 2011–12.

Percent of prison inmates reporting sexual victimization by level of coercion, by facility, National Inmate Survey, 2011–12

| Facility name | Inmate-on-inmate[a] | | Staff sexual misconduct[a] | | Without force or pressure[d] |
	Physically forced[b]	Pressured[c]	Physically forced[b]	Pressured[c]	
Total	1.3%	1.6%	0.8%	1.4%	1.4%
Alabama					
Bibb Corr. Fac.	2.0%	1.8%	0.3%	1.5%	2.9%
G.K. Fountain Corr. Fac./J.O. Davis Corr. Fac.	3.5	3.1	1.0	1.7	1.3
Julia Tutwiler Prison[e]	5.0	7.8	4.0	5.5	2.4
St. Clair Corr. Fac.	2.5	3.2	1.1	2.9	1.7
Alaska					
Anchorage Corr. Complex West	3.7%	2.3%	1.2%	1.2%	1.0%
Hiland Mountain Corr. Ctr.[e]	5.9	8.3	0.7	3.0	1.6
Arizona					
ASPC - Douglas	0.0%	0.0%	1.2%	0.4%	0.4%
ASPC - Eyman	1.3	1.8	1.8	1.7	1.7
ASPC - Perryville[e]	4.3	6.5	1.3	1.8	1.7
ASPC - Tuscon[f]	0.6	0.7	0.6	1.6	1.2
ASPC - Yuma	0.5	0.0	0.5	1.4	0.0
Florence Corr. Ctr.[f,g]	0.0	0.5	0.5	0.5	0.5
La Palma Corr. Ctr.[g]	0.0	0.0	0.0	0.0	0.0
Red Rock Corr. Ctr.[g]	0.0	0.0	0.0	0.0	2.9
Arkansas					
Ouachita River Corr. Unit	2.2%	3.0%	0.4%	0.4%	0.9%
California					
Avenal State Prison	1.2%	0.5%	0.0%	0.0%	0.0%
California Corr. Ctr.	0.8	1.4	0.0	0.0	0.7
California Corr. Inst.	0.9	2.9	0.3	2.0	0.0
California Inst. for Women[e]	1.9	3.0	0.6	3.7	1.2
California Men's Colony	1.1	1.5	0.0	0.0	0.0
California Rehabilitation Ctr.	0.4	1.0	0.0	1.1	0.0
Calipatria State Prison	0.7	0.7	0.7	0.7	0.9
Central California Women's Fac.[e]	7.5	5.4	1.5	2.1	0.0
Chuckawalla Valley State Prison	1.5	1.8	0.0	0.0	0.0
Corcoran State Prison	2.0	2.0	0.0	1.7	2.6
Corr. Training Fac.	1.2	0.8	1.8	1.1	2.2
Sacramento State Prison	1.4	2.4	0.0	2.2	0.0
Salinas Valley State Prison	2.2	2.2	1.4	2.0	1.0
San Quentin State Prison	1.7	1.7	1.4	1.9	1.9
Sierra Conservation Ctr.	0.0	0.4	0.0	0.4	0.5
Solano State Prison	0.0	0.5	0.4	0.9	1.1
Valley State Prison for Women[e]	8.8	10.7	3.1	3.6	0.7
Colorado					
Buena Vista Corr. Ctr.	1.5%	1.5%	1.2%	2.8%	0.8%
Denver Women's Corr. Fac.[e]	9.7	11.8	7.3	8.8	3.2
Skyline Corr. Inst.	0.0	0.0	0.6	1.8	1.9
Connecticut					
Manson Youth Inst.	0.5%	0.8%	1.6%	2.2%	2.7%
York Corr. Fac.[e]	7.2	9.1	0.4	2.4	0.3
Delaware					
Central Violation of Probation Ctr.	0.7%	0.7%	0.8%	1.5%	1.6%
Delores J. Baylor Women's Corr. Inst.[e]	6.0	5.8	0.6	5.2	3.2
James T. Vaughn Corr. Ctr.	3.2	2.5	0.0	0.8	0.9
Florida					
Apalachee Corr. Inst./West/East Unit/River Junction	5.0%	6.9%	1.3%	2.4%	5.7%
Broward Corr. Inst.[e]	2.3	3.6	4.7	3.5	1.3
Calhoun Corr. Inst. and Work Camp	1.4	1.0	0.7	1.1	2.4
Central Florida Reception Ctr. East and South	0.0	0.0	0.0	0.0	0.0
Florida State Prison and Work Camp	2.3	1.6	0.9	1.4	2.9

Percent of prison inmates reporting sexual victimization by level of coercion, by facility, National Inmate Survey, 2011–12

| Facility name | Inmate-on-inmate[a] | | Staff sexual misconduct[a] | | Without force or pressure[d] |
	Physically forced[b]	Pressured[c]	Physically forced[b]	Pressured[c]	
Jackson Corr. Inst. and Work Camp	0.8%	1.8%	1.8%	1.9%	0.3%
Lancaster Corr. Inst. and Work Camp	1.6	2.0	1.1	2.2	2.8
Lawtey Corr. Inst.	0.0	0.0	0.0	0.0	0.0
Levy Forestry Camp[e]	4.7	3.6	1.4	1.4	0.0
Marion Corr. Inst. and Work Camp	0.6	1.0	0.7	1.2	1.6
Martin Corr. Inst. and Work Camp	1.3	4.3	1.5	1.5	1.0
Northwest Florida Reception Ctr.	6.9	6.9	1.8	2.9	3.4
Santa Rosa Corr. Inst.	2.5	3.5	2.4	6.4	3.5
Taylor Corr. Inst. and Annex	0.4	0.4	1.2	1.2	1.0
Zephyrhills Corr. Inst.	1.9	2.5	1.9	2.0	3.4
Georgia					
Autry State Prison	0.7%	1.9%	0.8%	0.8%	4.2%
Burruss Corr. Training Ctr.	0.0	0.0	0.0	0.0	0.6
D. Ray James Prison[g]	0.0	0.5	0.0	0.0	0.0
Lee Arrendale State Prison[e]	2.5	4.4	0.0	0.0	0.0
Macon State Prison	1.3	1.3	1.5	2.9	3.8
Rogers State Prison	0.0	0.0	0.0	0.4	1.8
Valdosta State Prison	4.2	4.0	2.2	3.0	2.6
Ware State Prison	0.0	0.4	1.7	2.2	3.4
Washington State Prison	0.0	0.0	0.9	0.5	1.7
Hawaii					
Waiawa Corr. Fac.	2.6%	3.3%	0.7%	1.4%	1.4%
Idaho					
Idaho Max. Security Inst.	8.3%	4.8%	6.0%	6.0%	5.9%
St. Anthony Work Camp	0.0	0.0	0.0	2.3	0.0
Illinois					
Danville Corr. Ctr.	0.5%	0.3%	0.0%	0.3%	0.0%
Decatur Corr. Ctr.[e]	1.1	0.0	0.0	0.0	0.0
Dwight Corr. Ctr.[e]	6.8	6.9	2.6	3.7	0.5
Hill Corr. Ctr.	0.3	0.8	1.2	3.3	2.2
Menard Corr. Ctr.	0.4	0.0	0.6	1.3	1.3
Pittsfield Work Camp	0.0	0.0	0.0	0.0	0.0
Stateville Corr. Ctr.	0.0	0.0	0.0	0.3	0.8
Western Illinois Corr. Ctr.	0.8	2.2	0.8	2.3	0.9
Indiana					
Miami Corr. Fac.	0.9%	1.6%	0.0%	1.5%	1.2%
Reception-Diagnostic Ctr.	1.0	0.3	0.0	0.0	1.2
Rockville Corr. Fac.[e]	2.6	4.0	0.3	0.0	1.4
Wabash Valley Corr. Fac.	0.0	1.7	0.8	0.8	1.5
Iowa					
Anamosa State Penitentiary	1.3%	4.0%	0.5%	0.0%	0.5%
Kansas					
Lansing Corr. Fac.	2.4%	1.9%	2.8%	3.2%	3.1%
Norton Corr. Fac.	1.6	1.0	2.6	2.6	2.8
Kentucky					
Eastern Kentucky Corr. Complex	1.2%	2.0%	1.6%	2.9%	5.0%
Kentucky State Reformatory	2.1	2.6	0.5	3.1	3.6
Otter Creek Corr. Complex[g]	1.4	3.9	0.7	0.7	2.2
Louisiana					
B.B. Rayburn Corr. Ctr.	1.2%	2.7%	1.7%	1.1%	0.9%
Elayn Hunt Corr. Ctr.	2.7	1.3	1.6	3.8	1.2
Louisiana State Penitentiary	1.6	3.5	2.2	3.3	4.6
Maine					
Maine Corr. Ctr.[f]	3.1%	4.4%	0.0%	1.8%	1.0%

Percent of prison inmates reporting sexual victimization by level of coercion, by facility, National Inmate Survey, 2011–12

| Facility name | Inmate-on-inmate[a] | | Staff sexual misconduct[a] | | Without force or pressure[d] |
	Physically forced[b]	Pressured[c]	Physically forced[b]	Pressured[c]	
Maryland					
Maryland Corr. Inst. - Hagerstown	1.0%	1.5%	0.6%	0.6%	1.6%
Maryland Corr. Inst. for Women[e]	4.8	5.1	0.9	5.6	1.4
Maryland Corr. Training Ctr.	1.6	1.0	0.6	1.4	1.4
Metropolitan Transition Ctr.	0.8	0.8	1.8	1.8	2.2
Massachusetts					
Old Colony Corr. Ctr.	2.5%	1.6%	1.5%	2.0%	1.1%
Michigan					
Bellamy Creek Corr. Fac.	0.7%	0.7%	1.1%	2.0%	2.7%
Central Michigan Corr. Fac.	0.4	1.3	0.7	0.7	1.8
Lakeland Corr. Fac.	0.8	0.9	2.4	3.5	2.7
Saginaw Corr. Fac.	0.4	0.4	1.5	1.1	1.6
Thumb Corr. Fac.	1.4	0.7	1.5	2.5	1.0
Minnesota					
MCF - Moose Lake	0.4%	2.4%	1.5%	1.6%	2.1%
MCF - Shakopee[f]	7.3	10.2	0.2	0.5	0.0
Mississippi					
Pike Co. Community Work Ctr.	0.0%	0.0%	0.0%	0.0%	0.0%
Walnut Grove Youth Corr. Fac.[g]	0.4	0.0	1.5	2.7	8.8
Wilkinson Co. Corr. Fac.[g]	1.1	0.6	0.5	1.9	5.7
Missouri					
Algoa Corr. Ctr.	0.0%	0.0%	0.0%	0.0%	0.0%
Farmington Corr. Fac.	4.7	4.2	2.4	3.2	1.7
South Central Corr. Fac.	1.0	1.0	2.2	1.8	3.0
Tipton Corr. Ctr.	0.0	0.0	0.8	0.8	1.3
Western Missouri Corr. Ctr.	0.7	0.4	0.0	0.6	2.3
Western Reception, Diagnostic and Corr. Ctr.	0.0	0.0	0.0	0.5	1.0
Women's Eastern Reception, Diagnostic and Corr. Ctr.[e]	6.2	4.1	0.4	1.3	0.4
Montana					
Montana State Prison	7.1%	5.0%	3.5%	8.0%	2.3%
Nebraska					
Lincoln Corr. Ctr.	0.5%	0.0%	0.7%	1.1%	2.8%
Nevada					
Florence McClure Women's Corr. Ctr.[e]	12.0%	11.3%	0.4%	2.1%	0.0%
High Desert State Prison	0.0	1.3	0.8	0.8	1.2
Lovelock Corr. Ctr.	1.5	1.5	1.2	0.2	1.0
New Hampshire					
New Hampshire State Prison for Men	1.7%	1.2%	2.4%	2.4%	0.9%
New Hampshire State Prison for Women[e]	4.3	3.3	2.4	2.4	1.2
New Jersey					
Bayside State Prison	1.2%	2.0%	0.0%	1.4%	0.0%
Mountainview Youth Corr. Fac.	0.8	0.8	0.8	2.6	1.8
South Woods State Prison	2.9	3.5	1.0	2.3	2.8
New Mexico					
Lea Co. Corr. Fac.[g]	0.6%	1.3%	0.0%	2.4%	2.4%
New Mexico Women's Corr. Fac.[e,g]	6.8	8.9	4.5	5.3	2.4
New York					
Auburn Corr. Fac.	3.1%	2.8%	3.0%	2.9%	1.8%
Cayuga Corr. Fac.	0.0	0.0	1.6	2.1	1.6
Gowanda Corr. Fac.	0.4	1.1	1.8	1.9	0.3
Lakeview Shock Incarceration Corr. Fac.[f]	0.5	0.5	0.9	1.4	1.3
Otisville Corr. Fac.	0.8	3.7	3.3	0.8	3.5
Washington Corr. Fac.	0.6	0.4	1.8	2.5	0.4
Wyoming Corr. Fac.	0.4	1.4	0.4	1.2	0.5

Percent of prison inmates reporting sexual victimization by level of coercion, by facility, National Inmate Survey, 2011–12

Facility name	Inmate-on-inmate[a]		Staff sexual misconduct[a]		Without force or pressure[d]
	Physically forced[b]	Pressured[c]	Physically forced[b]	Pressured[c]	
North Carolina					
Harnett Corr. Inst.	0.8%	1.4%	1.0%	1.5%	1.0%
Lanesboro Corr. Inst.	0.0	0.0	1.2	1.2	3.3
Mary Frances Ctr.[e,g]	0.0	0.0	0.0	0.0	0.0
Maury Corr. Inst.	1.6	1.0	1.1	0.0	3.7
North Carolina Corr. Inst. for Women[e]	7.1	9.1	2.5	2.5	4.0
Odom Corr. Inst.	0.9	0.9	0.9	0.9	1.6
Western Youth Inst.	0.0	0.6	0.0	0.0	0.5
North Dakota					
North Dakota State Penitentiary	1.6%	1.4%	1.6%	1.1%	2.8%
Ohio					
Allen Corr. Inst.	1.5%	1.5%	0.9%	0.9%	1.7%
Belmont Corr. Inst.	1.0	1.2	0.7	0.7	0.7
Chillicothe Corr. Inst.	3.0	2.3	0.0	0.6	0.2
Franklin Medical Ctr.[f]	0.0	0.0	0.0	0.0	0.0
Madison Corr. Inst.	2.3	3.0	0.0	4.2	0.0
Noble Corr. Inst.	0.5	0.6	1.7	2.1	3.2
Northeast Pre-Release Ctr.[e]	2.4	4.7	0.0	2.4	0.0
Pickaway Corr. Fac.	1.9	2.3	0.3	1.6	0.5
Oklahoma					
Dr. Eddie Warrior Corr. Ctr.[e]	6.7%	6.5%	1.7%	2.4%	1.2%
Jackie Brannon Corr. Ctr.	0.0	0.5	0.0	0.0	0.0
Mabel Bassett Corr. Ctr.[e]	9.5	13.2	1.4	2.5	1.5
North Fork Corr. Fac.[g]	0.0	0.0	0.0	0.0	1.6
Oregon					
Coffee Creek Corr. Fac.[e]	5.5%	5.5%	1.1%	3.9%	1.3%
Deer Ridge Corr. Inst.	1.2	1.7	0.0	0.9	0.0
Oregon State Penitentiary	1.1	2.1	0.9	0.5	0.0
Pennsylvania					
Cambridge Springs State Corr. Inst.[e]	2.8%	3.0%	0.0%	0.4%	0.5%
Chester State Corr. Inst.	0.0	0.5	0.7	1.0	0.0
Houtzdale State Corr. Inst.	0.0	0.0	0.0	1.1	0.7
Mahanoy State Corr. Inst.	0.0	0.0	0.0	0.5	0.5
Muncy State Corr. Inst.[e]	5.7	6.0	1.0	3.2	0.3
Pine Grove State Corr. Inst.	1.5	2.0	1.8	1.8	5.6
Somerset State Corr. Inst.	1.9	1.4	1.5	2.0	2.1
Waymart State Corr. Inst.	0.0	1.0	0.4	0.4	0.0
Rhode Island					
Donald Price Med. Security Fac.	0.9%	0.5%	0.4%	1.7%	0.8%
South Carolina					
Camille Griffin Graham Corr. Inst.[e]	3.3%	4.4%	0.7%	1.1%	1.2%
Kershaw Corr. Inst.	1.9	2.6	0.4	1.3	2.2
Kirkland Reception and Evaluation Ctr.	0.5	1.5	0.5	1.0	1.4
Turbeville Corr. Inst.	0.5	1.0	1.6	1.9	1.9
Tyger River Corr. Inst.	0.5	0.9	0.3	0.3	1.0
South Dakota					
South Dakota Women's Prison[e]	7.9%	9.9%	0.0%	1.9%	0.7%
Tennessee					
Riverbend Max. Security Inst.	0.4%	0.4%	0.4%	0.4%	1.2%

Percent of prison inmates reporting sexual victimization by level of coercion, by facility, National Inmate Survey, 2011–12

Facility name	Inmate-on-inmate[a]		Staff sexual misconduct[a]		
	Physically forced[b]	Pressured[c]	Physically forced[b]	Pressured[c]	Without force or pressure[d]
Texas					
Byrd Unit	0.9%	0.4%	0.4%	0.4%	1.0%
Carole Young Medical Fac. Complex[e]	0.4	1.2	0.8	1.3	0.5
Clemens Unit	2.0	2.6	0.3	1.5	2.0
Clements Unit	4.9	5.7	8.1	8.7	2.5
Coffield Unit	0.7	0.4	2.0	3.5	3.8
Dawson State Jail[f,g]	1.4	1.4	1.6	1.0	0.6
Eastham Unit	1.4	2.3	1.9	1.9	1.8
Gist State Jail	0.6	0.6	0.0	0.6	0.3
Gurney Transfer Fac.	1.5	0.5	0.0	0.6	0.0
Henley State Jail[e]	1.7	0.0	0.0	0.8	0.0
Hodge Unit	1.9	1.9	0.5	0.5	0.2
Holliday Transfer Fac.	1.0	0.7	0.7	1.8	0.7
Huntsville Unit	0.0	0.5	0.3	0.3	0.0
McConnell Unit	3.0	2.9	1.0	1.6	1.1
Michael Unit	3.8	2.3	1.1	1.1	1.0
Montford Psychiatric Fac.	5.2	7.3	2.9	4.5	2.0
Murray Unit[e]	6.9	7.4	1.0	3.6	1.1
Plane State Jail[e]	1.7	1.1	1.0	2.3	0.0
Powledge Unit	1.3	0.5	1.1	1.1	1.1
Stiles Unit	4.5	6.3	0.9	2.5	4.9
Willacy Co. State Jail[g]	0.0	1.1	0.0	0.0	0.6
Woodman State Jail[e]	0.8	1.3	0.0	0.0	0.0
Utah					
Central Utah Corr. Fac.	3.7%	2.8%	2.2%	1.5%	1.8%
Utah State Prison[f]	2.4	4.7	0.0	1.2	0.0
Vermont					
Southeast State Corr. Fac.	2.2%	2.2%	2.2%	2.2%	5.1%
Southern State Corr. Fac.	3.3	7.7	2.2	4.1	1.3
Virginia					
Brunswick Women's Reception and Pre-Release Ctr.[e]	0.0%	0.0%	0.0%	0.0%	0.0%
Dillwyn Corr. Ctr.	0.0	0.8	0.6	0.0	3.2
Sussex II State Prison	1.3	1.3	0.8	2.1	2.8
Washington					
Clallam Bay Corr. Ctr.	0.8%	0.7%	1.4%	1.4%	2.6%
Monroe Corr. Complex	0.3	0.3	0.4	0.4	2.2
Washington State Penitentiary	3.3	3.3	0.0	1.3	0.7
West Virginia					
Huttonsville Corr. Ctr.	2.0%	1.6%	0.9%	2.8%	4.7%
Wisconsin					
Green Bay Corr. Inst.	1.6%	0.8%	0.9%	1.5%	1.9%
Oshkosh Corr. Ctr.	1.6	3.1	0.4	0.7	0.4
Wyoming					
Wyoming Honor Farm	1.0%	1.0%	0.0%	2.0%	0.8%

Percent of prison inmates reporting sexual victimization by level of coercion, by facility, National Inmate Survey, 2011–12

Facility name	Inmate-on-inmate[a]		Staff sexual misconduct[a]		
	Physically forced[b]	Pressured[c]	Physically forced[b]	Pressured[c]	Without force or pressure[d]
Federal Facilities (Bureau of Prisons)					
CI Eden[g]	0.0%	0.0%	0.0%	0.0%	0.0%
CI Reeves I and II[g]	0.0	0.0	0.0	0.0	0.0
CI Reeves III[g]	0.0	0.0	0.0	0.4	0.0
CI Rivers[g]	0.9	0.9	0.0	0.0	0.0
FCI Allenwood Low	0.0	0.5	0.7	1.4	0.0
FCI Big Spring Camp	0.0	0.0	1.2	1.2	0.0
FCI Butner Med. I Camp	0.0	0.0	0.0	0.0	0.0
FCI Butner Med. II	1.4	0.0	0.0	0.4	0.8
FCI Forrest City Med.	0.0	0.0	0.0	0.0	0.6
FCI Greenville Camp[e]	0.0	3.3	0.0	0.8	0.8
FCI Jesup	0.0	0.0	0.0	0.0	0.0
FCI Lompoc	0.0	0.0	0.0	0.0	0.6
FCI Manchester Camp	0.9	0.0	0.0	0.0	0.0
FCI Marianna Camp[e]	0.6	0.0	0.0	0.0	0.0
FCI Milan	0.5	1.2	0.5	0.5	0.8
FCI Seagoville	0.4	1.1	0.0	0.0	0.0
FCI Tallahassee[e]	1.7	3.5	0.0	0.8	1.5
FCI Terre Haute	0.0	0.5	1.7	1.6	0.0
FDC Philadelphia[f]	0.6	1.2	0.0	0.6	0.6
FMC Carswell[e]	1.5	4.2	0.0	0.4	0.0
FMC Devens	0.7	1.3	0.0	1.0	0.4
FMC Lexington Camp[e]	0.8	0.0	0.0	0.0	0.0
FPC Alderson[e]	1.3	2.3	0.4	0.4	0.0
Limestone Co. Det. Ctr.[g]	0.6	0.6	0.0	0.0	0.0
MCFP Springfield	1.2	0.6	0.6	0.0	0.0
USP Hazelton - Female[e]	3.3	3.6	0.8	0.8	0.0
USP Lee	0.9	0.9	0.0	0.7	0.0
USP Tucson	1.2	4.1	0.6	3.2	2.5

Note: Detail may sum to more than total victimization rate because victims may report on more than one incident involving different levels of coercion.

[a]Includes all types of sexual victimization, including oral, anal, or vaginal penetration, hand jobs, touching of the inmate's butt, thighs, penis, breasts, or vagina in a sexual way, and other sexual acts occurring in the past 12 months or since admission to the facility, if shorter.

[b]Physical force or threat of physical force reported.

[c]Includes incidents in which the perpetrator, without using force, pressured the inmate or made the inmate feel that they had to participate. (See *Methodology*.)

[d]Includes incidents in which the staff offered favors or privileges in exchange for sex or sexual contact and incidents in which the inmate reported that they willingly had sex or sexual contact with staff.

[e]Female facility.

[f]Facility housed both males and females; both were sampled at this facility.

[g]Privately operated facility.

Source: Bureau of Justice Statistics, National Inmate Survey, 2011–12.

Percent of prison inmates reporting nonconsensual sexual acts and abusive sexual contacts, by facility, National Inmate Survey, 2011–12

Facility name	Nonconsensual sexual acts[a]			Abusive sexual contacts only[b]		
		95%-confidence interval[c]			95%-confidence interval[c]	
	Percent victimized[d]	Lower bound	Upper bound	Percent victimized[d]	Lower bound	Upper bound
Total	1.3%	1.1%	1.6%	2.7%	2.4%	3.0%
Alabama						
Bibb Corr. Fac.	0.8%	0.2%	2.5%	5.1%	3.0%	8.5%
G.K. Fountain Corr. Fac./J.O. Davis Corr. Fac.	2.3	0.9	5.5	3.4	1.7	6.7
Julia Tutwiler Prison[e]	6.1	3.6	10.1	8.0	5.1	12.2
St. Clair Corr. Fac.	0.0	0.0	2.1	5.5	2.8	10.7
Alaska						
Anchorage Corr. Complex West	2.6%	1.0%	6.7%	3.2%	1.4%	7.1%
Hiland Mountain Corr. Ctr.[e]	6.2	3.8	9.9	6.7	3.4	12.8
Arizona						
ASPC - Douglas	0.0%	0.0%	2.3%	1.2%	0.3%	4.5%
ASPC - Eyman	0.0	0.0	1.9	4.1	2.0	8.2
ASPC - Perryville[e]	4.7	2.6	8.3	4.5	2.3	8.5
ASPC - Tuscon[f]	1.6	0.6	4.6	2.1	0.9	4.8
ASPC - Yuma	0.5	0.1	3.0	1.4	0.4	5.0
Florence Corr. Ctr.[f,g]	0.0	0.0	2.0	1.0	0.3	3.5
La Palma Corr. Ctr.[g]	0.0	0.0	2.3	0.0	0.0	2.3
Red Rock Corr. Ctr.[g]	0.0	0.0	5.8	2.9	0.8	10.0
Arkansas						
Ouachita River Corr. Unit	0.8%	0.1%	4.0%	3.5%	1.6%	7.4%
California						
Avenal State Prison	1.2%	0.3%	4.4%	0.0%	0.0%	2.1%
California Corr. Ctr.	1.4	0.4	5.0	0.7	0.1	3.9
California Corr. Inst.	4.5	1.8	10.4	0.9	0.2	4.8
California Inst. for Women[e]	1.4	0.4	4.6	5.3	2.9	9.5
California Men's Colony	0.0	0.0	2.2	1.5	0.6	4.2
California Rehabilitation Ctr.	1.5	0.4	5.9	1.0	0.2	5.1
Calipatria State Prison	1.4	0.4	4.9	0.9	0.2	4.7
Central California Women's Fac.[e]	4.8	2.6	8.6	5.3	2.8	9.8
Chuckawalla Valley State Prison	2.2	0.8	6.2	0.5	0.1	2.5
Corcoran State Prison	1.6	0.5	5.3	4.7	1.9	11.3
Corr. Training Fac.	0.9	0.2	3.0	2.4	1.1	5.2
Sacramento State Prison	0.9	0.2	4.7	2.4	0.8	7.6
Salinas Valley State Prison	1.0	0.3	3.6	2.7	1.2	6.3
San Quentin State Prison	0.0	0.0	2.4	3.8	1.6	8.6
Sierra Conservation Ctr.	0.0	0.0	2.0	1.4	0.5	3.9
Solano State Prison	0.5	0.1	2.5	1.5	0.5	4.4
Valley State Prison for Women[e]	6.1	3.4	10.7	5.4	2.8	10.0
Colorado						
Buena Vista Corr. Ctr.	1.2%	0.4%	4.1%	2.1%	0.7%	5.5%
Denver Women's Corr. Fac.[e]	7.0	3.8	12.6	12.2	8.0	18.3
Skyline Corr. Inst.	2.4	0.8	7.5	1.2	0.3	4.8
Connecticut						
Manson Youth Inst.	1.7%	0.8%	3.6%	3.5%	2.1%	5.8%
York Corr. Fac.[e]	6.5	4.1	10.3	5.5	3.0	10.0
Delaware						
Central Violation of Probation Ctr.	0.0%	0.0%	2.7%	3.0%	1.7%	5.3%
Delores J. Baylor Women's Corr. Inst.[e]	6.2	3.8	10.0	7.4	4.9	11.0
James T. Vaughn Corr. Ctr.	1.5	0.4	5.1	3.8	1.8	8.0

Percent of prison inmates reporting nonconsensual sexual acts and abusive sexual contacts, by facility, National Inmate Survey, 2011–12

Facility name	Nonconsensual sexual acts[a]			Abusive sexual contacts only[b]		
		95%-confidence interval[c]			95%-confidence interval[c]	
	Percent victimized[d]	Lower bound	Upper bound	Percent victimized[d]	Lower bound	Upper bound
Florida						
Apalachee Corr. Inst./West/East Unit/River Junction	4.5%	2.3%	8.6%	7.7%	4.4%	13.3%
Broward Corr. Inst.[e]	5.0	2.5	9.5	7.1	3.7	13.1
Calhoun Corr. Inst. and Work Camp	1.2	0.4	3.7	2.9	1.4	6.1
Central Florida Reception Ctr. East and South	0.0	0.0	3.4	0.0	0.0	3.4
Florida State Prison and Work Camp	1.9	0.5	6.7	3.3	1.5	7.1
Jackson Corr. Inst. and Work Camp	2.5	0.9	7.0	1.5	0.4	5.7
Lancaster Corr. Inst. and Work Camp	2.2	0.9	5.0	3.3	1.6	6.6
Lawtey Corr. Inst.	0.0	0.0	1.9	0.0	0.0	1.9
Levy Forestry Camp[e]	1.6	0.7	4.0	4.5	1.9	10.4
Marion Corr. Inst. and Work Camp	0.3	0.1	1.6	1.9	0.9	4.2
Martin Corr. Inst. and Work Camp	1.2	0.3	3.9	4.7	2.6	8.2
Northwest Florida Reception Ctr.	3.3	1.5	7.4	10.4	6.1	17.0
Santa Rosa Corr. Inst.	4.4	2.2	8.7	9.6	5.9	15.2
Taylor Corr. Inst. and Annex	1.1	0.3	3.7	1.6	0.5	4.5
Zephyrhills Corr. Inst.	0.5	0.1	2.5	7.4	4.3	12.4
Georgia						
Autry State Prison	0.0%	0.0%	2.8%	6.1%	3.3%	11.1%
Burruss Corr. Training Ctr.	0.0	0.0	1.9	0.6	0.1	2.6
D. Ray James Prison[g]	0.0	0.0	1.9	0.5	0.1	2.7
Lee Arrendale State Prison[e]	3.5	1.7	6.8	2.4	1.1	5.3
Macon State Prison	0.0	0.0	1.8	5.8	3.5	9.5
Rogers State Prison	0.0	0.0	1.6	2.2	1.0	4.8
Valdosta State Prison	4.0	1.9	8.4	6.5	3.4	12.0
Ware State Prison	0.0	0.0	1.7	4.6	2.7	7.8
Washington State Prison	0.0	0.0	1.7	2.1	1.0	4.7
Hawaii						
Waiawa Corr. Fac.	2.1%	1.1%	4.0%	4.0%	2.5%	6.3%
Idaho						
Idaho Max. Security Inst.	6.9%	2.6%	17.1%	7.0%	2.5%	18.0%
St. Anthony Work Camp	2.3	0.5	9.4	0.0	0.0	5.1
Illinois						
Danville Corr. Ctr.	0.5%	0.2%	1.8%	0.0%	0.0%	1.8%
Decatur Corr. Ctr.[e]	1.1	0.3	3.3	0.0	0.0	2.4
Dwight Corr. Ctr.[e]	4.0	2.1	7.4	6.7	3.9	11.0
Hill Corr. Ctr.	1.9	0.8	4.5	3.0	1.4	6.5
Menard Corr. Ctr.	1.0	0.3	3.5	1.6	0.5	4.6
Pittsfield Work Camp	0.0	0.0	4.6	0.0	0.0	4.6
Stateville Corr. Ctr.	0.3	0.1	1.5	0.8	0.2	2.7
Western Illinois Corr. Ctr.	0.0	0.0	2.4	3.7	1.6	8.1
Indiana						
Miami Corr. Fac.	0.0%	0.0%	1.9%	3.2%	1.5%	7.0%
Reception-Diagnostic Ctr.	1.2	0.3	3.9	1.3	0.4	3.6
Rockville Corr. Fac.[e]	4.1	2.0	8.3	3.5	1.5	8.1
Wabash Valley Corr. Fac.	0.8	0.1	4.0	2.4	0.9	6.7
Iowa						
Anamosa State Penitentiary	2.1%	0.7%	5.5%	2.5%	1.0%	5.9%
Kansas						
Lansing Corr. Fac.	2.1%	0.8%	5.2%	4.5%	2.4%	8.4%
Norton Corr. Fac.	2.2	0.8	5.8	2.9	1.2	7.1

Percent of prison inmates reporting nonconsensual sexual acts and abusive sexual contacts, by facility, National Inmate Survey, 2011–12

Facility name	Nonconsensual sexual acts[a]			Abusive sexual contacts only[b]		
		95%-confidence interval[c]			95%-confidence interval[c]	
	Percent victimized[d]	Lower bound	Upper bound	Percent victimized[d]	Lower bound	Upper bound
Kentucky						
Eastern Kentucky Corr. Complex	1.0%	0.3%	3.4%	5.4%	2.9%	9.7%
Kentucky State Reformatory	2.0	0.7	5.6	4.4	2.2	8.8
Otter Creek Corr. Complex[g]	1.3	0.4	4.2	5.7	2.9	10.9
Louisiana						
B.B. Rayburn Corr. Ctr.	1.0%	0.3%	3.1%	3.2%	1.4%	6.9%
Elayn Hunt Corr. Ctr.	2.5	0.9	6.3	4.0	2.1	7.6
Louisiana State Penitentiary	1.1	0.3	3.7	7.4	4.7	11.5
Maine						
Maine Corr. Ctr.[f]	2.6%	1.3%	5.4%	3.5%	1.6%	7.2%
Maryland						
Maryland Corr. Inst. - Hagerstown	0.0%	0.0%	2.1%	3.1%	1.5%	6.4%
Maryland Corr. Inst. for Women[e]	5.8	3.1	10.6	6.9	4.1	11.4
Maryland Corr. Training Ctr.	1.5	0.5	4.1	2.0	0.8	4.8
Metropolitan Transition Ctr.	0.0	0.0	3.5	3.2	1.4	7.6
Massachusetts						
Old Colony Corr. Ctr.	3.2%	1.6%	6.4%	2.4%	1.1%	5.1%
Michigan						
Bellamy Creek Corr. Fac.	0.7%	0.1%	3.4%	3.7%	1.7%	7.7%
Central Michigan Corr. Fac.	0.0	0.0	1.7	2.7	1.2	6.0
Lakeland Corr. Fac.	0.8	0.2	2.7	4.8	2.7	8.4
Saginaw Corr. Fac.	0.8	0.2	3.1	2.1	0.9	4.9
Thumb Corr. Fac.	1.5	0.5	4.9	1.7	0.5	5.4
Minnesota						
MCF - Moose Lake	2.5%	1.2%	5.4%	1.9%	0.8%	4.5%
MCF - Shakopee[e]	7.6	4.5	12.6	5.4	2.5	11.4
Mississippi						
Pike Co. Community Work Ctr.	0.0%	0.0%	11.7%	0.0%	0.0%	11.7%
Walnut Grove Youth Corr. Fac.[g]	1.2	0.5	3.1	8.7	6.1	12.2
Wilkinson Co. Corr. Fac.[g]	1.8	0.7	4.6	5.7	3.3	9.7
Missouri						
Algoa Corr. Ctr.	0.0%	0.0%	2.5%	0.0%	0.0%	2.5%
Farmington Corr. Fac.	3.0	1.5	5.7	4.9	2.9	8.3
South Central Corr. Fac.	2.0	0.7	5.7	5.1	2.7	9.5
Tipton Corr. Ctr.	0.6	0.1	2.8	0.8	0.2	3.9
Western Missouri Corr. Ctr.	0.7	0.1	3.7	2.7	1.3	5.8
Western Reception, Diagnostic and Corr. Ctr.	0.0	0.0	2.0	1.5	0.5	4.1
Women's Eastern Reception, Diagnostic and Corr. Ctr.[e]	6.0	3.4	10.5	2.6	1.1	6.4
Montana						
Montana State Prison	5.6%	3.2%	9.6%	8.3%	4.1%	16.1%
Nebraska						
Lincoln Corr. Ctr.	1.3%	0.5%	3.5%	3.2%	1.5%	6.6%
Nevada						
Florence McClure Women's Corr. Ctr.[e]	10.9%	6.3%	18.3%	5.4%	2.9%	9.6%
High Desert State Prison	0.5	0.1	2.5	2.1	0.7	5.9
Lovelock Corr. Ctr.	1.6	0.6	4.7	2.1	0.8	5.4
New Hampshire						
New Hampshire State Prison for Men	1.7%	0.6%	4.7%	3.8%	1.7%	8.4%
New Hampshire State Prison for Women[e]	4.3	2.4	7.6	3.9	2.2	6.7
New Jersey						
Bayside State Prison	0.0%	0.0%	3.1%	3.4%	1.3%	8.6%
Mountainview Youth Corr. Fac.	0.6	0.1	3.2	2.4	1.0	5.9
South Woods State Prison	1.3	0.2	6.6	4.0	1.6	9.3

Percent of prison inmates reporting nonconsensual sexual acts and abusive sexual contacts, by facility, National Inmate Survey, 2011–12

Facility name	Nonconsensual sexual acts[a]			Abusive sexual contacts only[b]		
		95%-confidence interval[c]			95%-confidence interval[c]	
	Percent victimized[d]	Lower bound	Upper bound	Percent victimized[d]	Lower bound	Upper bound
New Mexico						
Lea Co. Corr. Fac.[g]	0.9%	0.2%	4.4%	3.7%	1.6%	8.0%
New Mexico Women's Corr. Fac.[e,g]	5.2	2.9	9.2	9.1	5.8	14.0
New York						
Auburn Corr. Fac.	4.0%	2.1%	7.6%	5.8%	3.2%	10.0%
Cayuga Corr. Fac.	0.5	0.1	2.6	2.1	0.9	5.0
Gowanda Corr. Fac.	0.2	0.0	1.2	3.1	1.7	5.9
Lakeview Shock Incarceration Corr. Fac.[f]	0.0	0.0	1.8	1.9	0.8	4.3
Otisville Corr. Fac.	0.6	0.1	2.4	7.7	4.4	13.2
Washington Corr. Fac.	0.6	0.1	2.7	3.3	1.6	6.5
Wyoming Corr. Fac.	1.3	0.5	3.5	1.8	0.7	4.3
North Carolina						
Harnett Corr. Inst.	0.9%	0.3%	3.1%	2.7%	1.2%	5.9%
Lanesboro Corr. Inst.	0.0	0.0	2.3	3.3	1.5	7.1
Mary Frances Ctr.[e,g]	0.0	0.0	5.3	0.0	0.0	5.3
Maury Corr. Inst.	2.1	0.8	5.4	3.5	1.3	9.2
North Carolina Corr. Inst. for Women[e]	4.9	2.4	9.6	8.0	4.5	14.1
Odom Corr. Inst.	0.0	0.0	2.9	3.3	1.5	7.4
Western Youth Inst.	0.0	0.0	2.3	1.1	0.4	3.2
North Dakota						
North Dakota State Penitentiary	1.6%	0.6%	4.1%	3.6%	1.7%	7.5%
Ohio						
Allen Corr. Inst.	1.5%	0.3%	7.7%	1.7%	0.5%	5.7%
Belmont Corr. Inst.	0.5	0.1	2.5	1.9	0.7	5.3
Chillicothe Corr. Inst.	2.6	1.2	5.7	2.5	1.0	5.8
Franklin Medical Ctr.[f]	0.0	0.0	2.9	0.0	0.0	2.9
Madison Corr. Inst.	0.0	0.0	2.7	7.2	3.5	14.3
Noble Corr. Inst.	0.5	0.2	1.9	3.9	2.0	7.6
Northeast Pre-Release Ctr.[e]	4.7	2.7	8.3	2.8	1.1	7.3
Pickaway Corr. Fac.	2.9	1.2	6.5	2.5	1.1	5.5
Oklahoma						
Dr. Eddie Warrior Corr. Ctr.[e]	5.4%	3.2%	9.1%	4.0%	2.1%	7.3%
Jackie Brannon Corr. Ctr.	0.0	0.0	2.1	0.5	0.1	2.3
Mabel Bassett Corr. Ctr.[e]	8.5	5.6	12.8	8.9	5.8	13.4
North Fork Corr. Fac.[g]	0.0	0.0	7.7	1.6	0.3	8.7
Oregon						
Coffee Creek Corr. Fac.[e]	6.5%	4.1%	10.2%	4.3%	2.4%	7.6%
Deer Ridge Corr. Inst.	0.9	0.3	2.9	2.3	1.0	5.6
Oregon State Penitentiary	0.0	0.0	1.9	2.9	1.4	6.1
Pennsylvania						
Cambridge Springs State Corr. Inst.[e]	2.0%	0.9%	4.2%	2.2%	0.9%	5.1%
Chester State Corr. Inst.	1.2	0.3	3.8	0.4	0.1	1.8
Houtzdale State Corr. Inst.	0.8	0.2	4.2	1.0	0.3	3.8
Mahanoy State Corr. Inst.	0.5	0.1	2.4	0.5	0.1	2.5
Muncy State Corr. Inst.[e]	5.7	3.5	9.2	5.7	3.5	9.1
Pine Grove State Corr. Inst.	1.7	0.7	4.5	5.4	2.7	10.4
Somerset State Corr. Inst.	1.4	0.4	5.2	3.1	1.3	7.1
Waymart State Corr. Inst.	0.4	0.1	2.1	1.0	0.2	5.0
Rhode Island						
Donald Price Med. Security Fac.	1.2%	0.5%	3.0%	1.4%	0.7%	3.0%

Percent of prison inmates reporting nonconsensual sexual acts and abusive sexual contacts, by facility, National Inmate Survey, 2011–12

Facility name	Nonconsensual sexual acts[a]			Abusive sexual contacts only[b]		
		95%-confidence interval[c]			95%-confidence interval[c]	
	Percent victimized[d]	Lower bound	Upper bound	Percent victimized[d]	Lower bound	Upper bound
South Carolina						
Camille Griffin Graham Corr. Inst.[e]	4.4%	2.1%	9.1%	4.3%	2.2%	8.4%
Kershaw Corr. Inst.	1.3	0.5	3.6	4.3	2.2	8.2
Kirkland Reception and Evaluation Ctr.	0.4	0.1	2.2	2.4	1.1	5.2
Turbeville Corr. Inst.	0.9	0.3	2.8	2.3	1.0	5.2
Tyger River Corr. Inst.	0.3	0.1	1.3	1.6	0.6	4.5
South Dakota						
South Dakota Women's Prison[e]	8.6%	5.6%	13.1%	4.6%	2.7%	7.7%
Tennessee						
Riverbend Max. Security Inst.	0.8%	0.2%	3.9%	0.4%	0.1%	2.0%
Texas						
Byrd Unit	1.0%	0.3%	3.3%	0.8%	0.3%	2.7%
Carole Young Medical Fac. Complex[e]	1.3	0.5	3.1	0.4	0.1	1.5
Clemens Unit	1.5	0.5	4.6	4.9	2.1	11.2
Clements Unit	2.4	1.0	6.1	9.4	5.7	15.2
Coffield Unit	2.7	1.2	6.0	5.2	3.0	9.1
Dawson State Jail[f,g]	1.2	0.4	3.2	1.3	0.4	3.7
Eastham Unit	0.7	0.2	2.5	4.0	2.1	7.4
Gist State Jail	0.6	0.1	2.9	0.9	0.2	3.1
Gurney Transfer Fac.	0.4	0.1	2.1	1.1	0.3	3.7
Henley State Jail[e]	1.7	0.6	4.9	0.8	0.2	3.2
Hodge Unit	0.5	0.1	2.6	1.6	0.5	4.7
Holliday Transfer Fac.	1.0	0.3	3.7	1.8	0.5	6.1
Huntsville Unit	0.0	0.0	2.2	0.9	0.2	2.9
McConnell Unit	2.2	0.9	4.9	3.2	1.3	7.7
Michael Unit	3.2	1.5	6.8	2.7	1.2	6.1
Montford Psychiatric Fac.	3.4	1.7	6.8	6.8	4.0	11.3
Murray Unit[e]	7.0	4.0	11.9	8.3	5.0	13.4
Plane State Jail[e]	3.5	1.5	7.8	1.0	0.3	3.3
Powledge Unit	1.8	0.5	6.5	1.1	0.2	5.2
Stiles Unit	5.8	2.8	11.8	6.1	3.4	11.0
Willacy Co. State Jail[g]	0.0	0.0	2.5	1.1	0.3	3.8
Woodman State Jail[e]	1.3	0.4	4.3	0.0	0.0	2.7
Utah						
Central Utah Corr. Fac.	1.8%	0.7%	4.3%	3.7%	1.9%	7.1%
Utah State Prison[f]	2.8	1.3	5.8	3.6	1.8	7.2
Vermont						
Southeast State Corr. Fac.	0.0%	0.0%	6.2%	5.1%	2.3%	10.9%
Southern State Corr. Fac.	3.2	1.1	9.4	6.7	3.5	12.4
Virginia						
Brunswick Women's Reception and Pre-Release Ctr.[e]	0.0%	0.0%	3.9%	0.0%	0.0%	3.9%
Dillwyn Corr. Ctr.	1.5	0.5	5.0	3.0	1.3	7.0
Sussex II State Prison	1.3	0.4	4.3	4.1	2.1	7.8
Washington						
Clallam Bay Corr. Ctr.	2.3%	0.9%	6.1%	2.8%	1.2%	6.5%
Monroe Corr. Complex	1.9	0.6	6.0	1.0	0.3	3.5
Washington State Penitentiary	1.7	0.5	6.2	3.5	1.2	9.9
West Virginia						
Huttonsville Corr. Ctr.	2.2%	0.8%	6.1%	5.9%	2.8%	12.1%
Wisconsin						
Green Bay Corr. Inst.	1.8%	0.8%	4.2%	2.9%	1.5%	5.6%
Oshkosh Corr. Ctr.	1.7	0.7	4.0	3.1	1.5	6.1

Percent of prison inmates reporting nonconsensual sexual acts and abusive sexual contacts, by facility, National Inmate Survey, 2011–12

Facility name	Nonconsensual sexual acts[a]			Abusive sexual contacts only[b]		
		95%-confidence interval[c]			95%-confidence interval[c]	
	Percent victimized[d]	Lower bound	Upper bound	Percent victimized[d]	Lower bound	Upper bound
Wyoming						
Wyoming Honor Farm	0.0%	0.0%	3.8%	2.9%	1.5%	5.5%
Federal facilities (Bureau of Prisons)						
CI Eden[g]	0.0%	0.0%	2.0%	0.0%	0.0%	2.0%
CI Reeves I and II[g]	0.0	0.0	2.1	0.0	0.0	2.1
CI Reeves III[g]	0.4	0.1	2.0	0.0	0.0	2.0
CI Rivers[g]	0.0	0.0	2.4	0.9	0.2	4.7
FCI Allenwood Low	0.5	0.1	2.8	1.4	0.4	4.5
FCI Big Spring Camp	0.0	0.0	5.2	1.2	0.3	5.0
FCI Butner Med. I Camp	0.0	0.0	3.7	0.0	0.0	3.7
FCI Butner Med. II	1.4	0.3	7.0	0.8	0.2	2.7
FCI Forrest City Med.	0.0	0.0	2.5	0.6	0.1	2.9
FCI Greenville Camp[e]	3.3	1.5	7.0	0.8	0.2	3.2
FCI Jesup	0.0	0.0	2.8	0.0	0.0	2.8
FCI Lompoc	0.0	0.0	2.3	0.6	0.1	2.8
FCI Manchester Camp	0.9	0.2	4.1	0.0	0.0	3.4
FCI Marianna Camp[e]	0.6	0.2	2.1	0.0	0.0	2.2
FCI Milan	1.0	0.3	3.2	1.5	0.4	4.9
FCI Seagoville	0.0	0.0	1.9	1.1	0.4	3.1
FCI Tallahassee[e]	1.7	0.6	4.5	4.1	2.0	8.3
FCI Terre Haute	0.0	0.0	4.0	2.1	0.5	8.2
FDC Philadelphia[f]	0.6	0.1	3.0	1.2	0.4	4.0
FMC Carswell[e]	2.3	1.1	5.1	1.8	0.8	4.4
FMC Devens	1.3	0.4	4.1	1.4	0.5	3.8
FMC Lexington Camp[e]	0.8	0.2	2.7	0.0	0.0	2.5
FPC Alderson[e]	2.2	0.9	5.3	0.5	0.1	2.4
Limestone Co. Det. Ctr.[g]	0.0	0.0	2.4	0.6	0.1	3.1
MCFP Springfield	1.8	0.6	5.2	0.0	0.0	4.6
USP Hazelton - Female[e]	2.0	0.6	6.2	3.2	1.4	7.3
USP Lee	0.0	0.0	3.7	1.7	0.5	5.7
USP Tucson	2.6	0.9	7.8	4.7	2.2	9.8

Note: Detail may not sum to total due to rounding.

[a]Includes all inmates who reported unwanted contacts with another inmate or unwilling contacts with staff that involved oral sex, anal sex, vaginal sex, hand jobs, and other sexual acts occurring in the past 12 months or since admission to the facility, if shorter.

[b]Includes all inmates who reported unwanted contacts with another inmate or unwilling contacts with staff that involved touching of the inmate's butt, thighs, penis, breasts, or vagina in a sexual way occurring in the past 12 months or since admission to the facility, if shorter.

[c]Indicates that different samples in the same facility would yield prevalence rates falling between the lower and upper bound estimates 95 out of 100 times.

[d]Weights were applied so that inmates who responded accurately reflected the entire population of each facility on select characteristics, including age, sex, race, sentence length, and time served. (See *Methodology*.)

[e]Female facility.

[f]Facility housed both males and females; both were sampled at this facility.

[g]Privately operated facility.

Source: Bureau of Justice Statistics, National Inmate Survey, 2011–12.

Characteristics of jails and prevalence of sexual victimization, by facility, National Inmate Survey, 2011–12

| Facility name | Number of inmates in custody[c] | Respondents to sexual victimization survey[d] | Response rate[e] | Inmates reporting sexual victimization[a] | | |
| | | | | Percent[f] | 95%-confidence interval[b] | |
					Lower bound	Upper bound
Total	279,129	54,118	60.6%	3.2%	2.9%	3.5%
Alabama						
Barbour Co. Jail	95	47	65.9%	2.4%	0.7%	7.5%
Dallas Co. Jail	197	114	72.6	1.5	0.7	3.5
Lee Co. W.S. Buck Jones Det. Ctr.	384	165	79.9	2.9	1.6	5.2
Marshall Co. Jail	206	122	70.8	5.0	3.1	8.0
Tuscaloosa Co. Jail	626	216	77.1	3.5	2.0	5.9
Arizona						
Maricopa Co. Estrella Jail[g]	925	205	63.5%	3.7%	2.0%	6.8%
Maricopa Co. Fourth Avenue Jail	1,927	193	52.0	1.5	0.5	4.3
Maricopa Co. Towers Jail	167	85	63.9	5.4	3.0	9.5
Mariopa Co. Lower Buckeye Jail	1,989	234	52.8	4.3	2.4	7.7
Santa Cruz Co. Jail	228	52	34.7	0.0	0.0	6.9
Yuma Co. Det. Ctr.	620	162	57.5	2.1	0.8	5.1
Arkansas						
Crittenden Co. Jail	268	114	73.6%	6.3%	4.0%	9.9%
Mississippi Co. Det. Ctr.	177	86	67.1	0.9	0.3	2.8
Pope Co. Det. Ctr.	179	48	36.6	5.9	2.4	14.0
Pulaski Co. Regional Det. Ctr.	1,235	198	63.3	6.0	3.1	11.4
Sebastian Co. Adult Det. Ctr.	394	153	54.3	1.1	0.4	2.8
California						
Alameda Co. Santa Rita Jail	3,506	281	60.9%	3.0%	1.6%	5.5%
Contra Costa Co. Martinez Det. Fac.	766	143	42.5	7.0	4.1	11.7
Fresno Co. Downtown Det. Fac. - Main, North and South	1,883	190	51.9	3.5	1.8	6.7
Imperial Co. Jail	708	202	63.5	1.0	0.4	2.8
Kern Co. Lerdo Pre-Trial Fac.	1,287	163	46.7	3.8	1.8	8.0
Los Angeles Co. - Twin Towers Corr. Fac.	3,406	199	44.1	8.0	4.8	13.0
Los Angeles Co. Men's Central Jail	5,246	188	42.0	6.9	4.1	11.2
Los Angeles Co. North County Corr. Fac.	3,980	190	47.5	2.8	1.2	6.4
Napa Co. Jail	325	112	46.5	3.8	2.0	7.3
Orange Co. Central Jail Complex	2,525	169	53.6	1.4	0.4	4.7
Orange Co. Theo Lacy Fac.	2,999	241	58.4	4.7	2.5	8.7
Riverside Co. Indio Jail	387	133	56.3	2.8	1.3	5.8
Riverside Co. Larry D. Smith Corr. Ctr.	1,454	204	57.5	5.1	2.9	8.8
Riverside Co. Southwest Det. Ctr.[h]	888	149	46.8	0.6	0.1	3.0
Sacramento Co. Rio Cosumnes Corr. Ctr.	2,049	258	73.3	4.9	3.0	8.0
San Diego Co. East Mesa Med. Fac.	350	138	58.4	2.4	1.0	5.6
San Diego Co. George F. Bailey Det. Fac.	1,742	175	49.5	5.2	2.7	9.8
San Diego Co. Vista Det. Fac.	876	153	47.8	3.8	2.1	7.0
San Francisco Co. Jail Number 3	363	73	34.3	4.0	1.5	9.9
Santa Clara Co. Elmwood Fac. - Min. and Med.	1,920	219	54.4	2.4	1.1	5.4
Santa Clara Co. Main Jail	1,356	130	37.4	9.2	5.2	15.8
Santa Clara Co. Women's Corr. Ctr.[g]	518	141	50.3	2.1	0.9	5.2
Solano Co. Justice Ctr. Det. Fac.	660	195	71.6	5.2	3.1	8.4
Tulare Co. Jail	1,487	187	51.6	1.0	0.3	3.8
Ventura Co. Jail	722	199	65.0	2.8	1.4	5.3
Yolo Co. Leinberger Ctr.	77	44	73.1	2.1	0.7	6.0
Yuba Co. Jail	375	138	62.4	2.0	0.9	4.5
Colorado						
Chaffee Co. Jail	70	33	61.5%	0.0%	0.0%	10.4%
Denver Co. Jail	751	205	68.8	3.7	2.1	6.3
Denver Co. Van Cise-Simonet Det. Ctr.	1,211	158	44.0	2.1	0.8	5.6
Douglas Co. Jail	352	128	61.7	2.8	1.4	5.8
Fremont Co. Jail	205	105	63.8	3.0	1.6	5.7
Jefferson Co. Jail	1,165	205	62.0	0.0	0.0	1.8
Park Co. Jail	95	56	67.4	0.0	0.0	6.4

Characteristics of jails and prevalence of sexual victimization, by facility, National Inmate Survey, 2011–12

| Facility name | Number of inmates in custody[c] | Respondents to sexual victimization survey[d] | Response rate[e] | Inmates reporting sexual victimization[a] | 95%-confidence interval[b] | |
				Percent[f]	Lower bound	Upper bound
Florida						
Collier Co. Jail	939	154	45.9%	5.1%	2.6%	9.5%
Dixie Co. Jail	72	39	73.0	8.2	4.1	15.5
Escambia Co. Jail	1,562	222	54.3	2.5	1.2	5.2
Jacksonville City Montgomery Corr. Ctr.	488	179	68.8	2.4	1.1	4.9
Lake Co. Jail	920	172	54.8	2.8	0.8	9.4
Lee Co. Community Programs Unit	266	134	65.4	3.1	1.6	5.8
Leon Co. Det. Fac.	1,049	252	67.6	4.9	3.0	8.0
Manatee Co. Jail	1,141	226	64.5	5.2	3.1	8.5
Martin Co. Jail	569	165	60.2	3.1	1.5	6.3
Miami-Dade Co. Boot Camp	65	56	98.4	0.0	0.0	7.4
Miami-Dade Co. Metro West Det. Ctr.	2,091	218	58.4	2.6	1.3	5.1
Miami-Dade Co. Training and Treatment Ctr.	1,117	174	53.4	1.0	0.3	3.2
Miami-Dade Co. Turner Guilford Knight Corr. Ctr.	885	208	58.8	1.0	0.3	3.0
Okeechobee Co. Jail	232	105	57.7	1.1	0.3	3.9
Orange Co. 33rd Street Corr. Ctr.	2,896	278	66.2	3.5	1.7	6.9
Orange Co. Booking and Release Ctr.	711	43	42.7	2.9	1.2	6.8
Osceola Co. Jail	1,032	238	71.0	0.9	0.3	3.1
Palm Beach Co. Stockade	824	155	54.8	2.4	1.0	5.6
Pinellas Co. Central Division Fac.	938	155	48.4	2.4	0.9	6.4
Pinellas Co. South Division	1,294	181	48.3	3.2	1.5	7.0
Polk Co. - South Co. Jail	1,268	216	62.0	5.1	3.0	8.5
Sarasota North Co. Jail	952	207	65.0	0.0	0.0	1.9
Suwanee Co. Jail	155	83	64.7	0.9	0.3	3.0
Taylor Co. Jail	78	25	40.8	0.0	0.0	13.3
Georgia						
Candler Co. Jail	40	27	84.2%	0.0%	0.0%	12.5%
Carroll Co. Prison	203	150	82.7	2.7	1.6	4.3
Clayton Co. Jail	1,924	265	67.8	4.7	2.8	7.7
Dekalb Co. Jail	3,825	300	61.6	3.2	1.7	5.9
Douglas Co. Jail	908	272	66.1	2.8	1.5	5.1
Floyd Co. Jail	724	234	80.0	3.6	2.1	6.0
Floyd Co. Prison	351	180	75.7	2.8	1.5	5.0
Fulton Co. Jail	3,288	169	41.6	4.9	2.5	9.3
Gwinnett Co. Det. Ctr.	2,811	267	50.8	0.8	0.2	2.6
Hall Co. Det. Ctr.	1,350	193	57.3	3.0	1.5	6.0
Houston Co. Jail	524	176	71.2	7.1	4.6	10.8
Irwin Co. Jail	876	189	62.6	1.1	0.4	2.9
Murray County Jail	148	83	75.4	3.3	1.7	6.2
Newton Co. Jail	679	199	65.5	3.7	2.0	6.6
Screven Co. Jail	114	64	82.1	3.9	2.2	6.6
South Fulton Municipal Regional Jail	151	43	37.5	4.7	1.6	12.8
Spalding Co. Jail	507	138	50.6	5.1	2.7	9.2
Troup Co. Jail	440	174	68.7	2.2	1.0	4.4
Upson Co. Jail	160	108	82.3	2.6	1.5	4.6
Ware Co. Jail	429	201	84.3	2.2	1.2	3.9
Wilkinson Co. Jail	35	19	57.1	6.5	1.9	20.0
Idaho						
Bannock Co. Jail	298	114	55.8%	3.0%	1.3%	6.8%
Illinois						
Champaign Co. Satellite Jail[h]	313	58	42.5%	2.0%	0.5%	8.4%
Cook Co. - Division 1	1,206	284	82.5	4.3	2.7	6.9
Cook Co. - Division 11	1,552	289	75.6	7.7	5.3	11.0

Characteristics of jails and prevalence of sexual victimization, by facility, National Inmate Survey, 2011–12

Facility name	Number of inmates in custody[c]	Respondents to sexual victimization survey[d]	Response rate[e]	Inmates reporting sexual victimization[a]		
					95%-confidence interval[b]	
				Percent[f]	Lower bound	Upper bound
Cook Co. - Division 2	1,579	213	52.7%	5.8%	3.5%	9.4%
Cook Co. - Division 5	1,177	247	72.9	3.5	2.0	6.2
Cook Co. - Division 6	995	273	83.3	2.2	1.2	4.2
Kane Co. Adult Justice Ctr.	590	167	58.6	2.9	1.4	6.0
Kankakee Co. Jerome Combs Det. Ctr.	510	206	75.7	3.4	1.9	5.9
Kendall Co. Jail	111	61	68.4	5.1	2.8	9.2
McHenry Co. Jail	558	150	60.2	1.1	0.4	3.3
Sangamon Co. Jail	342	174	74.1	3.9	2.5	6.0
Indiana						
Bartholomew Co. Jail	183	120	79.9%	3.2%	1.9%	5.2%
Clinton Co. Jail	169	97	73.9	2.4	1.1	5.2
Dearborn Co. Jail	235	125	64.4	1.8	0.8	4.3
Delaware Co. Justice Ctr.	292	100	47.1	1.8	0.7	4.6
Elkhart Co. Corr. Ctr.	941	275	79.2	3.6	2.1	6.1
Hamilton Co. Jail	301	137	67.4	1.5	0.6	3.8
Jackson Co. Jail	169	91	63.5	1.0	0.3	3.4
Marion Co. Jail II[i]	1,223	197	58.8	3.4	1.4	8.1
Marion Co. Jail Intake Fac.	225	62	43.3	7.7	3.4	16.3
Noble Co. Jail	156	105	82.3	0.9	0.3	2.3
Ripley Co. Jail	84	52	89.2	7.9	5.1	11.9
Tippecanoe Co. Jail	271	119	55.7	2.5	1.1	5.7
Iowa						
Des Moines Co. Jail	75	30	58.9%	2.1%	0.6%	7.1%
Scott Co. Jail and Annex	301	141	66.7	3.2	1.6	6.1
Kansas						
Finney Co. Jail	124	73	78.4%	4.0%	2.3%	6.9%
Wilson Co. Jail	85	36	73.8	5.6	1.7	16.5
Kentucky						
Big Sandy Regional Det. Ctr.	262	144	74.3%	1.3%	0.6%	3.2%
Boyle Co. Det. Ctr.	308	150	84.5	1.9	0.6	5.7
Daviess Co. Det. Ctr.	628	202	69.3	3.6	2.1	6.2
Grayson Co. Det. Ctr.	497	213	76.8	2.2	1.2	4.1
Kenton Co. Det. Ctr.	524	137	53.9	1.1	0.4	3.0
Lexington-Fayette Co. Jail Det. Division	1,113	191	53.5	4.3	2.2	7.9
Madison Co. Det. Ctr.	263	139	67.2	3.8	2.3	6.2
McCracken Co. Jail	448	183	79.4	3.1	1.8	5.4
Meade Co. Jail	137	83	80.5	1.3	0.5	3.6
Pulaski Co. Det. Ctr.	269	97	57.2	1.6	0.6	4.2
Woodford Co. Det. Ctr.	100	34	50.7	0.1	0.0	0.6
Louisiana						
Assumption Parish Det. Ctr.	91	65	82.8%	4.6%	2.7%	7.9%
Bossier Parish Max. Security Fac.	349	177	74.8	0.9	0.4	2.3
Bossier Parish Med. Security Fac.	441	190	73.5	2.3	1.2	4.4
Caddo Parish Corr. Ctr.	1,285	273	80.5	2.0	0.9	4.2
East Baton Rouge Parish Prison	1,779	220	60.4	2.3	1.0	5.1
Iberia Parish Jail	546	198	67.5	3.9	2.3	6.6
Lafayette Parish Jail	972	213	63.6	3.2	1.7	6.0
Livingston Parish Det. Ctr.	560	219	78.7	1.4	0.6	3.2
Rapides Parish Det. Ctr. III	414	207	85.7	1.9	1.0	3.6
St. Landry Parish Jail	273	114	59.7	0.7	0.2	2.5
St. Martin Parish Corr. Ctr. 1	179	78	60.1	3.8	1.8	8.1
Webster Parish Bayou Dorcheat Corr. Fac.	464	192	78.1	3.3	1.9	5.8
Maine						
Penobscot Co. Jail	178	61	51.0%	4.3%	1.6%	11.4%

Characteristics of jails and prevalence of sexual victimization, by facility, National Inmate Survey, 2011–12

| | | | | Inmates reporting sexual victimization[a] | | |
| | | | | | 95%-confidence interval[b] | |
Facility name	Number of inmates in custody[c]	Respondents to sexual victimization survey[d]	Response rate[e]	Percent[f]	Lower bound	Upper bound
Maryland						
Allegany Co. Det. Ctr.	170	46	36.1%	2.3%	0.5%	9.6%
Anne Arundel Co. Jennifer Road Det. Ctr.	553	106	38.0	0.9	0.2	4.4
Baltimore City Det. Ctr.	2,574	268	65.9	6.7	4.3	10.2
Montgomery Co. Corr. Fac.	649	186	62.8	2.7	1.3	5.5
Wicomico Co. Det. Ctr.	325	147	73.5	0.6	0.2	2.1
Massachusetts						
Hampden Co. Corr. Ctr.	1,095	236	68.9%	1.9%	0.7%	5.0%
Middlesex Co. Jail and House of Corr.	1,204	232	70.1	2.1	0.9	4.7
Plymouth Co. Corr. Fac.	1,365	182	49.8	2.0	0.8	4.7
Suffolk Co. House of Corr.	1,510	228	65.5	6.2	3.8	9.9
Suffolk Co. Nashua Street Jail	775	150	48.7	1.9	0.7	4.9
Worcester Co. Jail and House of Corr.	1,172	266	77.0	4.4	2.7	7.3
Michigan						
Berrien Co. Jail	503	213	79.7%	4.3%	2.9%	6.5%
Calhoun Co. Jail	547	167	46.8	5.1	2.7	9.6
Huron Co. Jail	52	29	70.2	0.0	0.0	12.1
Kalamazoo Co. Jail	355	164	71.9	5.7	3.7	8.7
Macomb Co. Jail	1,154	157	40.6	1.9	0.8	4.5
Oakland Co. East Annex	443	177	71.9	2.5	1.3	5.0
Oakland Co. Law Enforcement Complex	779	151	48.7	7.3	4.1	12.6
Ottawa Co. Jail	344	120	53.3	0.6	0.2	2.5
Wayne Co. Andrew C. Baird Det. Fac.	1,354	127	32.4	4.1	2.0	8.3
Wayne Co. William Dickerson Det. - Division III	996	175	54.2	0.4	0.1	2.1
Minnesota						
Anoka Co. Jail	220	95	58.7%	2.0%	0.9%	4.5%
Hennepin Co. Adult Det. Ctr.	793	156	51.7	1.5	0.6	3.8
Mille Lacs Co. Jail	70	35	64.9	1.8	0.6	5.5
Ramsey Co. Corr. Fac.	383	167	71.6	0.9	0.3	2.2
Mississippi						
Covington Co. Jail	35	11	44.4%	0.0%	0.0%	25.9%
Harrison Co. Adult Det. Ctr.	909	258	73.7	5.1	3.0	8.7
Hinds Co. Jackson Det. Ctr.	161	92	79.5	3.0	1.6	5.6
Hinds Co. Raymond Det. Ctr.	684	209	69.8	5.2	3.1	8.6
Holmes-Humphreys Co. Regional Corr. Fac.	359	147	64.6	2.5	1.1	5.6
Madison Co. Jail	325	146	65.7	3.2	1.7	5.9
Marshall Co. Jail	87	47	64.2	0.0	0.0	7.6
Pike Co. Jail	144	92	75.2	0.0	0.0	4.1
Missouri						
Boone Co. Jail	219	71	47.1%	4.0%	1.6%	9.9%
LaClede Co. Jail	133	90	90.3	7.6	5.2	10.8
St. Charles Co. Jail	448	150	60.1	6.0	3.5	10.1
St. Louis Co. Jail	1,424	212	61.8	3.5	1.7	7.0
St. Louis Med. Security Inst.	837	224	57.6	6.7	4.2	10.4
Washington Co. Jail	41	20	59.0	3.3	0.9	11.3
Montana						
Cascade Co. Regional Jail	377	167	62.8%	5.2%	3.3%	8.3%
Hill Co. Jail	53	27	60.9	0.0	0.0	12.5
Missoula Co. Jail	350	155	67.7	2.5	1.3	4.9
Nebraska						
Douglas Co. Dept. of Corr.	1,517	207	55.5%	4.0%	1.9%	8.3%
Saline Co. Jail	93	63	73.0	4.0	1.9	8.1

Characteristics of jails and prevalence of sexual victimization, by facility, National Inmate Survey, 2011–12

Facility name	Number of inmates in custody[c]	Respondents to sexual victimization survey[d]	Response rate[e]	Percent[f]	Inmates reporting sexual victimization[a] 95%-confidence interval[b] Lower bound	Upper bound
Nevada						
Clark Co. Det. Ctr.	3,967	240	55.6%	1.0%	0.3%	2.8%
Nye Co. Jail - Pahrump	44	14	43.9	0.0	0.0	21.5
Washoe Co. Det. Ctr.	1,100	210	62.1	3.2	1.6	6.4
New Hampshire						
Coos Co. Jail	36	19	63.9%	4.4%	1.2%	14.3%
Hillsborough Co. House of Corr.	618	132	38.3	6.0	3.3	10.6
New Jersey						
Bergen Co. Jail	785	238	79.1%	2.7%	1.5%	4.8%
Burlington Co. Min. Security Jail/Corr. and Work Release Ctr.	203	61	48.6	0.0	0.0	5.9
Essex Co. Corr. Fac.	2,620	174	34.1	2.2	0.9	4.9
Hudson Co. Corr. Fac.	2,068	279	57.4	2.0	0.9	4.1
Mercer Co. Corr. Ctr.	910	145	55.6	7.3	4.3	12.0
Middlesex Co. Adult Corr. Ctr.	1,111	256	75.5	1.3	0.5	2.9
Ocean Co. Justice Complex	643	149	67.5	2.0	0.8	5.1
Passaic Co. Jail	1,020	197	61.1	2.6	1.3	5.0
Salem Co. Corr. Fac.	359	115	51.4	2.5	1.0	5.7
New Mexico						
Dona Ana Co. Det. Ctr.	849	212	66.4%	4.8%	2.9%	7.9%
San Juan Co. Adult Det. Ctr.	693	140	45.1	3.0	1.3	6.9
Santa Fe Co. Adult Det. Fac.[i]	496	136	47.0	3.5	1.6	7.5
New York						
Albany Co. Corr. Fac.	702	193	60.6%	4.2%	2.4%	7.2%
Allegany Co. Jail	138	69	56.8	4.6	2.1	9.6
Broome Co. Jail	536	167	54.7	5.3	2.8	9.7
Dutchess Co. Jail	305	129	60.3	1.5	0.5	3.8
Erie Co. Corr. Fac.	892	205	61.3	4.3	2.3	7.7
Erie Co. Holding Fac.	850	71	38.5	4.5	0.9	19.6
Jefferson Co. Jail	186	78	52.9	5.2	2.5	10.5
New York City Anna M. Kross Ctr.	2,739	161	42.1	5.6	3.1	10.0
New York City George Motchan Det. Ctr.	1,424	220	57.0	5.3	3.2	8.8
New York City Otis Bantum Corr. Ctr.	1,780	175	43.6	6.2	3.3	11.1
New York City Robert N Davoren Complex	2,166	273	50.2	3.4	1.8	6.3
New York City Rose M. Singer Ctr.[g]	1,004	215	63.4	8.6	5.8	12.6
Niagara Co. Jail	490	170	61.2	1.8	0.7	4.1
Oneida Co. Corr. Fac.	510	158	59.6	3.1	1.4	6.5
Orange Co. Corr. Fac.	611	199	62.6	1.9	0.9	4.2
Putnam Co. Corr. Fac.	129	68	63.4	1.1	0.3	3.7
Rockland Co. Corr. Ctr.	253	146	68.0	4.1	2.1	7.9
Schenectady Co. Jail	353	173	67.6	4.8	3.1	7.6
Seneca Co. Law Enforcement Ctr.	79	56	81.3	4.9	2.8	8.5
Ulster Co. Law Enforcement Ctr.	332	159	67.9	6.9	4.3	11.0
Washington Co. Corr. Fac.	102	63	72.9	0.0	0.0	5.8
Westchester Co. Jail	938	150	43.0	2.9	1.3	6.4
Westchester Co. Penitentiary - Dept. of Corr.	569	167	59.9	2.2	1.0	4.4

Characteristics of jails and prevalence of sexual victimization, by facility, National Inmate Survey, 2011–12

Facility name	Number of inmates in custody[c]	Respondents to sexual victimization survey[d]	Response rate[e]	Inmates reporting sexual victimization[a]		
					95%-confidence interval[b]	
				Percent[f]	Lower bound	Upper bound
North Carolina						
Buncombe Co. Det. Fac.	433	154	63.6%	1.9%	0.8%	4.3%
Cherokee Co. Jail	81	45	65.8	2.5	0.8	7.8
Durham Co. Jail	538	180	76.4	2.3	1.1	4.8
Edgecombe Co. Det. Ctr.	249	138	67.2	6.3	4.2	9.5
Forsyth Co. Adult Det. Ctr.	705	153	40.5	3.2	1.5	6.8
Granville Co. Det. Ctr.	83	35	52.1	6.5	2.3	17.1
Guilford Co. High Point Det. Fac.	329	162	57.8	1.1	0.4	2.7
Guilford Co. Prison Farm	60	36	66.1	0.0	0.0	9.6
Mecklenburg Co. Jail North	510	146	45.5	2.0	0.8	4.9
New Hanover Det. Fac.	415	155	60.1	1.9	0.8	4.3
Robeson Co. Jail	488	147	52.4	7.5	4.8	11.5
Scotland Co. Jail	187	93	58.2	5.4	3.1	9.3
Wake Co. John H. Baker, Jr. Public Safety Ctr.	1,380	200	57.1	4.2	1.9	8.8
North Dakota						
Burleigh Co. Det. Ctr.	151	82	75.2%	3.5%	1.9%	6.5%
Ohio						
Bedford Heights City Jail	143	35	34.7%	0.0%	0.0%	9.9%
Cuyahoga Co. Corr. Ctr.	2,321	315	72.3	2.4	1.3	4.4
Delaware Co. Jail	214	108	61.1	0.0	0.0	3.4
Franklin Co. Jail	628	155	53.4	4.1	2.1	7.9
Hamilton Co. Justice Ctr.	1,245	219	64.9	1.8	0.8	4.3
Hamilton Co. Reading Road Fac.	183	105	70.7	2.4	1.3	4.3
Lorain Co. Jail	432	174	66.4	2.2	1.1	4.3
Miami Co. Jail	125	68	73.8	0.0	0.0	5.3
Montgomery Co. Jail	942	202	59.2	1.3	0.5	3.3
Richland Co. Jail	226	130	75.8	2.9	1.7	4.7
Oklahoma						
Dewey Co. Jail	14	13	100.0%	0.0%	0.0%	22.8%
Kay Co. Jail	182	110	75.6	2.6	1.4	4.9
Nowata Co. Jail	53	24	63.8	2.4	0.7	8.3
Oregon						
Lane Co. Jail	489	171	72.9%	0.8%	0.3%	2.1%
Marion Co. Corr. Fac.	597	212	77.3	1.9	0.9	3.8
Washington Co. Jail	604	153	49.4	0.5	0.1	2.4
Yamhill Co. Corr. Fac.	235	127	77.8	4.7	2.8	7.7
Pennsylvania						
Allegheny Co. Jail	2,792	233	50.1%	3.0%	1.6%	5.6%
Blair Co. Prison	335	100	45.3	5.3	2.3	11.5
Fayette Co. Prison	310	97	39.3	4.9	2.6	9.1
Indiana Co. Jail	229	70	44.8	3.9	1.5	9.4
Luzerne Co. Corr. Fac.	727	181	52.2	3.0	1.6	5.7
Montgomery Co. Prison Corr. Fac.	1,838	236	66.4	3.7	2.0	6.6
Philadelphia City Alternative and Special Det. Fac.	768	173	55.0	0.8	0.3	2.5
Philadelphia City Curran/Fromhold Corr. Fac.	3,217	221	54.8	4.5	2.5	7.9
Philadelphia City Industrial Corr. Ctr.	1,052	241	68.7	9.5	6.4	13.7
Philadelphia City Riverside Corr. Fac.[g]	801	195	58.4	8.6	5.7	12.9
Schuykill Co. Prison	292	136	74.3	2.7	1.4	5.0
Westmoreland Co. Prison	566	145	51.3	3.3	1.5	7.0
York Co. Prison	2,559	237	59.6	5.4	3.1	9.1

Characteristics of jails and prevalence of sexual victimization, by facility, National Inmate Survey, 2011–12

Facility name	Number of inmates in custody[c]	Respondents to sexual victimization survey[d]	Response rate[e]	Inmates reporting sexual victimization[a]		
					95%-confidence interval[b]	
				Percent[f]	Lower bound	Upper bound
South Carolina						
Charleston Co. Det. Ctr.	1,450	213	55.7%	1.9%	0.9%	4.3%
Florence Co. Det. Ctr.	389	165	74.9	1.2	0.5	3.1
Lexington Co. Jail	781	193	59.9	1.6	0.6	4.0
Spartanburg Co. Det. Fac.	908	212	66.7	1.1	0.4	3.5
Sumter-Lee Regional Det. Ctr.	364	149	67.3	5.1	3.0	8.4
York Co. Det. Ctr.	397	133	48.7	2.1	0.8	5.3
South Dakota						
Pennington Co. Jail	399	154	68.0%	2.5%	1.2%	5.1%
Tennessee						
Lincoln Co. Jail	117	78	80.0%	3.0%	1.4%	6.1%
Madison Co. Jail	404	186	80.7	5.3	2.8	10.0
McMinn Co. Jail	248	161	78.4	3.4	2.2	5.2
Montgomery Co. Jail	542	122	45.8	0.7	0.2	3.3
Obion Co. Jail	154	98	75.0	0.0	0.0	3.8
Robertson Co. Det. Ctr.	398	171	71.7	2.8	1.5	5.3
Shelby Co. Corr. Ctr.	2,564	276	76.1	3.4	1.9	5.9
Shelby Co. Jail	2,715	286	72.6	1.8	0.8	3.7
Sumner Co. Jail	730	220	73.0	6.1	3.9	9.4
Tipton Co. Jail	137	74	64.6	1.5	0.5	5.0
Van Buren Co. Jail	30	15	77.8	0.0	0.0	20.4
Washington Co. Det. Ctr.	592	243	77.9	2.9	1.6	5.0
Texas						
Bexar Co. Adult Det. Ctr.	3,557	201	42.3%	5.1%	2.6%	9.5%
Bowie Co. Corr. Ctr.	643	174	55.9	2.5	1.2	5.5
Brazoria Co. Jail and Det. Ctr.	761	222	69.6	0.9	0.3	2.6
Brown Co. Jail	147	78	70.3	0.0	0.0	4.7
Cameron Co. Carrizales-Rucker Det. Ctr.	1,518	286	72.1	0.3	0.1	1.6
Dallas Co. Kays Det. Fac.	2,120	212	57.0	2.1	0.9	4.6
Denton Co. Det. Ctr.	1,176	274	76.1	2.4	1.2	4.8
Eastland Co. Jail	58	36	90.2	0.0	0.0	9.9
El Paso Co. Det. Fac. Annex	1,354	195	52.0	2.9	1.4	5.9
El Paso Co. Downtown Det. Fac.	1,014	173	55.4	3.0	1.2	7.6
Ellis Co. Wayne McCollum Det. Ctr.	428	186	75.3	3.6	2.2	5.9
Gregg Co. Jail	679	238	80.9	1.5	0.7	3.2
Harris Co. Jail - 1200 Baker Street Jail	4,602	276	58.3	7.6	4.5	12.5
Harris Co. Jail - 1307 Baker Street Jail	454	194	65.5	1.4	0.6	3.1
Harris Co. Jail - 701 North San Jacinto Street Jail[h]	4,441	296	61.7	3.2	1.7	6.0
Harris Co. Jail - 711 North San Jacinto Jail	127	64	58.8	1.5	0.4	4.9
Hays Co. Jail	318	93	43.5	3.9	1.6	9.4
Jefferson Co. Corr. Fac.	1,026	241	70.3	2.1	1.1	4.2
Johnson Co. Jail	361	178	83.5	5.2	3.4	7.9
Tarrant Co. Corr. Ctr.	1,933	182	60.6	2.9	1.3	6.3
Taylor Co. Jail	513	169	63.9	3.0	1.5	5.9
Titus Co. Jail	162	64	52.7	0.0	0.0	5.7
Travis Co. Corr. Fac.	2,346	121	22.8	2.7	0.9	7.6
Travis Co. Jail	345	25	19.0	0.0	0.0	13.3
Uvalde Co. Jail	50	17	42.6	3.6	0.9	14.1
Victoria Co. Jail	473	41	43.8	1.6	0.4	6.6
Washington Co. Jail	109	77	84.3	2.7	1.4	5.1
Webb Co. Jail	475	110	38.8	0.6	0.1	2.7
Utah						
Box Elder Co. Jail	51	40	87.8%	0.0%	0.0%	8.8%
Davis Co. Jail	652	170	54.4	4.8	2.7	8.4
Weber Co. Corr. Fac.	830	193	60.3	3.7	1.9	6.9

Characteristics of jails and prevalence of sexual victimization, by facility, National Inmate Survey, 2011–12

Facility name	Number of inmates in custody[c]	Respondents to sexual victimization survey[d]	Response rate[e]	Inmates reporting sexual victimization[a] Percent[f]	95%-confidence interval[b] Lower bound	95%-confidence interval[b] Upper bound
Virginia						
Alexandria Det. Ctr.	470	119	47.8%	0.6%	0.1%	2.6%
Arlington Co. Det. Fac.	472	161	65.3	0.8	0.2	3.2
Bristol City Jail	157	101	79.2	0.8	0.3	2.3
Hampton Corr. Fac.	423	189	76.3	1.0	0.4	2.7
Henrico Co. Regional Jail West	593	177	64.1	2.7	1.4	5.2
Mecklenburg Co. Jail	123	67	77.2	0.0	0.0	5.4
Montgomery Co. Jail	108	60	84.6	0.0	0.0	6.0
Newport News City Jail	525	197	73.7	3.5	2.0	6.0
Piedmont Regional Jail	611	188	64.9	2.3	1.1	4.7
Rappahannock Regional Jail	1,878	266	75.6	4.5	2.7	7.3
Richmond City Jail	1,429	230	68.8	3.4	1.9	6.3
Riverside Regional Jail	1,391	256	75.2	4.9	3.0	8.0
Virginia Beach Municipal Corr. Ctr.	1,518	268	73.6	2.4	1.3	4.6
Washington						
Benton Co. Jail	820	153	54.7%	2.3%	0.9%	6.0%
Cowlitz Co. Jail	359	173	79.3	1.7	0.8	3.6
King Co. Regional Justice Ctr.	791	179	53.7	1.3	0.5	3.5
Snohomish Co. Jail	1,385	230	64.3	1.0	0.3	3.1
Sunnyside City Jail	55	17	51.4	0.0	0.0	18.4
Whatcom Co. Jail	364	154	65.1	2.9	1.5	5.6
Yakima City Jail	76	39	65.2	1.8	0.5	5.9
West Virginia						
Eastern Regional Jail	470	130	50.7%	6.5%	3.7%	11.2%
South Central Regional Jail	622	102	37.8	5.9	3.0	11.2
Western Regional Jail	658	215	68.0	4.8	3.0	7.7
Wisconsin						
Brown Co. Jail	470	167	62.4%	4.1%	2.2%	7.8%
Columbia Co. Jail	101	40	50.0	4.1	1.6	10.4
Milwaukee Co. Corr. Fac. South	1,701	207	55.8	4.2	2.3	7.5
Oconto Co. Jail	50	18	45.0	0.0	0.0	18.4
Rock Co. Jail	661	164	60.9	3.3	1.7	6.4
Walworth Co. Jail	188	100	73.3	2.5	1.3	5.0
Washington Co. Jail	110	67	68.3	4.5	2.4	8.6
Wood Co. Jail	69	26	69.0	0.0	0.0	12.9
Wyoming						
Lincoln Co. Jail	23	11	81.3%	0.0%	0.0%	25.9%

[a]Includes all types of sexual victimization, including oral, anal, or vaginal penetration, hand jobs, touching of the inmate's butt, thighs, penis, breasts, or vagina in a sexual way, and other sexual acts occurring in the past 12 months or since admission to the facility, if shorter.

[b]Indicates that different samples in the same facility would yield prevalence rates falling between the lower and upper bound estimates 95 out of 100 times.

[c]Number of inmates in the facility on the day of the roster plus any new inmates admitted prior to the first day of data collection.

[d]Number of respondents consenting to the sexual victimization survey on NIS. (See *Methodology*.)

[e]Response rate is equal to the number of respondents divided by the number of eligible inmates sampled times 100 percent.

[f]Weights were applied so that inmates who responded accurately reflected the entire population of each facility on select characteristics, including age, sex, race, sentence length, and time served. (See *Methodology*.)

[g]Female facility.

[h]Facility housed both males and females; only males were sampled at this facility.

[i]Privately operated facility.

Source: Bureau of Justice Statistics, National Inmate Survey, 2011–12.

Percent of jail inmates reporting victimization, by type of incident and facility, National Inmate Survey, 2011–12

Facility name	Inmate-on-inmate[a]			Staff sexual misconduct[a]		
		95%-confidence interval[b]			95%-confidence interval[b]	
	Percent victimized[c]	Lower bound	Upper bound	Percent victimized[c]	Lower bound	Upper bound
Total	1.6%	1.4%	1.9%	1.8%	1.7%	2.0%
Alabama						
Barbour Co. Jail	2.3%	0.7%	7.5%	0.0%	0.0%	7.6%
Dallas Co. Jail	1.5	0.7	3.5	0.0	0.0	3.3
Lee Co. W.S. Buck Jones Det. Ctr.	2.4	1.3	4.6	1.0	0.4	2.5
Marshall Co. Jail	2.5	1.3	4.9	3.4	1.9	6.0
Tuscaloosa Co. Jail	0.8	0.3	2.3	2.7	1.4	4.9
Arizona						
Maricopa Co. Estrella Jail[d]	3.7%	2.0%	6.8%	0.3%	0.1%	1.5%
Maricopa Co. Fourth Avenue Jail	0.6	0.1	3.2	0.9	0.3	3.2
Maricopa Co. Towers Jail	1.1	0.3	3.7	4.3	2.2	8.1
Mariopa Co. Lower Buckeye Jail	2.4	1.1	4.9	2.8	1.3	5.9
Santa Cruz Co. Jail	0.0	0.0	6.9	0.0	0.0	6.9
Yuma Co. Det. Ctr.	0.6	0.1	2.9	1.4	0.5	4.2
Arkansas						
Crittenden Co. Jail	3.5%	1.9%	6.4%	2.8%	1.4%	5.7%
Mississippi Co. Det. Ctr.	0.0	0.0	4.3	0.8	0.3	2.8
Pope Co. Det. Ctr.	3.6	1.2	10.3	2.3	0.5	9.6
Pulaski Co. Regional Det. Ctr.	3.5	1.3	9.1	2.5	1.1	5.4
Sebastian Co. Adult Det. Ctr.	0.5	0.1	2.0	0.6	0.1	2.0
California						
Alameda Co. Santa Rita Jail	1.2%	0.5%	3.0%	2.0%	1.0%	4.3%
Contra Costa Co. Martinez Det. Fac.	2.0	0.8	5.1	5.9	3.2	10.4
Fresno Co. Downtown Det. Fac. - Main, North and South	1.6	0.7	4.0	1.9	0.8	4.6
Imperial Co. Jail	0.4	0.1	1.2	0.6	0.1	2.6
Kern Co. Lerdo Pre-Trial Fac.	2.5	1.0	6.1	1.7	0.6	5.1
Los Angeles Co. - Twin Towers Corr. Fac.	4.9	2.6	9.1	4.4	2.3	8.5
Los Angeles Co. Men's Central Jail	4.2	2.1	8.0	3.3	1.6	6.6
Los Angeles Co. North County Corr. Fac.	1.8	0.6	5.2	2.4	0.9	6.0
Napa Co. Jail	2.3	1.0	5.4	2.5	1.1	5.7
Orange Co. Central Jail Complex	1.4	0.4	4.7	0.7	0.1	3.8
Orange Co. Theo Lacy Fac.	3.2	1.4	6.8	1.5	0.5	4.4
Riverside Co. Indio Jail	2.8	1.3	5.8	0.6	0.2	2.5
Riverside Co. Larry D. Smith Corr. Ctr.	4.0	2.1	7.5	2.0	0.8	4.8
Riverside Co. Southwest Det. Ctr.[e]	0.0	0.0	2.5	0.6	0.1	3.0
Sacramento Co. Rio Cosumnes Corr. Ctr.	2.6	1.3	5.1	2.6	1.3	5.1
San Diego Co. East Mesa Med. Fac.	1.2	0.3	4.7	1.1	0.4	3.1
San Diego Co. George F. Bailey Det. Fac.	4.1	1.9	8.4	1.7	0.6	4.6
San Diego Co. Vista Det. Fac.	1.6	0.6	4.3	2.6	1.3	5.2
San Francisco Co. Jail Number 3	2.4	0.8	7.3	1.6	0.3	7.0
Santa Clara Co. Elmwood Fac. - Min. and Med.	1.3	0.5	3.6	1.1	0.3	3.7
Santa Clara Co. Main Jail	3.5	1.5	7.9	6.2	3.0	12.5
Santa Clara Co. Women's Corr. Ctr.[d]	1.4	0.5	4.2	0.7	0.2	3.1
Solano Co. Justice Ctr. Det. Fac.	2.4	1.2	4.9	3.7	2.1	6.7
Tulare Co. Jail	0.0	0.0	2.0	1.0	0.3	3.8
Ventura Co. Jail	0.9	0.3	2.7	1.9	0.8	4.2
Yolo Co. Leinberger Ctr.	2.1	0.7	6.0	0.0	0.0	8.0
Yuba Co. Jail	1.5	0.5	3.9	1.2	0.4	3.2
Colorado						
Chaffee Co. Jail	0.0%	0.0%	10.4%	0.0%	0.0%	10.4%
Denver Co. Jail	2.9	1.6	5.4	1.1	0.5	2.8
Denver Co. Van Cise-Simonet Det. Ctr.	0.5	0.1	2.5	1.6	0.5	5.1
Douglas Co. Jail	0.0	0.0	2.9	2.8	1.4	5.8
Fremont Co. Jail	3.0	1.6	5.7	0.8	0.2	2.5
Jefferson Co. Jail	0.0	0.0	1.8	0.0	0.0	1.8
Park Co. Jail	0.0	0.0	6.4	0.0	0.0	6.4

Percent of jail inmates reporting victimization, by type of incident and facility, National Inmate Survey, 2011–12

| Facility name | Inmate-on-inmate[a] | | | Staff sexual misconduct[a] | | |
| | Percent victimized[c] | 95%-confidence interval[b] | | Percent victimized[c] | 95%-confidence interval[b] | |
		Lower bound	Upper bound		Lower bound	Upper bound
Florida						
Collier Co. Jail	2.4%	1.1%	5.5%	2.6%	1.0%	6.8%
Dixie Co. Jail	4.9	2.1	10.8	5.7	2.5	12.6
Escambia Co. Jail	2.0	0.9	4.5	0.5	0.1	2.3
Jacksonville City Montgomery Corr. Ctr.	1.3	0.4	3.6	1.6	0.7	3.6
Lake Co. Jail	0.3	0.1	1.7	2.5	0.6	9.4
Lee Co. Community Programs Unit	2.4	1.1	5.0	1.6	0.7	4.1
Leon Co. Det. Fac.	2.0	1.0	4.3	3.7	2.0	6.5
Manatee Co. Jail	3.4	1.8	6.4	2.3	1.1	4.8
Martin Co. Jail	1.1	0.4	3.4	2.6	1.2	5.8
Miami-Dade Co. Boot Camp	0.0	0.0	7.4	0.0	0.0	7.4
Miami-Dade Co. Metro West Det. Ctr.	1.0	0.3	3.4	1.6	0.7	3.5
Miami-Dade Co. Training and Treatment Ctr.	0.0	0.0	2.2	1.0	0.3	3.2
Miami-Dade Co. Turner Guilford Knight Corr. Ctr.	1.0	0.3	3.0	0.0	0.0	2.3
Okeechobee Co. Jail	0.0	0.0	3.7	1.1	0.3	3.9
Orange Co. 33rd Street Corr. Ctr.	1.3	0.4	3.7	2.2	0.9	5.3
Orange Co. Booking and Release Ctr.	1.0	0.2	3.9	2.9	1.2	6.8
Osceola Co. Jail	0.9	0.3	3.1	0.7	0.1	3.0
Palm Beach Co. Stockade	1.3	0.4	4.3	1.6	0.6	4.2
Pinellas Co. Central Division Fac.	2.4	0.9	6.4	1.0	0.2	4.8
Pinellas Co. South Division	2.0	0.7	5.4	1.3	0.4	4.1
Polk Co. - South Co. Jail	2.3	1.1	5.0	3.7	2.0	6.8
Sarasota North Co. Jail	0.0	0.0	1.9	0.0	0.0	1.9
Suwanee Co. Jail	0.9	0.3	3.0	0.0	0.0	4.5
Taylor Co. Jail	0.0	0.0	13.3	0.0	0.0	13.3
Georgia						
Candler Co. Jail	0.0%	0.0%	12.5%	0.0%	0.0%	12.5%
Carroll Co. Prison	0.0	0.0	2.5	2.7	1.6	4.3
Clayton Co. Jail	2.3	1.1	4.7	3.3	1.7	6.1
Dekalb Co. Jail	2.0	0.9	4.5	1.9	0.9	4.0
Douglas Co. Jail	2.3	1.2	4.3	0.5	0.1	2.2
Floyd Co. Jail	2.4	1.3	4.6	1.2	0.5	2.8
Floyd Co. Prison	0.6	0.2	2.0	2.2	1.2	4.3
Fulton Co. Jail	3.3	1.5	7.4	1.6	0.5	4.5
Gwinnett Co. Det. Ctr.	0.8	0.2	2.6	0.0	0.0	1.5
Hall Co. Det. Ctr.	3.0	1.5	6.0	0.0	0.0	2.0
Houston Co. Jail	2.2	1.1	4.7	6.0	3.7	9.6
Irwin Co. Jail	0.0	0.0	2.0	1.1	0.4	2.9
Murray County Jail	2.4	1.1	5.3	0.8	0.3	2.5
Newton Co. Jail	2.2	1.1	4.4	1.5	0.6	4.0
Screven Co. Jail	1.4	0.6	3.5	2.4	1.3	4.7
South Fulton Municipal Regional Jail	0.0	0.0	8.2	4.7	1.6	12.8
Spalding Co. Jail	1.8	0.7	4.5	3.3	1.4	7.2
Troup Co. Jail	2.2	1.0	4.4	0.0	0.0	2.2
Upson Co. Jail	1.7	0.8	3.4	1.9	0.9	3.7
Ware Co. Jail	1.7	0.9	3.4	0.8	0.3	2.0
Wilkinson Co. Jail	6.5	1.9	20.0	0.0	0.0	16.8
Idaho						
Bannock Co. Jail	0.0%	0.0%	3.3%	3.0%	1.3%	6.8%

Percent of jail inmates reporting victimization, by type of incident and facility, National Inmate Survey, 2011–12

| Facility name | Inmate-on-inmate[a] | | | Staff sexual misconduct[a] | | |
| | Percent victimized[c] | 95%-confidence interval[b] | | Percent victimized[c] | 95%-confidence interval[b] | |
		Lower bound	Upper bound		Lower bound	Upper bound
Illinois						
Champaign Co. Satellite Jail[e]	0.0%	0.0%	6.4%	2.0%	0.5%	8.4%
Cook Co. - Division 1	0.7	0.2	2.1	4.0	2.4	6.5
Cook Co. - Division 11	5.5	3.5	8.4	3.3	1.8	5.7
Cook Co. - Division 2	2.5	1.1	5.4	4.2	2.3	7.5
Cook Co. - Division 5	0.9	0.3	2.7	2.6	1.3	5.1
Cook Co. - Division 6	1.1	0.4	2.7	1.5	0.7	3.3
Kane Co. Adult Justice Ctr.	1.5	0.6	3.8	2.1	0.8	5.1
Kankakee Co. Jerome Combs Det. Ctr.	1.6	0.7	3.8	2.6	1.5	4.7
Kendall Co. Jail	2.6	1.1	5.9	2.5	1.1	5.8
McHenry Co. Jail	0.5	0.1	2.2	0.6	0.1	2.6
Sangamon Co. Jail	2.4	1.3	4.2	2.0	1.1	3.5
Indiana						
Bartholomew Co. Jail	3.2%	1.9%	5.2%	0.8%	0.3%	2.0%
Clinton Co. Jail	1.6	0.5	4.4	0.8	0.3	2.4
Dearborn Co. Jail	0.7	0.2	2.4	1.1	0.3	3.5
Delaware Co. Justice Ctr.	0.2	0.0	0.7	1.7	0.6	4.5
Elkhart Co. Corr. Ctr.	1.7	0.7	3.8	1.9	1.0	3.7
Hamilton Co. Jail	1.5	0.6	3.8	0.9	0.3	3.3
Jackson Co. Jail	1.0	0.3	3.4	0.0	0.0	4.1
Marion Co. Jail II[f]	0.5	0.1	2.5	2.9	1.0	7.7
Marion Co. Jail Intake Fac.	0.0	0.0	5.8	7.7	3.4	16.3
Noble Co. Jail	0.0	0.0	3.5	0.9	0.3	2.3
Ripley Co. Jail	7.9	5.1	11.9	2.0	0.8	4.5
Tippecanoe Co. Jail	2.5	1.1	5.7	0.0	0.0	3.2
Iowa						
Des Moines Co. Jail	0.0%	0.0%	11.4%	2.1%	0.6%	7.1%
Scott Co. Jail and Annex	0.0	0.0	2.7	3.2	1.6	6.1
Kansas						
Finney Co. Jail	1.0%	0.3%	2.9%	3.0%	1.6%	5.7%
Wilson Co. Jail	0.0	0.0	9.6	5.6	1.7	16.5
Kentucky						
Big Sandy Regional Det. Ctr.	1.3%	0.6%	3.2%	0.0%	0.0%	2.6%
Boyle Co. Det. Ctr.	1.9	0.6	5.7	0.0	0.0	2.5
Daviess Co. Det. Ctr.	2.1	1.1	4.2	1.9	0.9	4.1
Grayson Co. Det. Ctr.	0.9	0.3	2.4	1.3	0.6	2.9
Kenton Co. Det. Ctr.	1.1	0.4	3.0	0.1	0.0	0.6
Lexington-Fayette Co. Jail Det. Division	3.1	1.4	6.6	3.3	1.6	6.7
Madison Co. Det. Ctr.	2.1	1.1	4.2	1.7	0.8	3.5
McCracken Co. Jail	1.5	0.7	3.2	1.6	0.8	3.5
Meade Co. Jail	1.3	0.5	3.6	1.3	0.5	3.6
Pulaski Co. Det. Ctr.	1.6	0.6	4.2	0.8	0.2	2.9
Woodford Co. Det. Ctr.	0.1	0.0	0.6	0.0	0.0	10.2
Louisiana						
Assumption Parish Det. Ctr.	3.1%	1.6%	6.0%	1.5%	0.6%	3.9%
Bossier Parish Max. Security Fac.	0.9	0.4	2.3	0.0	0.0	2.2
Bossier Parish Med. Security Fac.	1.4	0.6	3.1	1.5	0.7	3.4
Caddo Parish Corr. Ctr.	1.1	0.4	3.0	1.1	0.4	3.0
East Baton Rouge Parish Prison	2.3	1.0	5.1	0.6	0.1	3.1
Iberia Parish Jail	2.4	1.2	4.7	2.5	1.3	4.9
Lafayette Parish Jail	1.8	0.8	4.1	2.4	1.1	4.9
Livingston Parish Det. Ctr.	1.0	0.4	2.7	0.4	0.1	1.5
Rapides Parish Det. Ctr. III	1.4	0.7	3.0	0.5	0.1	1.6
St. Landry Parish Jail	0.7	0.2	2.5	0.7	0.2	2.5
St. Martin Parish Corr. Ctr. 1	1.3	0.4	4.6	2.6	1.0	6.4
Webster Parish Bayou Dorcheat Corr. Fac.	1.8	0.9	3.6	2.1	1.0	4.5

Percent of jail inmates reporting victimization, by type of incident and facility, National Inmate Survey, 2011–12

Facility name	Inmate-on-inmate[a]			Staff sexual misconduct[a]		
	Percent victimized[c]	95%-confidence interval[b]		Percent victimized[c]	95%-confidence interval[b]	
		Lower bound	Upper bound		Lower bound	Upper bound
Maine						
Penobscot Co. Jail	0.0%	0.0%	5.9%	4.3%	1.6%	11.4%
Maryland						
Allegany Co. Det. Ctr.	2.3%	0.5%	9.6%	0.0%	0.0%	7.7%
Anne Arundel Co. Jennifer Road Det. Ctr.	0.0	0.0	3.6	0.9	0.2	4.4
Baltimore City Det. Ctr.	0.7	0.2	2.4	6.7	4.3	10.2
Montgomery Co. Corr. Fac.	1.8	0.7	4.5	1.6	0.6	4.1
Wicomico Co. Det. Ctr.	0.6	0.2	2.1	0.0	0.0	2.5
Massachusetts						
Hampden Co. Corr. Ctr.	0.0%	0.0%	1.7%	1.9%	0.7%	5.0%
Middlesex Co. Jail and House of Corr.	1.5	0.5	4.0	0.6	0.2	2.1
Plymouth Co. Corr. Fac.	0.6	0.1	2.9	2.0	0.8	4.7
Suffolk Co. House of Corr.	4.1	2.2	7.6	3.5	1.9	6.6
Suffolk Co. Nashua Street Jail	0.6	0.1	2.7	1.3	0.4	4.2
Worcester Co. Jail and House of Corr.	1.9	0.9	4.0	2.9	1.5	5.5
Michigan						
Berrien Co. Jail	0.9%	0.4%	2.3%	3.4%	2.1%	5.3%
Calhoun Co. Jail	2.7	1.1	6.5	3.5	1.7	7.3
Huron Co. Jail	0.0	0.0	12.1	0.0	0.0	12.1
Kalamazoo Co. Jail	3.6	2.0	6.5	3.5	2.0	5.8
Macomb Co. Jail	1.1	0.3	3.6	1.2	0.4	3.3
Oakland Co. East Annex	1.9	0.9	4.2	1.2	0.5	3.2
Oakland Co. Law Enforcement Complex	3.0	1.4	6.5	5.9	3.0	11.1
Ottawa Co. Jail	0.0	0.0	3.1	0.6	0.2	2.5
Wayne Co. Andrew C. Baird Det. Fac.	4.1	2.0	8.3	0.5	0.1	2.5
Wayne Co. William Dickerson Det. - Division III	0.0	0.0	2.2	0.4	0.1	2.1
Minnesota						
Anoka Co. Jail	1.5%	0.6%	3.9%	1.1%	0.4%	2.8%
Hennepin Co. Adult Det. Ctr.	0.9	0.3	2.8	0.6	0.1	2.7
Mille Lacs Co. Jail	0.0	0.0	9.9	1.8	0.6	5.5
Ramsey Co. Corr. Fac.	0.0	0.0	2.2	0.9	0.3	2.2
Mississippi						
Covington Co. Jail	0.0%	0.0%	25.9%	0.0%	0.0%	25.9%
Harrison Co. Adult Det. Ctr.	0.7	0.2	1.9	4.4	2.4	8.0
Hinds Co. Jackson Det. Ctr.	0.5	0.2	1.5	2.4	1.2	5.0
Hinds Co. Raymond Det. Ctr.	2.5	1.1	5.5	3.6	1.9	6.8
Holmes-Humphreys Co. Regional Corr. Fac.	1.0	0.2	3.6	1.5	0.6	4.1
Madison Co. Jail	0.0	0.0	2.7	3.2	1.7	5.9
Marshall Co. Jail	0.0	0.0	7.6	0.0	0.0	7.6
Pike Co. Jail	0.0	0.0	4.1	0.0	0.0	4.1
Missouri						
Boone Co. Jail	3.1%	1.0%	9.2%	0.9%	0.2%	3.5%
LaClede Co. Jail	3.1	1.8	5.3	4.5	2.7	7.3
St. Charles Co. Jail	2.0	0.8	4.7	4.5	2.4	8.3
St. Louis Co. Jail	1.2	0.4	3.2	2.4	0.9	5.7
St. Louis Med. Security Inst.	0.8	0.3	2.3	6.3	3.9	10.0
Washington Co. Jail	3.3	0.9	11.3	0.0	0.0	16.1
Montana						
Cascade Co. Regional Jail	3.3%	1.9%	5.8%	3.6%	2.0%	6.3%
Hill Co. Jail	0.0	0.0	12.5	0.0	0.0	12.5
Missoula Co. Jail	1.8	0.8	4.0	1.4	0.5	3.5
Nebraska						
Douglas Co. Dept. of Corr.	0.7%	0.1%	3.6%	3.3%	1.4%	7.4%
Saline Co. Jail	1.6	0.6	4.5	2.3	0.9	6.2

Percent of jail inmates reporting victimization, by type of incident and facility, National Inmate Survey, 2011–12

Facility name	Inmate-on-inmate[a]			Staff sexual misconduct[a]		
	Percent victimized[c]	95%-confidence interval[b]		Percent victimized[c]	95%-confidence interval[b]	
		Lower bound	Upper bound		Lower bound	Upper bound
Nevada						
Clark Co. Det. Ctr.	0.6%	0.2%	1.9%	0.4%	0.1%	2.2%
Nye Co. Jail - Pahrump	0.0	0.0	21.5	0.0	0.0	21.5
Washoe Co. Det. Ctr.	1.1	0.3	3.5	2.1	0.9	4.9
New Hampshire						
Coos Co. Jail	0.0%	0.0%	16.8%	4.4%	1.2%	14.3%
Hillsborough Co. House of Corr.	4.1	1.9	8.5	3.3	1.6	6.6
New Jersey						
Bergen Co. Jail	1.6%	0.7%	3.3%	1.5%	0.7%	3.2%
Burlington Co. Min. Security Jail/Corr. and Work Release Ctr.	0.0	0.0	5.9	0.0	0.0	5.9
Essex Co. Corr. Fac.	0.8	0.2	2.8	1.7	0.7	4.2
Hudson Co. Corr. Fac.	1.0	0.4	2.7	1.7	0.8	3.8
Mercer Co. Corr. Ctr.	4.1	2.0	8.2	5.1	2.8	9.2
Middlesex Co. Adult Corr. Ctr.	1.0	0.4	2.5	0.7	0.2	2.2
Ocean Co. Justice Complex	1.2	0.4	3.7	0.8	0.2	3.6
Passaic Co. Jail	1.6	0.7	3.8	2.6	1.3	5.0
Salem Co. Corr. Fac.	0.7	0.2	3.0	1.7	0.6	4.8
New Mexico						
Dona Ana Co. Det. Ctr.	3.0%	1.7%	5.4%	2.5%	1.2%	5.3%
San Juan Co. Adult Det. Ctr.	3.0	1.3	6.9	1.8	0.6	5.5
Santa Fe Co. Adult Det. Fac.[f]	2.3	1.0	5.3	1.8	0.6	5.5
New York						
Albany Co. Corr. Fac.	2.7%	1.4%	5.2%	2.4%	1.2%	5.0%
Allegany Co. Jail	3.0	1.2	7.5	1.5	0.4	5.3
Broome Co. Jail	2.9	1.3	6.5	3.4	1.5	7.6
Dutchess Co. Jail	0.7	0.2	2.7	1.4	0.5	3.8
Erie Co. Corr. Fac.	0.4	0.1	2.0	3.9	2.0	7.2
Erie Co. Holding Fac.	0.0	0.0	5.3	4.5	0.9	19.6
Jefferson Co. Jail	1.0	0.3	3.9	4.2	1.8	9.4
New York City Anna M. Kross Ctr.	2.4	1.0	6.0	3.7	1.8	7.4
New York City George Motchan Det. Ctr.	1.4	0.5	3.6	4.0	2.2	7.1
New York City Otis Bantum Corr. Ctr.	0.6	0.1	3.0	5.6	2.9	10.5
New York City Robert N Davoren Complex	0.3	0.1	1.8	3.1	1.6	5.8
New York City Rose M. Singer Ctr.[d]	5.0	2.9	8.4	5.9	3.7	9.4
Niagara Co. Jail	0.7	0.2	2.8	1.1	0.4	3.0
Oneida Co. Corr. Fac.	0.0	0.0	2.5	3.0	1.4	6.5
Orange Co. Corr. Fac.	1.4	0.6	3.5	1.4	0.6	3.4
Putnam Co. Corr. Fac.	0.0	0.0	5.4	1.1	0.3	3.7
Rockland Co. Corr. Ctr.	2.1	0.7	6.5	2.0	1.1	3.6
Schenectady Co. Jail	4.4	2.7	7.0	2.9	1.7	5.0
Seneca Co. Law Enforcement Ctr.	3.6	1.8	7.0	3.3	1.6	6.6
Ulster Co. Law Enforcement Ctr.	1.5	0.7	3.5	6.1	3.6	10.2
Washington Co. Corr. Fac.	0.0	0.0	5.8	0.0	0.0	5.8
Westchester Co. Jail	0.5	0.1	2.3	2.5	1.0	5.9
Westchester Co. Penitentiary - Dept. of Corr.	0.9	0.3	2.5	1.3	0.5	3.3
North Carolina						
Buncombe Co. Det. Fac.	0.7%	0.2%	2.5%	1.3%	0.5%	3.4%
Cherokee Co. Jail	0.0	0.0	7.9	2.5	0.8	7.8
Durham Co. Jail	0.7	0.2	2.7	1.6	0.7	3.7
Edgecombe Co. Det. Ctr.	2.6	1.4	4.8	3.8	2.2	6.5
Forsyth Co. Adult Det. Ctr.	1.2	0.3	3.8	2.9	1.2	6.5
Granville Co. Det. Ctr.	0.4	0.1	1.7	6.0	2.0	16.9
Guilford Co. High Point Det. Fac.	0.0	0.0	2.4	1.1	0.4	2.7
Guilford Co. Prison Farm	0.0	0.0	9.6	0.0	0.0	9.6

Percent of jail inmates reporting victimization, by type of incident and facility, National Inmate Survey, 2011–12

Facility name	Inmate-on-inmate[a]			Staff sexual misconduct[a]		
	Percent victimized[c]	95%-confidence interval[b]		Percent victimized[c]	95%-confidence interval[b]	
		Lower bound	Upper bound		Lower bound	Upper bound
Mecklenburg Co. Jail North	0.6%	0.1%	2.4%	2.0%	0.8%	4.9%
New Hanover Det. Fac.	0.6	0.2	2.6	1.2	0.4	3.4
Robeson Co. Jail	2.4	1.1	5.0	5.2	3.0	8.7
Scotland Co. Jail	1.0	0.3	3.5	4.4	2.4	8.1
Wake Co. John H. Baker, Jr. Public Safety Ctr.	3.4	1.4	8.1	1.4	0.5	3.7
North Dakota						
Burleigh Co. Det. Ctr.	0.0%	0.0%	4.5%	3.5%	1.9%	6.5%
Ohio						
Bedford Heights City Jail	0.0%	0.0%	9.9%	0.0%	0.0%	9.9%
Cuyahoga Co. Corr. Ctr.	1.2	0.5	2.8	1.2	0.5	2.9
Delaware Co. Jail	0.0	0.0	3.4	0.0	0.0	3.4
Franklin Co. Jail	3.1	1.5	6.4	1.0	0.2	4.3
Hamilton Co. Justice Ctr.	0.0	0.0	1.8	1.8	0.8	4.3
Hamilton Co. Reading Road Fac.	2.1	1.1	4.0	0.3	0.1	0.9
Lorain Co. Jail	1.1	0.4	2.9	1.1	0.4	2.8
Miami Co. Jail	0.0	0.0	5.3	0.0	0.0	5.3
Montgomery Co. Jail	0.4	0.1	2.0	0.9	0.3	2.7
Richland Co. Jail	1.4	0.7	2.9	1.4	0.7	2.9
Oklahoma						
Dewey Co. Jail	0.0%	0.0%	22.8%	0.0%	0.0%	22.8%
Kay Co. Jail	1.7	0.8	3.7	0.9	0.3	2.5
Nowata Co. Jail	0.0	0.0	13.8	2.4	0.7	8.3
Oregon						
Lane Co. Jail	0.5%	0.1%	1.9%	0.8%	0.3%	2.1%
Marion Co. Corr. Fac.	0.5	0.1	1.8	1.4	0.6	3.2
Washington Co. Jail	0.0	0.0	2.5	0.5	0.1	2.4
Yamhill Co. Corr. Fac.	4.3	2.5	7.4	0.4	0.1	1.0
Pennsylvania						
Allegheny Co. Jail	2.0%	0.9%	4.3%	1.5%	0.6%	3.7%
Blair Co. Prison	3.5	1.2	10.1	1.7	0.6	4.9
Fayette Co. Prison	2.6	1.0	6.1	3.9	1.9	7.7
Indiana Co. Jail	3.9	1.5	9.4	0.0	0.0	5.2
Luzerne Co. Corr. Fac.	2.4	1.2	4.9	0.6	0.1	2.5
Montgomery Co. Prison Corr. Fac.	1.4	0.6	3.4	2.6	1.3	5.3
Philadelphia City Alternative and Special Det. Fac.	0.0	0.0	2.2	0.8	0.3	2.5
Philadelphia City Curran/Fromhold Corr. Fac.	1.2	0.4	3.9	3.4	1.8	6.5
Philadelphia City Industrial Corr. Ctr.	3.5	1.8	6.6	6.3	3.9	10.0
Philadelphia City Riverside Corr. Fac.[d]	6.7	4.2	10.7	3.7	2.0	6.8
Schuykill Co. Prison	1.0	0.3	3.2	2.7	1.4	5.0
Westmoreland Co. Prison	2.1	0.8	5.1	2.2	0.8	6.1
York Co. Prison	3.5	1.8	6.8	1.8	0.8	4.4
South Carolina						
Charleston Co. Det. Ctr.	0.7%	0.2%	2.3%	1.7%	0.7%	4.0%
Florence Co. Det. Ctr.	0.0	0.0	2.3	1.2	0.5	3.1
Lexington Co. Jail	1.1	0.3	3.2	0.6	0.1	2.5
Spartanburg Co. Det. Fac.	0.0	0.0	1.8	1.1	0.4	3.5
Sumter-Lee Regional Det. Ctr.	0.4	0.1	1.5	4.7	2.7	8.0
York Co. Det. Ctr.	0.0	0.0	2.9	2.1	0.8	5.3
South Dakota						
Pennington Co. Jail	2.0%	0.9%	4.6%	0.9%	0.3%	2.4%

Percent of jail inmates reporting victimization, by type of incident and facility, National Inmate Survey, 2011–12

Facility name	Inmate-on-inmate[a]			Staff sexual misconduct[a]		
	Percent victimized[c]	95%-confidence interval[b]		Percent victimized[c]	95%-confidence interval[b]	
		Lower bound	Upper bound		Lower bound	Upper bound
Tennessee						
Lincoln Co. Jail	3.0%	1.4%	6.1%	1.3%	0.5%	3.6%
Madison Co. Jail	1.5	0.7	3.3	4.4	2.1	9.3
McMinn Co. Jail	2.8	1.8	4.5	1.0	0.5	2.1
Montgomery Co. Jail	0.0	0.0	3.1	0.7	0.2	3.3
Obion Co. Jail	0.0	0.0	3.8	0.0	0.0	3.8
Robertson Co. Det. Ctr.	1.1	0.4	2.9	1.7	0.8	3.9
Shelby Co. Corr. Ctr.	1.1	0.4	3.1	3.1	1.7	5.5
Shelby Co. Jail	0.6	0.2	2.2	1.1	0.5	2.8
Sumner Co. Jail	4.2	2.5	7.1	3.0	1.5	5.6
Tipton Co. Jail	1.5	0.5	5.0	0.0	0.0	4.9
Van Buren Co. Jail	0.0	0.0	20.4	0.0	0.0	20.4
Washington Co. Det. Ctr.	2.8	1.5	4.9	0.7	0.2	2.1
Texas						
Bexar Co. Adult Det. Ctr.	1.6%	0.6%	4.0%	4.3%	2.1%	8.6%
Bowie Co. Corr. Ctr.	0.6	0.1	2.7	1.9	0.8	4.7
Brazoria Co. Jail and Det. Ctr.	0.4	0.1	2.0	0.4	0.1	2.0
Brown Co. Jail	0.0	0.0	4.7	0.0	0.0	4.7
Cameron Co. Carrizales-Rucker Det. Ctr.	0.3	0.1	1.6	0.0	0.0	1.4
Dallas Co. Kays Det. Fac.	0.4	0.1	2.2	2.1	0.9	4.6
Denton Co. Det. Ctr.	0.7	0.2	2.1	1.7	0.8	3.9
Eastland Co. Jail	0.0	0.0	9.9	0.0	0.0	9.9
El Paso Co. Det. Fac. Annex	2.2	1.0	4.9	1.0	0.3	3.3
El Paso Co. Downtown Det. Fac.	1.0	0.3	3.4	2.7	1.0	7.4
Ellis Co. Wayne McCollum Det. Ctr.	1.8	0.9	3.6	1.8	0.9	3.5
Gregg Co. Jail	0.3	0.1	1.4	1.2	0.5	2.8
Harris Co. Jail - 1200 Baker Street Jail	6.3	3.4	11.2	1.5	0.7	3.2
Harris Co. Jail - 1307 Baker Street Jail	1.0	0.4	2.5	0.5	0.1	1.7
Harris Co. Jail - 701 North San Jacinto Street Jail[e]	0.9	0.3	2.5	2.9	1.5	5.6
Harris Co. Jail - 711 North San Jacinto Jail	0.0	0.0	5.7	1.5	0.4	4.9
Hays Co. Jail	0.8	0.2	3.3	3.1	1.1	8.7
Jefferson Co. Corr. Fac.	1.0	0.4	2.5	1.8	0.8	3.7
Johnson Co. Jail	2.7	1.5	4.8	3.0	1.7	5.3
Tarrant Co. Corr. Ctr.	1.0	0.3	3.4	2.3	0.9	5.5
Taylor Co. Jail	1.7	0.7	4.2	1.3	0.4	3.6
Titus Co. Jail	0.0	0.0	5.7	0.0	0.0	5.7
Travis Co. Corr. Fac.	1.7	0.5	5.9	1.0	0.2	5.3
Travis Co. Jail	0.0	0.0	13.3	0.0	0.0	13.3
Uvalde Co. Jail	0.0	0.0	18.4	3.6	0.9	14.1
Victoria Co. Jail	1.6	0.4	6.6	0.0	0.0	8.6
Washington Co. Jail	2.6	1.4	5.1	0.0	0.0	4.8
Webb Co. Jail	0.0	0.0	3.4	0.6	0.1	2.7
Utah						
Box Elder Co. Jail	0.0%	0.0%	8.8%	0.0%	0.0%	8.8%
Davis Co. Jail	4.0	2.1	7.6	0.8	0.3	2.4
Weber Co. Corr. Fac.	2.4	1.1	5.1	1.8	0.7	4.4

Percent of jail inmates reporting victimization, by type of incident and facility, National Inmate Survey, 2011–12

Facility name	Inmate-on-inmate[a]			Staff sexual misconduct[a]		
		95%-confidence interval[b]			95%-confidence interval[b]	
	Percent victimized[c]	Lower bound	Upper bound	Percent victimized[c]	Lower bound	Upper bound
Virginia						
Alexandria Det. Ctr.	0.6%	0.1%	2.6%	0.6%	0.1%	2.6%
Arlington Co. Det. Fac.	0.0	0.0	2.3	0.8	0.2	3.2
Bristol City Jail	0.8	0.3	2.3	0.0	0.0	3.7
Hampton Corr. Fac.	0.5	0.1	1.8	0.5	0.1	2.0
Henrico Co. Regional Jail West	0.7	0.2	2.0	2.0	0.9	4.4
Mecklenburg Co. Jail	0.0	0.0	5.4	0.0	0.0	5.4
Montgomery Co. Jail	0.0	0.0	6.0	0.0	0.0	6.0
Newport News City Jail	1.0	0.3	2.8	2.5	1.3	4.8
Piedmont Regional Jail	1.4	0.5	3.5	0.9	0.3	2.7
Rappahannock Regional Jail	1.2	0.4	3.2	3.3	1.8	5.8
Richmond City Jail	2.1	1.0	4.5	1.8	0.8	4.2
Riverside Regional Jail	1.6	0.7	3.7	3.7	2.1	6.5
Virginia Beach Municipal Corr. Ctr.	1.0	0.4	2.6	1.4	0.6	3.4
Washington						
Benton Co. Jail	1.2%	0.3%	5.0%	1.1%	0.4%	3.6%
Cowlitz Co. Jail	0.7	0.2	2.3	1.0	0.4	2.5
King Co. Regional Justice Ctr.	0.0	0.0	2.2	1.3	0.5	3.5
Snohomish Co. Jail	0.5	0.1	2.3	0.5	0.1	2.3
Sunnyside City Jail	0.0	0.0	18.4	0.0	0.0	18.4
Whatcom Co. Jail	2.9	1.5	5.6	0.3	0.1	1.0
Yakima City Jail	0.0	0.0	9.0	1.8	0.5	5.9
West Virginia						
Eastern Regional Jail	6.0%	3.3%	10.6%	1.5%	0.6%	3.6%
South Central Regional Jail	3.6	1.6	8.1	2.3	0.8	6.4
Western Regional Jail	4.8	3.0	7.7	1.6	0.6	3.8
Wisconsin						
Brown Co. Jail	1.7%	0.7%	4.4%	3.9%	2.0%	7.6%
Columbia Co. Jail	2.1	0.6	7.5	2.1	0.6	7.5
Milwaukee Co. Corr. Fac. South	1.3	0.5	3.7	2.9	1.4	5.9
Oconto Co. Jail	0.0	0.0	18.4	0.0	0.0	18.4
Rock Co. Jail	2.6	1.2	5.5	2.0	0.9	4.7
Walworth Co. Jail	0.8	0.3	2.6	2.5	1.3	5.0
Washington Co. Jail	3.1	1.4	6.9	3.0	1.3	6.5
Wood Co. Jail	0.0	0.0	12.9	0.0	0.0	12.9
Wyoming						
Lincoln Co. Jail	0.0%	0.0%	25.9%	0.0%	0.0%	25.9%

Note: Detail may sum to more than total victimization rate because victims may have reported both inmate-on-inmate and staff-on-inmate sexual victimization.

[a]Includes all types of sexual victimization, including oral, anal, or vaginal penetration, hand jobs, touching of the inmate's butt, thighs, penis, breasts, or vagina in a sexual way, and other sexual acts occurring in the past 12 months or since admission to the facility, if shorter.

[b]Indicates that different samples in the same facility would yield prevalence rates falling between the lower and upper bound estimates 95 out of 100 times.

[c]Weights were applied so that inmates who responded accurately reflected the entire population of each facility on select characteristics, including age, sex, race, sentence length, and time served. (See *Methodology*.)

[d]Female facility.

[e]Facility housed both males and females; only males were sampled at this facility.

[f]Privately operated facility.

Source: Bureau of Justice Statistics, National Inmate Survey, 2011–12.

Percent of jail inmates reporting sexual victimization, by level of coercion and facility, National Inmate Survey, 2011–12

Facility name	Inmate-on-inmate[a]		Staff sexual misconduct[a]		
	Physically forced[b]	Pressured[c]	Physically forced[b]	Pressured[c]	Without force or pressure[d]
Total	1.2%	1.1%	0.8%	1.2%	0.9%
Alabama					
Barbour Co. Jail	2.3%	0.0%	0.0%	0.0%	0.0%
Dallas Co. Jail	1.5	0.0	0.0	0.0	0.0
Lee Co. W.S. Buck Jones Det. Ctr.	2.4	0.0	0.0	0.5	0.5
Marshall Co. Jail	2.5	0.0	1.7	3.4	0.0
Tuscaloosa Co. Jail	0.8	0.0	1.0	0.8	1.9
Arizona					
Maricopa Co. Estrella Jail[e]	2.3%	2.1%	0.3%	0.3%	0.3%
Maricopa Co. Fourth Avenue Jail	0.6	0.0	0.9	0.9	0.9
Maricopa Co. Towers Jail	1.1	0.0	1.8	1.8	2.5
Mariopa Co. Lower Buckeye Jail	0.7	2.0	1.1	2.1	1.8
Santa Cruz Co. Jail	0.0	0.0	0.0	0.0	0.0
Yuma Co. Det. Ctr.	0.0	0.6	0.6	0.6	1.4
Arkansas					
Crittenden Co. Jail	2.7%	0.8%	1.9%	1.1%	1.0%
Mississippi Co. Det. Ctr.	0.0	0.0	0.8	0.0	0.0
Pope Co. Det. Ctr.	3.6	1.8	0.0	0.0	2.3
Pulaski Co. Regional Det. Ctr.	3.1	3.0	0.4	1.5	1.5
Sebastian Co. Adult Det. Ctr.	0.0	0.5	0.0	0.0	0.6
California					
Alameda Co. Santa Rita Jail	0.9%	1.0%	1.3%	1.7%	0.6%
Contra Costa Co. Martinez Det. Fac.	1.4	2.0	3.2	5.2	3.7
Fresno Co. Downtown Det. Fac. - Main, North and South	1.2	0.5	1.5	1.4	0.4
Imperial Co. Jail	0.4	0.2	0.6	0.6	0.6
Kern Co. Lerdo Pre-Trial Fac.	2.5	1.5	0.4	1.4	1.3
Los Angeles Co. - Twin Towers Corr. Fac.	4.9	2.0	2.9	2.6	0.3
Los Angeles Co. Men's Central Jail	1.5	3.6	2.1	2.9	2.1
Los Angeles Co. North County Corr. Fac.	1.4	1.8	1.8	2.4	1.8
Napa Co. Jail	1.6	1.3	1.8	2.5	1.8
Orange Co. Central Jail Complex	0.0	1.4	0.7	0.7	0.0
Orange Co. Theo Lacy Fac.	1.7	1.9	1.1	1.1	0.5
Riverside Co. Indio Jail	2.8	2.1	0.6	0.6	0.0
Riverside Co. Larry D. Smith Corr. Ctr.	4.0	2.7	1.5	2.0	0.6
Riverside Co. Southwest Det. Ctr.[f]	0.0	0.0	0.6	0.6	0.6
Sacramento Co. Rio Cosumnes Corr. Ctr.	1.4	1.7	0.6	1.7	1.2
San Diego Co. East Mesa Med. Fac.	1.2	0.0	1.1	1.1	0.0
San Diego Co. George F. Bailey Det. Fac.	3.1	3.5	1.1	1.7	0.0
San Diego Co. Vista Det. Fac.	0.7	1.2	1.2	2.1	1.6
San Francisco Co. Jail Number 3	1.0	2.4	0.0	1.6	0.0
Santa Clara Co. Elmwood Fac. - Min. and Med.	1.3	0.9	0.4	1.1	0.0
Santa Clara Co. Main Jail	2.1	2.5	4.8	3.6	1.6
Santa Clara Co. Women's Corr. Ctr.[e]	0.7	1.4	0.7	0.7	0.0
Solano Co. Justice Ctr. Det. Fac.	1.5	2.4	2.6	2.6	2.3
Tulare Co. Jail	0.0	0.0	0.0	0.8	0.3
Ventura Co. Jail	0.4	0.9	0.9	1.9	0.0
Yolo Co. Leinberger Ctr.	2.1	0.0	0.0	0.0	0.0
Yuba Co. Jail	0.7	1.5	0.5	0.7	0.0
Colorado					
Chaffee Co. Jail	0.0%	0.0%	0.0%	0.0%	0.0%
Denver Co. Jail	2.9	0.8	0.7	0.3	0.8
Denver Co. Van Cise-Simonet Det. Ctr.	0.0	0.5	0.8	0.0	0.8
Douglas Co. Jail	0.0	0.0	1.7	2.8	1.2
Fremont Co. Jail	3.0	1.4	0.8	0.8	0.0
Jefferson Co. Jail	0.0	0.0	0.0	0.0	0.0
Park Co. Jail	0.0	0.0	0.0	0.0	0.0

Percent of jail inmates reporting sexual victimization, by level of coercion and facility, National Inmate Survey, 2011–12

Facility name	Inmate-on-inmate[a]		Staff sexual misconduct[a]		
	Physically forced[b]	Pressured[c]	Physically forced[b]	Pressured[c]	Without force or pressure[d]
Florida					
Collier Co. Jail	1.6%	1.2%	2.6%	2.2%	0.4%
Dixie Co. Jail	2.4	4.9	0.0	2.4	3.3
Escambia Co. Jail	1.6	1.5	0.5	0.5	0.0
Jacksonville City Montgomery Corr. Ctr.	1.3	0.5	1.1	1.1	0.9
Lake Co. Jail	0.3	0.3	0.0	2.1	0.4
Lee Co. Community Programs Unit	2.4	2.4	1.6	1.6	0.9
Leon Co. Det. Fac.	1.7	1.1	0.8	1.4	2.3
Manatee Co. Jail	2.4	2.0	2.3	1.9	1.4
Martin Co. Jail	0.7	1.1	2.6	2.2	1.4
Miami-Dade Co. Boot Camp	0.0	0.0	0.0	0.0	0.0
Miami-Dade Co. Metro West Det. Ctr.	0.5	0.5	0.6	1.2	0.6
Miami-Dade Co. Training and Treatment Ctr.	0.0	0.0	0.5	0.5	0.5
Miami-Dade Co. Turner Guilford Knight Corr. Ctr.	0.5	0.5	0.0	0.0	0.0
Okeechobee Co. Jail	0.0	0.0	0.0	1.1	0.0
Orange Co. 33rd Street Corr. Ctr.	0.7	1.3	0.6	1.9	0.3
Orange Co. Booking and Release Ctr.	1.0	0.0	1.0	1.0	1.9
Osceola Co. Jail	0.9	0.9	0.0	0.0	0.7
Palm Beach Co. Stockade	1.3	1.3	1.1	1.6	0.0
Pinellas Co. Central Division Fac.	2.4	1.6	0.0	1.0	0.0
Pinellas Co. South Division	2.0	2.0	1.3	1.3	1.3
Polk Co. - South Co. Jail	2.3	1.8	0.9	2.0	2.3
Sarasota North Co. Jail	0.0	0.0	0.0	0.0	0.0
Suwanee Co. Jail	0.9	0.0	0.0	0.0	0.0
Taylor Co. Jail	0.0	0.0	0.0	0.0	0.0
Georgia					
Candler Co. Jail	0.0%	0.0%	0.0%	0.0%	0.0%
Carroll Co. Prison	0.0	0.0	1.3	2.0	2.0
Clayton Co. Jail	1.8	1.4	2.6	1.4	1.2
Dekalb Co. Jail	2.0	1.4	0.3	1.2	1.3
Douglas Co. Jail	1.1	1.9	0.5	0.5	0.0
Floyd Co. Jail	2.4	0.4	0.4	0.8	0.4
Floyd Co. Prison	0.6	0.6	1.1	1.7	1.1
Fulton Co. Jail	2.5	2.0	0.6	0.6	1.0
Gwinnett Co. Det. Ctr.	0.4	0.4	0.0	0.0	0.0
Hall Co. Det. Ctr.	2.6	2.0	0.0	0.0	0.0
Houston Co. Jail	2.2	1.0	1.1	3.1	5.4
Irwin Co. Jail	0.0	0.0	0.8	0.8	0.7
Murray County Jail	1.1	1.3	0.0	0.8	0.0
Newton Co. Jail	1.7	1.8	0.3	1.5	0.9
Screven Co. Jail	1.4	1.4	2.4	2.4	1.2
South Fulton Municipal Regional Jail	0.0	0.0	2.3	4.7	4.7
Spalding Co. Jail	0.6	1.2	1.5	1.0	1.8
Troup Co. Jail	0.9	2.2	0.0	0.0	0.0
Upson Co. Jail	0.7	1.7	0.0	1.0	0.9
Ware Co. Jail	1.0	1.7	0.0	0.8	0.0
Wilkinson Co. Jail	0.0	6.5	0.0	0.0	0.0
Idaho					
Bannock Co. Jail	0.0%	0.0%	1.8%	1.2%	0.0%
Illinois					
Champaign Co. Satellite Jail[f]	0.0%	0.0%	0.0%	2.0%	2.0%
Cook Co. - Division 1	0.7	0.7	1.5	2.2	2.5
Cook Co. - Division 11	4.0	3.3	2.6	2.9	1.4
Cook Co. - Division 2	2.5	2.0	1.8	2.9	2.3
Cook Co. - Division 5	0.4	0.5	1.4	1.6	1.8

Percent of jail inmates reporting sexual victimization, by level of coercion and facility, National Inmate Survey, 2011–12

Facility name	Inmate-on-inmate[a]		Staff sexual misconduct[a]		
	Physically forced[b]	Pressured[c]	Physically forced[b]	Pressured[c]	Without force or pressure[d]
Cook Co. - Division 6	1.1%	1.1%	0.7%	1.1%	1.1%
Kane Co. Adult Justice Ctr.	1.1	1.0	1.3	2.1	0.6
Kankakee Co. Jerome Combs Det. Ctr.	0.9	1.2	1.3	1.4	0.8
Kendall Co. Jail	1.7	2.6	0.9	0.9	1.7
McHenry Co. Jail	0.0	0.5	0.0	0.6	0.0
Sangamon Co. Jail	1.9	2.4	0.5	1.6	0.9
Indiana					
Bartholomew Co. Jail	1.4%	2.4%	0.8%	0.8%	0.8%
Clinton Co. Jail	1.6	1.6	0.0	0.0	0.8
Dearborn Co. Jail	0.7	0.7	1.1	1.1	0.0
Delaware Co. Justice Ctr.	0.2	0.2	0.0	0.5	1.2
Elkhart Co. Corr. Ctr.	1.3	1.0	1.3	1.6	0.7
Hamilton Co. Jail	1.5	1.5	0.0	0.0	0.9
Jackson Co. Jail	1.0	0.0	0.0	0.0	0.0
Marion Co. Jail II[g]	0.5	0.5	2.1	1.3	1.7
Marion Co. Jail Intake Fac.	0.0	0.0	3.7	4.9	2.7
Noble Co. Jail	0.0	0.0	0.0	0.9	0.0
Ripley Co. Jail	5.9	7.9	2.0	2.0	2.0
Tippecanoe Co. Jail	2.5	0.0	0.0	0.0	0.0
Iowa					
Des Moines Co. Jail	0.0%	0.0%	0.0%	0.0%	2.1%
Scott Co. Jail and Annex	0.0	0.0	0.6	1.3	1.9
Kansas					
Finney Co. Jail	0.0%	1.0%	3.0%	2.0%	0.0%
Wilson Co. Jail	0.0	0.0	5.6	0.0	0.0
Kentucky					
Big Sandy Regional Det. Ctr.	1.3%	0.9%	0.0%	0.0%	0.0%
Boyle Co. Det. Ctr.	1.9	1.9	0.0	0.0	0.0
Daviess Co. Det. Ctr.	1.3	2.1	0.9	1.5	0.9
Grayson Co. Det. Ctr.	0.4	0.5	0.5	1.3	0.0
Kenton Co. Det. Ctr.	1.0	0.5	0.0	0.0	0.1
Lexington-Fayette Co. Jail Det. Division	2.1	2.4	1.7	2.7	1.3
Madison Co. Det. Ctr.	2.1	0.7	0.7	0.9	1.0
McCracken Co. Jail	1.0	0.9	1.1	1.1	0.6
Meade Co. Jail	1.3	1.3	0.0	1.3	0.0
Pulaski Co. Det. Ctr.	1.6	0.0	0.8	0.8	0.0
Woodford Co. Det. Ctr.	0.1	0.0	0.0	0.0	0.0
Louisiana					
Assumption Parish Det. Ctr.	3.1%	0.0%	0.0%	0.0%	1.5%
Bossier Parish Max. Security Fac.	0.9	0.0	0.0	0.0	0.0
Bossier Parish Med. Security Fac.	1.0	0.8	1.0	1.0	0.5
Caddo Parish Corr. Ctr.	1.1	1.1	0.0	0.8	0.4
East Baton Rouge Parish Prison	1.4	1.3	0.0	0.0	0.6
Iberia Parish Jail	2.0	0.9	1.0	1.5	1.5
Lafayette Parish Jail	1.0	1.8	0.0	0.5	1.9
Livingston Parish Det. Ctr.	0.5	1.0	0.0	0.0	0.4
Rapides Parish Det. Ctr. III	1.4	0.5	0.5	0.5	0.0
St. Landry Parish Jail	0.7	0.7	0.7	0.7	0.7
St. Martin Parish Corr. Ctr. 1	1.3	0.0	1.3	1.3	2.6
Webster Parish Bayou Dorcheat Corr. Fac.	1.8	1.4	0.6	0.6	1.5
Maine					
Penobscot Co. Jail	0.0%	0.0%	0.0%	1.8%	2.6%

Percent of jail inmates reporting sexual victimization, by level of coercion and facility, National Inmate Survey, 2011–12

Facility name	Inmate-on-inmate[a]		Staff sexual misconduct[a]		
	Physically forced[b]	Pressured[c]	Physically forced[b]	Pressured[c]	Without force or pressure[d]
Maryland					
Allegany Co. Det. Ctr.	2.3%	2.3%	0.0%	0.0%	0.0%
Anne Arundel Co. Jennifer Road Det. Ctr.	0.0	0.0	0.0	0.0	0.9
Baltimore City Det. Ctr.	0.4	0.7	2.8	3.1	5.2
Montgomery Co. Corr. Fac.	1.8	0.6	0.5	1.2	0.4
Wicomico Co. Det. Ctr.	0.6	0.0	0.0	0.0	0.0
Massachusetts					
Hampden Co. Corr. Ctr.	0.0%	0.0%	0.0%	0.5%	1.4%
Middlesex Co. Jail and House of Corr.	1.5	0.7	0.4	0.4	0.6
Plymouth Co. Corr. Fac.	0.6	0.0	0.5	1.5	0.5
Suffolk Co. House of Corr.	1.8	3.8	1.9	2.0	2.3
Suffolk Co. Nashua Street Jail	0.6	0.0	0.0	0.6	1.3
Worcester Co. Jail and House of Corr.	1.2	1.2	0.4	2.3	1.2
Michigan					
Berrien Co. Jail	0.9%	0.9%	1.3%	3.0%	0.9%
Calhoun Co. Jail	1.3	2.7	3.1	3.5	0.7
Huron Co. Jail	0.0	0.0	0.0	0.0	0.0
Kalamazoo Co. Jail	3.6	3.1	3.5	1.5	1.0
Macomb Co. Jail	1.1	1.1	0.9	0.0	0.3
Oakland Co. East Annex	1.3	1.9	1.2	1.2	0.0
Oakland Co. Law Enforcement Complex	3.0	1.9	5.2	2.9	2.2
Ottawa Co. Jail	0.0	0.0	0.0	0.6	0.0
Wayne Co. Andrew C. Baird Det. Fac.	4.1	0.8	0.0	0.0	0.5
Wayne Co. William Dickerson Det. - Division III	0.0	0.0	0.4	0.4	0.0
Minnesota					
Anoka Co. Jail	1.5%	0.5%	1.1%	0.5%	0.6%
Hennepin Co. Adult Det. Ctr.	0.9	0.4	0.0	0.6	0.6
Mille Lacs Co. Jail	0.0	0.0	0.0	0.0	1.8
Ramsey Co. Corr. Fac.	0.0	0.0	0.0	0.4	0.5
Mississippi					
Covington Co. Jail	0.0%	0.0%	0.0%	0.0%	0.0%
Harrison Co. Adult Det. Ctr.	0.7	0.7	0.9	3.4	0.7
Hinds Co. Jackson Det. Ctr.	0.5	0.0	0.0	1.3	1.1
Hinds Co. Raymond Det. Ctr.	1.9	2.2	0.5	1.5	2.6
Holmes-Humphreys Co. Regional Corr. Fac.	1.0	0.0	0.8	0.8	0.8
Madison Co. Jail	0.0	0.0	1.2	1.8	1.4
Marshall Co. Jail	0.0	0.0	0.0	0.0	0.0
Pike Co. Jail	0.0	0.0	0.0	0.0	0.0
Missouri					
Boone Co. Jail	0.0%	3.1%	0.0%	0.9%	0.0%
LaClede Co. Jail	1.8	1.3	3.0	4.5	0.0
St. Charles Co. Jail	2.0	0.5	3.0	4.0	1.4
St. Louis Co. Jail	0.9	0.3	0.3	1.9	0.8
St. Louis Med. Security Inst.	0.4	0.8	3.6	4.0	4.1
Washington Co. Jail	0.0	3.3	0.0	0.0	0.0
Montana					
Cascade Co. Regional Jail	2.2%	2.2%	1.9%	3.6%	2.4%
Hill Co. Jail	0.0	0.0	0.0	0.0	0.0
Missoula Co. Jail	1.2	1.8	0.7	0.7	0.7
Nebraska					
Douglas Co. Dept. of Corr.	0.7%	0.7%	1.4%	2.8%	1.9%
Saline Co. Jail	0.0	1.6	0.0	0.0	2.3
Nevada					
Clark Co. Det. Ctr.	0.6%	0.3%	0.4%	0.4%	0.4%
Nye Co. Jail - Pahrump	0.0	0.0	0.0	0.0	0.0
Washoe Co. Det. Ctr.	1.1	1.1	1.5	1.7	0.0

Percent of jail inmates reporting sexual victimization, by level of coercion and facility, National Inmate Survey, 2011–12

Facility name	Inmate-on-inmate[a]		Staff sexual misconduct[a]		
	Physically forced[b]	Pressured[c]	Physically forced[b]	Pressured[c]	Without force or pressure[d]
New Hampshire					
Coos Co. Jail	0.0%	0.0%	0.0%	4.4%	0.0%
Hillsborough Co. House of Corr.	3.2	2.3	3.3	2.0	1.0
New Jersey					
Bergen Co. Jail	1.6%	1.1%	1.2%	1.5%	0.0%
Burlington Co. Min. Security Jail/Corr. and Work Release Ctr.	0.0	0.0	0.0	0.0	0.0
Essex Co. Corr. Fac.	0.8	0.4	1.2	1.2	0.8
Hudson Co. Corr. Fac.	1.0	0.7	1.0	1.3	0.8
Mercer Co. Corr. Ctr.	4.1	1.3	2.0	3.1	3.7
Middlesex Co. Adult Corr. Ctr.	1.0	0.7	0.4	0.4	0.3
Ocean Co. Justice Complex	0.0	1.2	0.0	0.8	0.0
Passaic Co. Jail	1.2	1.3	2.6	2.3	1.2
Salem Co. Corr. Fac.	0.0	0.7	0.0	1.7	0.0
New Mexico					
Dona Ana Co. Det. Ctr.	1.6%	2.5%	1.4%	1.9%	0.8%
San Juan Co. Adult Det. Ctr.	3.0	2.5	0.7	0.7	1.8
Santa Fe Co. Adult Det. Fac.[g]	1.2	2.3	0.0	0.6	1.2
New York					
Albany Co. Corr. Fac.	2.7%	1.3%	1.2%	1.2%	2.0%
Allegany Co. Jail	3.0	3.0	1.5	1.5	0.0
Broome Co. Jail	1.4	2.9	1.5	2.8	1.9
Dutchess Co. Jail	0.7	0.7	0.7	1.4	0.0
Erie Co. Corr. Fac.	0.4	0.4	2.8	2.8	2.7
Erie Co. Holding Fac.	0.0	0.0	4.5	4.5	0.0
Jefferson Co. Jail	1.0	1.0	4.2	1.0	1.6
New York City Anna M. Kross Ctr.	2.4	0.5	1.2	2.1	1.5
New York City George Motchan Det. Ctr.	0.9	0.8	0.4	1.8	2.1
New York City Otis Bantum Corr. Ctr.	0.0	0.6	2.7	3.1	4.6
New York City Robert N Davoren Complex	0.3	0.3	0.6	1.3	2.3
New York City Rose M. Singer Ctr.[e]	4.1	2.3	2.3	5.6	2.9
Niagara Co. Jail	0.7	0.7	0.0	1.1	0.0
Oneida Co. Corr. Fac.	0.0	0.0	2.1	3.0	1.6
Orange Co. Corr. Fac.	0.4	1.0	0.0	0.9	0.9
Putnam Co. Corr. Fac.	0.0	0.0	1.1	1.1	1.1
Rockland Co. Corr. Ctr.	0.0	2.1	1.6	1.6	0.9
Schenectady Co. Jail	2.2	3.1	0.5	2.5	1.4
Seneca Co. Law Enforcement Ctr.	3.6	0.0	1.3	1.3	2.0
Ulster Co. Law Enforcement Ctr.	0.7	1.5	3.8	3.5	3.0
Washington Co. Corr. Fac.	0.0	0.0	0.0	0.0	0.0
Westchester Co. Jail	0.0	0.5	1.0	1.6	0.9
Westchester Co. Penitentiary - Dept. of Corr.	0.4	0.9	0.5	1.3	0.3
North Carolina					
Buncombe Co. Det. Fac.	0.7%	0.0%	0.6%	1.3%	0.0%
Cherokee Co. Jail	0.0	0.0	2.5	2.5	2.5
Durham Co. Jail	0.7	0.7	0.0	0.5	1.1
Edgecombe Co. Det. Ctr.	1.1	1.5	0.9	1.7	2.9
Forsyth Co. Adult Det. Ctr.	0.8	0.4	2.2	1.4	2.0
Granville Co. Det. Ctr.	0.4	0.4	1.2	1.2	4.8
Guilford Co. High Point Det. Fac.	0.0	0.0	0.0	0.0	1.1
Guilford Co. Prison Farm	0.0	0.0	0.0	0.0	0.0
Mecklenburg Co. Jail North	0.6	0.6	0.0	1.3	1.4
New Hanover Det. Fac.	0.6	0.6	0.7	1.2	0.0
Robeson Co. Jail	2.4	1.3	1.2	3.3	2.6
Scotland Co. Jail	0.0	1.0	1.9	3.0	2.5
Wake Co. John H. Baker, Jr. Public Safety Ctr.	2.9	2.2	0.4	0.9	0.4

Percent of jail inmates reporting sexual victimization, by level of coercion and facility, National Inmate Survey, 2011–12

Facility name	Inmate-on-inmate[a]		Staff sexual misconduct[a]		
	Physically forced[b]	Pressured[c]	Physically forced[b]	Pressured[c]	Without force or pressure[d]
North Dakota					
Burleigh Co. Det. Ctr.	0.0%	0.0%	2.5%	3.5%	0.0%
Ohio					
Bedford Heights City Jail	0.0%	0.0%	0.0%	0.0%	0.0%
Cuyahoga Co. Corr. Ctr.	0.9	1.2	0.7	0.7	1.2
Delaware Co. Jail	0.0	0.0	0.0	0.0	0.0
Franklin Co. Jail	2.6	1.2	0.0	1.0	0.0
Hamilton Co. Justice Ctr.	0.0	0.0	1.1	1.8	0.0
Hamilton Co. Reading Road Fac.	0.8	1.3	0.0	0.0	0.3
Lorain Co. Jail	0.6	1.1	1.1	1.1	0.0
Miami Co. Jail	0.0	0.0	0.0	0.0	0.0
Montgomery Co. Jail	0.4	0.0	0.9	0.9	0.0
Richland Co. Jail	1.4	1.4	0.0	0.7	0.7
Oklahoma					
Dewey Co. Jail	0.0%	0.0%	0.0%	0.0%	0.0%
Kay Co. Jail	1.7	0.9	0.0	0.0	0.9
Nowata Co. Jail	0.0	0.0	0.0	2.4	0.0
Oregon					
Lane Co. Jail	0.5%	0.5%	0.5%	0.8%	0.0%
Marion Co. Corr. Fac.	0.5	0.5	0.9	0.5	0.9
Washington Co. Jail	0.0	0.0	0.0	0.0	0.5
Yamhill Co. Corr. Fac.	3.2	4.3	0.0	0.4	0.4
Pennsylvania					
Allegheny Co. Jail	1.5%	1.0%	0.2%	1.0%	1.0%
Blair Co. Prison	0.0	3.5	0.0	1.7	0.0
Fayette Co. Prison	1.6	2.6	2.1	2.9	2.3
Indiana Co. Jail	1.7	2.1	0.0	0.0	0.0
Luzerne Co. Corr. Fac.	1.5	2.4	0.0	0.6	0.0
Montgomery Co. Prison Corr. Fac.	0.7	1.4	1.0	2.2	0.5
Philadelphia City Alternative and Special Det. Fac.	0.0	0.0	0.4	0.8	0.0
Philadelphia City Curran/Fromhold Corr. Fac.	1.2	0.5	1.3	2.0	1.7
Philadelphia City Industrial Corr. Ctr.	3.5	1.9	2.3	3.4	3.4
Philadelphia City Riverside Corr. Fac.[e]	6.7	4.5	3.1	3.2	0.0
Schuykill Co. Prison	1.0	1.0	1.0	1.6	1.1
Westmoreland Co. Prison	0.7	1.8	1.0	2.2	0.0
York Co. Prison	2.4	2.2	0.0	1.8	0.0
South Carolina					
Charleston Co. Det. Ctr.	0.4%	0.7%	0.9%	0.8%	0.4%
Florence Co. Det. Ctr.	0.0	0.0	0.5	0.0	0.7
Lexington Co. Jail	1.1	0.6	0.6	0.6	0.0
Spartanburg Co. Det. Fac.	0.0	0.0	0.0	1.1	0.5
Sumter-Lee Regional Det. Ctr.	0.0	0.4	2.4	3.2	3.0
York Co. Det. Ctr.	0.0	0.0	1.8	2.1	0.0
South Dakota					
Pennington Co. Jail	2.0%	0.7%	0.4%	0.9%	0.0%
Tennessee					
Lincoln Co. Jail	3.0%	3.0%	1.3%	1.3%	0.0%
Madison Co. Jail	1.0	0.5	1.7	3.0	1.0
McMinn Co. Jail	1.9	2.8	0.6	0.6	1.0
Montgomery Co. Jail	0.0	0.0	0.7	0.7	0.7
Obion Co. Jail	0.0	0.0	0.0	0.0	0.0
Robertson Co. Det. Ctr.	0.6	0.5	0.0	1.2	0.6
Shelby Co. Corr. Ctr.	1.1	0.4	1.1	1.1	2.8
Shelby Co. Jail	0.6	0.3	0.6	1.1	0.8
Sumner Co. Jail	3.4	1.9	1.7	2.0	1.0

Percent of jail inmates reporting sexual victimization, by level of coercion and facility, National Inmate Survey, 2011–12

Facility name	Inmate-on-inmate[a]		Staff sexual misconduct[a]		
	Physically forced[b]	Pressured[c]	Physically forced[b]	Pressured[c]	Without force or pressure[d]
Tipton Co. Jail	0.0%	1.5%	0.0%	0.0%	0.0%
Van Buren Co. Jail	0.0	0.0	0.0	0.0	0.0
Washington Co. Det. Ctr.	1.9	2.2	0.5	0.7	0.0
Texas					
Bexar Co. Adult Det. Ctr.	0.8%	1.1%	1.8%	3.1%	1.2%
Bowie Co. Corr. Ctr.	0.6	0.6	0.5	1.1	1.3
Brazoria Co. Jail and Det. Ctr.	0.0	0.4	0.0	0.4	0.0
Brown Co. Jail	0.0	0.0	0.0	0.0	0.0
Cameron Co. Carrizales-Rucker Det. Ctr.	0.0	0.3	0.0	0.0	0.0
Dallas Co. Kays Det. Fac.	0.0	0.4	0.4	0.9	1.2
Denton Co. Det. Ctr.	0.0	0.7	0.4	1.4	1.3
Eastland Co. Jail	0.0	0.0	0.0	0.0	0.0
El Paso Co. Det. Fac. Annex	2.2	1.5	0.3	0.3	0.6
El Paso Co. Downtown Det. Fac.	1.0	1.0	1.4	1.4	1.3
Ellis Co. Wayne McCollum Det. Ctr.	1.8	0.9	0.5	1.8	0.4
Gregg Co. Jail	0.3	0.3	0.0	0.3	0.8
Harris Co. Jail - 1200 Baker Street Jail	5.0	2.6	0.4	1.1	0.2
Harris Co. Jail - 1307 Baker Street Jail	1.0	0.5	0.0	0.5	0.0
Harris Co. Jail - 701 North San Jacinto Street Jail[f]	0.6	0.6	0.3	1.4	1.4
Harris Co. Jail - 711 North San Jacinto Jail	0.0	0.0	0.0	0.0	1.5
Hays Co. Jail	0.8	0.8	1.8	3.1	1.8
Jefferson Co. Corr. Fac.	1.0	0.2	1.0	1.4	0.7
Johnson Co. Jail	2.3	1.6	0.5	2.5	1.1
Tarrant Co. Corr. Ctr.	0.6	1.0	0.0	1.0	1.2
Taylor Co. Jail	1.0	1.1	0.0	1.3	0.7
Titus Co. Jail	0.0	0.0	0.0	0.0	0.0
Travis Co. Corr. Fac.	1.0	0.8	0.0	0.0	1.0
Travis Co. Jail	0.0	0.0	0.0	0.0	0.0
Uvalde Co. Jail	0.0	0.0	0.0	3.6	0.0
Victoria Co. Jail	0.0	1.6	0.0	0.0	0.0
Washington Co. Jail	2.6	2.6	0.0	0.0	0.0
Webb Co. Jail	0.0	0.0	0.0	0.6	0.0
Utah					
Box Elder Co. Jail	0.0%	0.0%	0.0%	0.0%	0.0%
Davis Co. Jail	2.2	2.8	0.0	0.8	0.5
Weber Co. Corr. Fac.	1.2	1.6	0.7	1.8	0.5
Virginia					
Alexandria Det. Ctr.	0.0%	0.6%	0.0%	0.6%	0.0%
Arlington Co. Det. Fac.	0.0	0.0	0.8	0.8	0.0
Bristol City Jail	0.0	0.8	0.0	0.0	0.0
Hampton Corr. Fac.	0.5	0.0	0.5	0.5	0.0
Henrico Co. Regional Jail West	0.4	0.3	0.9	1.5	0.6
Mecklenburg Co. Jail	0.0	0.0	0.0	0.0	0.0
Montgomery Co. Jail	0.0	0.0	0.0	0.0	0.0
Newport News City Jail	0.4	0.6	1.9	2.5	1.5
Piedmont Regional Jail	0.0	1.4	0.5	0.9	0.5
Rappahannock Regional Jail	1.2	0.0	2.3	1.9	0.6
Richmond City Jail	1.7	0.8	0.4	0.8	1.0
Riverside Regional Jail	0.8	1.6	1.4	3.2	0.9
Virginia Beach Municipal Corr. Ctr.	1.0	0.4	1.1	0.7	0.7

APPENDIX TABLE 7 (continued)
Percent of jail inmates reporting sexual victimization, by level of coercion and facility, National Inmate Survey, 2011–12

Facility name	Inmate-on-inmate[a]		Staff sexual misconduct[a]		
	Physically forced[b]	Pressured[c]	Physically forced[b]	Pressured[c]	Without force or pressure[d]
Washington					
Benton Co. Jail	0.1%	1.1%	0.0%	1.1%	1.1%
Cowlitz Co. Jail	0.7	0.0	0.6	1.0	0.0
King Co. Regional Justice Ctr.	0.0	0.0	0.9	0.6	0.8
Snohomish Co. Jail	0.5	0.0	0.5	0.5	0.0
Sunnyside City Jail	0.0	0.0	0.0	0.0	0.0
Whatcom Co. Jail	2.7	2.9	0.0	0.0	0.3
Yakima City Jail	0.0	0.0	0.0	1.8	0.0
West Virginia					
Eastern Regional Jail	4.7%	4.0%	0.9%	1.5%	0.4%
South Central Regional Jail	2.9	3.0	1.7	1.1	0.5
Western Regional Jail	4.4	3.6	0.9	1.6	0.4
Wisconsin					
Brown Co. Jail	1.7%	0.5%	2.1%	2.1%	1.4%
Columbia Co. Jail	0.0	2.1	2.1	2.1	0.0
Milwaukee Co. Corr. Fac. South	1.3	1.3	1.4	2.4	1.0
Oconto Co. Jail	0.0	0.0	0.0	0.0	0.0
Rock Co. Jail	1.3	2.1	0.8	1.3	0.7
Walworth Co. Jail	0.8	0.8	1.7	1.7	2.5
Washington Co. Jail	3.1	3.1	1.4	3.0	3.0
Wood Co. Jail	0.0	0.0	0.0	0.0	0.0
Wyoming					
Lincoln Co. Jail	0.0%	0.0%	0.0%	0.0%	0.0%

[a]Includes all types of sexual victimization, including oral, anal, or vaginal penetration, hand jobs, touching of the inmate's butt, thighs, penis, breasts, or vagina in a sexual way, and other sexual acts occurring in the past 12 months or since admission to the facility, if shorter.

[b]Physical force or threat of physical force reported.

[c]Includes incidents in which the perpetrator, without using force, pressured the inmate or made the inmate feel that they had to participate. (See *Methodology*.)

[d]Includes incidents in which the staff offered favors or privileges in exchange for sex or sexual contact and incidents in which the inmate reported that they willingly had sex or sexual contact with staff.

[e]Female facility.

[f]Facility housed both males and females; only males were sampled at this facility.

[g]Privately operated facility.

Source: Bureau of Justice Statistics, National Inmate Survey, 2011–12.

Percent of jail inmates reporting nonconsensual sexual acts and abusive sexual contacts, by facility, National Inmate Survey, 2011–12

Facility name	Nonconsensual sexual acts[a]			Abusive sexual contacts only[b]		
		95%-confidence interval[c]			95%-confidence interval[c]	
	Percent victimized[d]	Lower bound	Upper bound	Percent victimized[d]	Lower bound	Upper bound
Total	1.2%	1.0%	1.4%	1.9%	1.7%	2.2%
Alabama						
Barbour Co. Jail	2.3%	0.7%	7.5%	0.0%	0.0%	7.6%
Dallas Co. Jail	0.7	0.2	2.1	0.9	0.3	2.7
Lee Co. W.S. Buck Jones Det. Ctr.	1.4	0.5	3.3	1.6	0.8	3.3
Marshall Co. Jail	1.7	0.7	3.8	3.4	1.9	6.0
Tuscaloosa Co. Jail	1.7	0.8	3.6	1.8	0.8	3.8
Arizona						
Maricopa Co. Estrella Jail[e]	2.9%	1.4%	5.8%	0.8%	0.3%	2.6%
Maricopa Co. Fourth Avenue Jail	0.6	0.1	3.2	0.9	0.3	3.2
Maricopa Co. Towers Jail	2.0	0.8	4.9	3.4	1.6	7.1
Mariopa Co. Lower Buckeye Jail	0.9	0.3	2.9	3.4	1.8	6.6
Santa Cruz Co. Jail	0.0	0.0	6.9	0.0	0.0	6.9
Yuma Co. Det. Ctr.	0.0	0.0	2.4	2.1	0.8	5.1
Arkansas						
Crittenden Co. Jail	4.5%	2.6%	7.6%	1.9%	0.8%	4.4%
Mississippi Co. Det. Ctr.	0.0	0.0	4.3	0.8	0.3	2.8
Pope Co. Det. Ctr.	4.1	1.4	11.7	1.8	0.4	7.7
Pulaski Co. Regional Det. Ctr.	5.0	2.4	10.5	1.0	0.3	3.2
Sebastian Co. Adult Det. Ctr.	0.0	0.0	2.5	1.1	0.4	2.8
California						
Alameda Co. Santa Rita Jail	0.3%	0.0%	1.3%	2.7%	1.4%	5.2%
Contra Costa Co. Martinez Det. Fac.	0.6	0.1	2.8	6.4	3.7	11.0
Fresno Co. Downtown Det. Fac. - Main, North and South	2.7	1.3	5.7	0.8	0.2	2.7
Imperial Co. Jail	0.2	0.0	0.8	0.8	0.3	2.7
Kern Co. Lerdo Pre-Trial Fac.	1.0	0.2	4.9	2.8	1.2	6.3
Los Angeles Co. - Twin Towers Corr. Fac.	3.3	1.5	7.2	4.6	2.4	8.9
Los Angeles Co. Men's Central Jail	1.3	0.5	3.8	5.6	3.1	9.7
Los Angeles Co. North County Corr. Fac.	0.8	0.2	2.9	1.9	0.7	5.5
Napa Co. Jail	0.0	0.0	3.3	3.8	2.0	7.3
Orange Co. Central Jail Complex	0.6	0.1	3.4	0.7	0.1	3.8
Orange Co. Theo Lacy Fac.	1.7	0.6	4.8	3.0	1.4	6.4
Riverside Co. Indio Jail	2.1	0.9	5.0	0.7	0.2	2.6
Riverside Co. Larry D. Smith Corr. Ctr.	2.3	1.1	5.0	2.7	1.2	6.0
Riverside Co. Southwest Det. Ctr.[f]	0.0	0.0	2.5	0.6	0.1	3.0
Sacramento Co. Rio Cosumnes Corr. Ctr.	1.8	0.8	3.9	3.1	1.6	5.8
San Diego Co. East Mesa Med. Fac.	0.0	0.0	2.7	2.4	1.0	5.6
San Diego Co. George F. Bailey Det. Fac.	3.1	1.4	7.0	2.1	0.7	5.8
San Diego Co. Vista Det. Fac.	0.4	0.1	1.7	3.5	1.8	6.6
San Francisco Co. Jail Number 3	0.0	0.0	5.0	4.0	1.5	9.9
Santa Clara Co. Elmwood Fac. - Min. and Med.	1.3	0.5	3.6	1.1	0.3	3.7
Santa Clara Co. Main Jail	6.0	2.8	12.4	3.2	1.4	7.2
Santa Clara Co. Women's Corr. Ctr.[e]	1.4	0.5	4.2	0.7	0.2	3.1
Solano Co. Justice Ctr. Det. Fac.	1.5	0.6	3.5	3.7	2.0	6.6
Tulare Co. Jail	0.8	0.1	3.8	0.3	0.1	1.4
Ventura Co. Jail	1.9	0.8	4.2	0.9	0.3	2.7
Yolo Co. Leinberger Ctr.	2.1	0.7	6.0	0.0	0.0	8.0
Yuba Co. Jail	0.8	0.2	2.9	1.2	0.4	3.2

Percent of jail inmates reporting nonconsensual sexual acts and abusive sexual contacts, by facility, National Inmate Survey, 2011–12

Facility name	Nonconsensual sexual acts[a]			Abusive sexual contacts only[b]		
		95%-confidence interval[c]			95%-confidence interval[c]	
	Percent victimized[d]	Lower bound	Upper bound	Percent victimized[d]	Lower bound	Upper bound
Colorado						
Chaffee Co. Jail	0.0%	0.0%	10.4%	0.0%	0.0%	10.4%
Denver Co. Jail	2.1	1.0	4.4	1.5	0.7	3.4
Denver Co. Van Cise-Simonet Det. Ctr.	1.3	0.4	4.4	0.8	0.1	3.8
Douglas Co. Jail	0.7	0.2	2.6	2.2	0.9	5.0
Fremont Co. Jail	2.3	1.1	4.7	0.8	0.2	2.5
Jefferson Co. Jail	0.0	0.0	1.8	0.0	0.0	1.8
Park Co. Jail	0.0	0.0	6.4	0.0	0.0	6.4
Florida						
Collier Co. Jail	2.0%	0.9%	4.2%	3.1%	1.2%	7.6%
Dixie Co. Jail	2.4	0.8	7.4	5.7	2.5	12.6
Escambia Co. Jail	1.4	0.6	3.4	1.1	0.3	3.6
Jacksonville City Montgomery Corr. Ctr.	0.8	0.2	3.1	1.6	0.7	3.6
Lake Co. Jail	0.3	0.1	1.7	2.5	0.6	9.4
Lee Co. Community Programs Unit	0.7	0.2	2.4	2.4	1.1	5.0
Leon Co. Det. Fac.	2.3	1.1	4.8	2.6	1.3	5.1
Manatee Co. Jail	2.0	0.8	4.6	3.2	1.7	5.9
Martin Co. Jail	1.3	0.4	3.8	1.9	0.7	4.6
Miami-Dade Co. Boot Camp	0.0	0.0	7.4	0.0	0.0	7.4
Miami-Dade Co. Metro West Det. Ctr.	0.5	0.1	2.6	2.1	1.0	4.4
Miami-Dade Co. Training and Treatment Ctr.	0.0	0.0	2.2	1.0	0.3	3.2
Miami-Dade Co. Turner Guilford Knight Corr. Ctr.	0.5	0.1	2.4	0.5	0.1	2.2
Okeechobee Co. Jail	1.1	0.3	3.9	0.0	0.0	3.7
Orange Co. 33rd Street Corr. Ctr.	0.5	0.1	2.6	3.0	1.4	6.3
Orange Co. Booking and Release Ctr.	1.0	0.2	3.9	1.9	0.7	5.4
Osceola Co. Jail	0.3	0.1	1.2	0.7	0.1	3.0
Palm Beach Co. Stockade	0.5	0.1	2.3	1.9	0.7	5.0
Pinellas Co. Central Division Fac.	0.0	0.0	2.4	2.4	0.9	6.4
Pinellas Co. South Division	0.8	0.2	3.9	2.4	1.0	5.8
Polk Co. - South Co. Jail	1.2	0.4	3.2	3.9	2.1	7.1
Sarasota North Co. Jail	0.0	0.0	1.9	0.0	0.0	1.9
Suwanee Co. Jail	0.9	0.3	3.0	0.0	0.0	4.5
Taylor Co. Jail	0.0	0.0	13.3	0.0	0.0	13.3
Georgia						
Candler Co. Jail	0.0%	0.0%	12.5%	0.0%	0.0%	12.5%
Carroll Co. Prison	0.7	0.3	1.7	2.0	1.1	3.5
Clayton Co. Jail	2.1	1.0	4.4	2.5	1.2	5.1
Dekalb Co. Jail	0.9	0.3	2.4	2.4	1.1	4.8
Douglas Co. Jail	2.2	1.1	4.3	0.7	0.2	1.9
Floyd Co. Jail	2.1	1.0	4.2	1.5	0.7	3.2
Floyd Co. Prison	0.0	0.0	2.1	2.8	1.5	5.0
Fulton Co. Jail	2.9	1.2	6.5	2.0	0.7	5.6
Gwinnett Co. Det. Ctr.	0.8	0.2	2.6	0.0	0.0	1.5
Hall Co. Det. Ctr.	1.4	0.5	3.8	1.6	0.6	4.2
Houston Co. Jail	2.2	1.0	4.6	4.9	2.8	8.3
Irwin Co. Jail	0.0	0.0	2.0	1.1	0.4	2.9
Murray County Jail	1.1	0.4	3.3	2.2	1.0	4.7
Newton Co. Jail	1.7	0.8	3.7	2.0	0.9	4.6
Screven Co. Jail	2.7	1.4	5.1	1.2	0.5	3.0
South Fulton Municipal Regional Jail	2.3	0.5	9.5	2.3	0.5	9.5
Spalding Co. Jail	1.1	0.4	3.3	4.0	1.9	8.0
Troup Co. Jail	1.1	0.4	2.9	1.1	0.4	2.9
Upson Co. Jail	0.0	0.0	3.4	2.6	1.5	4.6
Ware Co. Jail	0.8	0.3	2.1	1.4	0.6	2.9
Wilkinson Co. Jail	6.5	1.9	20.0	0.0	0.0	16.8

Percent of jail inmates reporting nonconsensual sexual acts and abusive sexual contacts, by facility, National Inmate Survey, 2011–12

Facility name	Nonconsensual sexual acts[a]			Abusive sexual contacts only[b]		
		95%-confidence interval[c]			95%-confidence interval[c]	
	Percent victimized[d]	Lower bound	Upper bound	Percent victimized[d]	Lower bound	Upper bound
Idaho						
Bannock Co. Jail	0.0%	0.0%	3.3%	3.0%	1.3%	6.8%
Illinois						
Champaign Co. Satellite Jail[f]	2.0%	0.5%	8.4%	0.0%	0.0%	6.4%
Cook Co. - Division 1	1.1	0.4	2.7	3.3	1.9	5.6
Cook Co. - Division 11	3.3	1.9	5.8	4.4	2.7	7.1
Cook Co. - Division 2	0.6	0.1	3.0	5.1	3.0	8.6
Cook Co. - Division 5	1.2	0.5	3.1	2.3	1.1	4.7
Cook Co. - Division 6	0.4	0.1	1.6	1.9	0.9	3.7
Kane Co. Adult Justice Ctr.	0.8	0.3	2.6	2.1	0.8	5.1
Kankakee Co. Jerome Combs Det. Ctr.	1.7	0.7	3.9	1.7	0.8	3.4
Kendall Co. Jail	3.4	1.7	6.8	1.7	0.5	5.1
McHenry Co. Jail	0.6	0.1	2.6	0.5	0.1	2.2
Sangamon Co. Jail	1.6	0.8	3.0	2.3	1.3	4.1
Indiana						
Bartholomew Co. Jail	0.5%	0.2%	1.3%	2.6%	1.5%	4.7%
Clinton Co. Jail	1.6	0.5	4.4	0.8	0.3	2.4
Dearborn Co. Jail	0.0	0.0	3.0	1.8	0.8	4.3
Delaware Co. Justice Ctr.	1.6	0.6	4.4	0.2	0.1	0.9
Elkhart Co. Corr. Ctr.	1.2	0.5	3.2	2.4	1.3	4.4
Hamilton Co. Jail	0.5	0.2	1.9	0.9	0.3	3.3
Jackson Co. Jail	1.0	0.3	3.4	0.0	0.0	4.1
Marion Co. Jail II[g]	1.2	0.4	3.3	2.2	0.6	7.3
Marion Co. Jail Intake Fac.	2.7	0.7	10.7	4.9	1.9	12.2
Noble Co. Jail	0.0	0.0	3.5	0.9	0.3	2.3
Ripley Co. Jail	0.0	0.0	7.0	7.9	5.1	11.9
Tippecanoe Co. Jail	2.5	1.1	5.7	0.0	0.0	3.2
Iowa						
Des Moines Co. Jail	0.0%	0.0%	11.4%	2.1%	0.6%	7.1%
Scott Co. Jail and Annex	2.4	1.1	5.1	0.8	0.2	2.8
Kansas						
Finney Co. Jail	3.0%	1.6%	5.6%	1.0%	0.3%	2.9%
Wilson Co. Jail	0.0	0.0	9.6	5.6	1.7	16.5
Kentucky						
Big Sandy Regional Det. Ctr.	0.0%	0.0%	2.6%	1.3%	0.6%	3.2%
Boyle Co. Det. Ctr.	0.0	0.0	2.5	1.9	0.6	5.7
Daviess Co. Det. Ctr.	0.7	0.3	2.1	2.9	1.5	5.4
Grayson Co. Det. Ctr.	0.8	0.3	2.2	1.4	0.6	3.1
Kenton Co. Det. Ctr.	0.4	0.1	1.8	0.7	0.2	2.5
Lexington-Fayette Co. Jail Det. Division	0.6	0.2	2.0	3.6	1.8	7.3
Madison Co. Det. Ctr.	2.1	1.1	4.2	1.7	0.8	3.4
McCracken Co. Jail	1.1	0.4	2.8	2.0	1.0	3.9
Meade Co. Jail	0.0	0.0	4.4	1.3	0.5	3.6
Pulaski Co. Det. Ctr.	0.9	0.2	3.1	0.8	0.2	2.9
Woodford Co. Det. Ctr.	0.1	0.0	0.6	0.0	0.0	10.2
Louisiana						
Assumption Parish Det. Ctr.	1.5%	0.6%	3.9%	3.1%	1.6%	6.0%
Bossier Parish Max. Security Fac.	0.9	0.4	2.3	0.0	0.0	2.2
Bossier Parish Med. Security Fac.	0.4	0.1	1.5	2.0	1.0	4.0
Caddo Parish Corr. Ctr.	0.4	0.1	1.8	1.6	0.7	3.7
East Baton Rouge Parish Prison	1.4	0.5	3.8	0.9	0.3	3.2
Iberia Parish Jail	1.4	0.6	3.2	2.5	1.3	4.9
Lafayette Parish Jail	0.5	0.1	2.2	2.8	1.4	5.4

Percent of jail inmates reporting nonconsensual sexual acts and abusive sexual contacts, by facility, National Inmate Survey, 2011–12

| Facility name | Nonconsensual sexual acts[a] | | | Abusive sexual contacts only[b] | | |
| | Percent victimized[d] | 95%-confidence interval[c] | | Percent victimized[d] | 95%-confidence interval[c] | |
		Lower bound	Upper bound		Lower bound	Upper bound
Livingston Parish Det. Ctr.	0.0%	0.0%	1.7%	1.4%	0.6%	3.2%
Rapides Parish Det. Ctr. III	1.4	0.7	3.0	0.5	0.1	1.6
St. Landry Parish Jail	0.0	0.0	3.3	0.7	0.2	2.5
St. Martin Parish Corr. Ctr. 1	2.6	1.0	6.4	1.3	0.4	4.6
Webster Parish Bayou Dorcheat Corr. Fac.	1.2	0.6	2.6	2.1	1.0	4.5
Maine						
Penobscot Co. Jail	1.8%	0.4%	6.7%	2.6%	0.7%	9.6%
Maryland						
Allegany Co. Det. Ctr.	2.3%	0.5%	9.6%	0.0%	0.0%	7.7%
Anne Arundel Co. Jennifer Road Det. Ctr.	0.0	0.0	3.6	0.9	0.2	4.4
Baltimore City Det. Ctr.	1.2	0.4	3.3	5.5	3.4	8.8
Montgomery Co. Corr. Fac.	1.6	0.6	3.9	1.1	0.4	3.5
Wicomico Co. Det. Ctr.	0.6	0.2	2.1	0.0	0.0	2.5
Massachusetts						
Hampden Co. Corr. Ctr.	0.0%	0.0%	1.7%	1.9%	0.7%	5.0%
Middlesex Co. Jail and House of Corr.	0.7	0.2	3.5	1.4	0.6	3.2
Plymouth Co. Corr. Fac.	0.0	0.0	2.1	2.0	0.8	4.7
Suffolk Co. House of Corr.	1.5	0.6	3.5	4.7	2.6	8.3
Suffolk Co. Nashua Street Jail	0.0	0.0	2.5	1.9	0.7	4.9
Worcester Co. Jail and House of Corr.	0.7	0.2	2.2	3.7	2.1	6.5
Michigan						
Berrien Co. Jail	0.8%	0.3%	1.9%	3.5%	2.2%	5.6%
Calhoun Co. Jail	0.3	0.1	1.2	4.8	2.4	9.4
Huron Co. Jail	0.0	0.0	12.1	0.0	0.0	12.1
Kalamazoo Co. Jail	1.6	0.8	3.2	4.1	2.4	7.0
Macomb Co. Jail	0.0	0.0	2.5	1.9	0.8	4.5
Oakland Co. East Annex	1.2	0.5	3.2	1.3	0.5	3.5
Oakland Co. Law Enforcement Complex	3.7	1.8	7.5	3.6	1.5	8.5
Ottawa Co. Jail	0.0	0.0	3.1	0.6	0.2	2.5
Wayne Co. Andrew C. Baird Det. Fac.	2.8	1.2	6.4	1.3	0.4	4.6
Wayne Co. William Dickerson Det. - Division III	0.0	0.0	2.2	0.4	0.1	2.1
Minnesota						
Anoka Co. Jail	0.9%	0.3%	3.3%	1.1%	0.4%	2.8%
Hennepin Co. Adult Det. Ctr.	0.6	0.1	2.7	0.9	0.3	2.8
Mille Lacs Co. Jail	0.0	0.0	9.9	1.8	0.6	5.5
Ramsey Co. Corr. Fac.	0.0	0.0	2.2	0.9	0.3	2.2
Mississippi						
Covington Co. Jail	0.0%	0.0%	25.9%	0.0%	0.0%	25.9%
Harrison Co. Adult Det. Ctr.	1.0	0.4	2.5	4.1	2.2	7.6
Hinds Co. Jackson Det. Ctr.	1.8	0.8	4.0	1.1	0.4	3.1
Hinds Co. Raymond Det. Ctr.	1.6	0.7	3.9	3.5	1.8	6.6
Holmes-Humphreys Co. Regional Corr. Fac.	1.7	0.6	4.6	0.8	0.2	3.0
Madison Co. Jail	1.8	0.8	3.9	1.4	0.5	3.6
Marshall Co. Jail	0.0	0.0	7.6	0.0	0.0	7.6
Pike Co. Jail	0.0	0.0	4.1	0.0	0.0	4.1
Missouri						
Boone Co. Jail	1.7%	0.6%	4.6%	2.3%	0.6%	8.8%
LaClede Co. Jail	3.1	1.8	5.3	4.5	2.7	7.3
St. Charles Co. Jail	2.4	1.0	5.6	3.6	1.8	7.0
St. Louis Co. Jail	1.8	0.7	4.8	1.7	0.6	4.4
St. Louis Med. Security Inst.	3.5	1.7	6.8	3.2	1.7	5.9
Washington Co. Jail	3.3	0.9	11.3	0.0	0.0	16.1

Percent of jail inmates reporting nonconsensual sexual acts and abusive sexual contacts, by facility, National Inmate Survey, 2011–12

Facility name	Nonconsensual sexual acts[a]			Abusive sexual contacts only[b]		
		95%-confidence interval[c]			95%-confidence interval[c]	
	Percent victimized[d]	Lower bound	Upper bound	Percent victimized[d]	Lower bound	Upper bound
Montana						
Cascade Co. Regional Jail	1.7%	0.7%	3.7%	3.6%	2.0%	6.3%
Hill Co. Jail	0.0	0.0	12.5	0.0	0.0	12.5
Missoula Co. Jail	1.2	0.4	3.0	1.4	0.5	3.5
Nebraska						
Douglas Co. Dept. of Corr.	1.4%	0.4%	4.9%	2.6%	1.1%	6.4%
Saline Co. Jail	2.3	0.9	6.2	1.6	0.6	4.5
Nevada						
Clark Co. Det. Ctr.	0.6%	0.2%	1.9%	0.4%	0.1%	2.2%
Nye Co. Jail - Pahrump	0.0	0.0	21.5	0.0	0.0	21.5
Washoe Co. Det. Ctr.	2.8	1.3	5.9	0.4	0.1	2.1
New Hampshire						
Coos Co. Jail	0.0%	0.0%	16.8%	4.4%	1.2%	14.3%
Hillsborough Co. House of Corr.	2.9	1.2	6.8	3.1	1.4	6.7
New Jersey						
Bergen Co. Jail	0.8%	0.3%	2.3%	1.9%	0.9%	3.7%
Burlington Co. Min. Security Jail/Corr. and Work Release Ctr.	0.0	0.0	5.9	0.0	0.0	5.9
Essex Co. Corr. Fac.	0.5	0.1	2.4	1.7	0.7	4.2
Hudson Co. Corr. Fac.	1.3	0.5	3.1	0.7	0.2	2.4
Mercer Co. Corr. Ctr.	2.8	1.2	6.5	4.4	2.3	8.4
Middlesex Co. Adult Corr. Ctr.	0.3	0.1	1.4	1.0	0.4	2.5
Ocean Co. Justice Complex	2.0	0.8	5.1	0.0	0.0	2.5
Passaic Co. Jail	0.7	0.2	2.1	1.9	0.9	4.2
Salem Co. Corr. Fac.	1.8	0.6	4.9	0.7	0.2	2.8
New Mexico						
Dona Ana Co. Det. Ctr.	2.3%	1.2%	4.4%	2.5%	1.2%	5.3%
San Juan Co. Adult Det. Ctr.	1.7	0.5	5.3	1.4	0.4	4.1
Santa Fe Co. Adult Det. Fac.[g]	3.5	1.6	7.5	0.0	0.0	2.7
New York						
Albany Co. Corr. Fac.	1.8%	0.8%	4.1%	2.4%	1.1%	4.9%
Allegany Co. Jail	1.5	0.4	5.3	3.0	1.2	7.5
Broome Co. Jail	0.9	0.3	2.7	4.3	2.1	8.8
Dutchess Co. Jail	0.0	0.0	3.0	1.4	0.5	3.8
Erie Co. Corr. Fac.	0.0	0.0	2.1	4.3	2.3	7.7
Erie Co. Holding Fac.	0.0	0.0	5.3	4.5	0.9	19.6
Jefferson Co. Jail	1.6	0.4	6.0	3.6	1.6	8.2
New York City Anna M. Kross Ctr.	1.9	0.7	5.4	3.7	1.8	7.4
New York City George Motchan Det. Ctr.	1.8	0.7	4.1	3.6	1.9	6.6
New York City Otis Bantum Corr. Ctr.	0.0	0.0	2.2	6.2	3.3	11.1
New York City Robert N Davoren Complex	0.4	0.1	1.9	3.0	1.6	5.8
New York City Rose M. Singer Ctr.[e]	2.4	1.1	5.1	6.2	3.9	9.7
Niagara Co. Jail	0.0	0.0	2.3	1.8	0.7	4.1
Oneida Co. Corr. Fac.	0.9	0.2	3.8	2.1	0.9	5.1
Orange Co. Corr. Fac.	0.5	0.1	2.3	1.4	0.6	3.4
Putnam Co. Corr. Fac.	0.0	0.0	5.4	1.1	0.3	3.7
Rockland Co. Corr. Ctr.	0.6	0.2	1.8	3.5	1.7	7.4
Schenectady Co. Jail	1.9	0.9	4.1	2.9	1.7	5.0
Seneca Co. Law Enforcement Ctr.	1.6	0.6	4.0	3.3	1.6	6.6
Ulster Co. Law Enforcement Ctr.	0.9	0.3	2.2	6.1	3.6	10.1
Washington Co. Corr. Fac.	0.0	0.0	5.8	0.0	0.0	5.8
Westchester Co. Jail	0.9	0.3	2.8	2.1	0.8	5.5
Westchester Co. Penitentiary - Dept. of Corr.	0.4	0.1	1.9	1.7	0.8	3.8

Percent of jail inmates reporting nonconsensual sexual acts and abusive sexual contacts, by facility, National Inmate Survey, 2011–12

Facility name	Nonconsensual sexual acts[a]			Abusive sexual contacts only[b]		
	Percent victimized[d]	95%-confidence interval[c]		Percent victimized[d]	95%-confidence interval[c]	
		Lower bound	Upper bound		Lower bound	Upper bound
North Carolina						
Buncombe Co. Det. Fac.	0.7%	0.2%	2.5%	1.3%	0.5%	3.4%
Cherokee Co. Jail	0.0	0.0	7.9	2.5	0.8	7.8
Durham Co. Jail	0.7	0.2	2.7	1.6	0.7	3.7
Edgecombe Co. Det. Ctr.	3.1	1.8	5.4	3.2	1.7	5.9
Forsyth Co. Adult Det. Ctr.	1.2	0.4	4.0	2.0	0.8	5.1
Granville Co. Det. Ctr.	5.3	1.5	16.5	1.2	0.3	4.4
Guilford Co. High Point Det. Fac.	0.0	0.0	2.4	1.1	0.4	2.7
Guilford Co. Prison Farm	0.0	0.0	9.6	0.0	0.0	9.6
Mecklenburg Co. Jail North	0.0	0.0	3.1	2.0	0.8	4.9
New Hanover Det. Fac.	0.0	0.0	2.4	1.9	0.8	4.3
Robeson Co. Jail	2.4	1.1	5.1	5.1	3.0	8.6
Scotland Co. Jail	4.0	2.0	7.7	1.4	0.5	3.6
Wake Co. John H. Baker, Jr. Public Safety Ctr.	2.3	0.7	7.3	1.8	0.8	4.3
North Dakota						
Burleigh Co. Det. Ctr.	0.0%	0.0%	4.5%	3.5%	1.9%	6.5%
Ohio						
Bedford Heights City Jail	0.0%	0.0%	9.9%	0.0%	0.0%	9.9%
Cuyahoga Co. Corr. Ctr.	0.7	0.3	2.0	1.6	0.7	3.6
Delaware Co. Jail	0.0	0.0	3.4	0.0	0.0	3.4
Franklin Co. Jail	2.6	1.2	5.8	1.5	0.5	4.6
Hamilton Co. Justice Ctr.	0.0	0.0	1.8	1.8	0.8	4.3
Hamilton Co. Reading Road Fac.	0.9	0.4	2.1	1.6	0.7	3.3
Lorain Co. Jail	0.6	0.1	2.1	1.6	0.7	3.6
Miami Co. Jail	0.0	0.0	5.3	0.0	0.0	5.3
Montgomery Co. Jail	0.9	0.3	2.7	0.4	0.1	2.0
Richland Co. Jail	1.4	0.7	2.9	1.4	0.7	2.9
Oklahoma						
Dewey Co. Jail	0.0%	0.0%	22.8%	0.0%	0.0%	22.8%
Kay Co. Jail	0.8	0.3	2.4	1.8	0.8	3.8
Nowata Co. Jail	0.0	0.0	13.8	2.4	0.7	8.3
Oregon						
Lane Co. Jail	0.0%	0.0%	2.2%	0.8%	0.3%	2.1%
Marion Co. Corr. Fac.	0.0	0.0	1.8	1.8	0.9	3.8
Washington Co. Jail	0.0	0.0	2.5	0.5	0.1	2.4
Yamhill Co. Corr. Fac.	2.8	1.4	5.8	1.8	0.9	3.5
Pennsylvania						
Allegheny Co. Jail	0.5%	0.1%	1.7%	2.5%	1.2%	5.1%
Blair Co. Prison	3.5	1.2	10.1	1.7	0.6	4.9
Fayette Co. Prison	1.0	0.2	4.1	3.9	1.9	7.7
Indiana Co. Jail	1.7	0.6	4.8	2.1	0.5	8.2
Luzerne Co. Corr. Fac.	2.4	1.2	4.9	0.6	0.1	2.7
Montgomery Co. Prison Corr. Fac.	1.9	0.8	4.1	1.8	0.8	4.3
Philadelphia City Alternative and Special Det. Fac.	0.0	0.0	2.2	0.8	0.3	2.5
Philadelphia City Curran/Fromhold Corr. Fac.	1.5	0.5	4.3	3.0	1.5	5.9
Philadelphia City Industrial Corr. Ctr.	2.7	1.2	5.6	6.8	4.3	10.6
Philadelphia City Riverside Corr. Fac.[e]	4.1	2.3	7.3	4.5	2.5	8.1
Schuykill Co. Prison	0.0	0.0	2.7	2.7	1.4	5.0
Westmoreland Co. Prison	2.1	0.8	5.2	1.2	0.3	4.4
York Co. Prison	1.5	0.6	4.2	3.8	2.0	7.1

Percent of jail inmates reporting nonconsensual sexual acts and abusive sexual contacts, by facility, National Inmate Survey, 2011–12

Facility name	Nonconsensual sexual acts[a]			Abusive sexual contacts only[b]		
	Percent victimized[d]	95%-confidence interval[c]		Percent victimized[d]	95%-confidence interval[c]	
		Lower bound	Upper bound		Lower bound	Upper bound
South Carolina						
Charleston Co. Det. Ctr.	0.3%	0.1%	1.3%	1.7%	0.7%	4.0%
Florence Co. Det. Ctr.	0.0	0.0	2.3	1.2	0.5	3.1
Lexington Co. Jail	1.1	0.3	3.2	0.6	0.1	2.5
Spartanburg Co. Det. Fac.	0.0	0.0	1.8	1.1	0.4	3.5
Sumter-Lee Regional Det. Ctr.	1.0	0.4	2.7	4.1	2.2	7.3
York Co. Det. Ctr.	0.7	0.2	2.7	1.4	0.4	4.6
South Dakota						
Pennington Co. Jail	1.6%	0.6%	4.2%	0.9%	0.3%	2.4%
Tennessee						
Lincoln Co. Jail	3.0%	1.4%	6.1%	0.0%	0.0%	4.7%
Madison Co. Jail	0.4	0.1	1.4	4.9	2.4	9.7
McMinn Co. Jail	1.0	0.5	2.0	2.4	1.4	4.1
Montgomery Co. Jail	0.0	0.0	3.1	0.7	0.2	3.3
Obion Co. Jail	0.0	0.0	3.8	0.0	0.0	3.8
Robertson Co. Det. Ctr.	1.1	0.4	2.9	1.7	0.8	3.9
Shelby Co. Corr. Ctr.	0.3	0.1	1.6	3.1	1.7	5.5
Shelby Co. Jail	0.2	0.0	0.9	1.6	0.7	3.5
Sumner Co. Jail	3.1	1.7	5.7	2.9	1.5	5.6
Tipton Co. Jail	0.0	0.0	4.9	1.5	0.5	5.0
Van Buren Co. Jail	0.0	0.0	20.4	0.0	0.0	20.4
Washington Co. Det. Ctr.	1.5	0.7	3.4	1.4	0.6	2.9
Texas						
Bexar Co. Adult Det. Ctr.	4.6%	2.3%	9.0%	0.4%	0.1%	2.4%
Bowie Co. Corr. Ctr.	1.2	0.4	3.6	1.3	0.4	3.8
Brazoria Co. Jail and Det. Ctr.	0.0	0.0	1.7	0.9	0.3	2.6
Brown Co. Jail	0.0	0.0	4.7	0.0	0.0	4.7
Cameron Co. Carrizales-Rucker Det. Ctr.	0.0	0.0	1.4	0.3	0.1	1.6
Dallas Co. Kays Det. Fac.	0.7	0.2	2.6	1.3	0.5	3.7
Denton Co. Det. Ctr.	1.3	0.5	3.3	1.1	0.4	2.9
Eastland Co. Jail	0.0	0.0	9.9	0.0	0.0	9.9
El Paso Co. Det. Fac. Annex	1.4	0.5	3.9	1.5	0.5	4.0
El Paso Co. Downtown Det. Fac.	0.0	0.0	2.2	3.0	1.2	7.6
Ellis Co. Wayne McCollum Det. Ctr.	1.3	0.6	2.9	2.3	1.2	4.3
Gregg Co. Jail	1.0	0.4	2.4	0.5	0.1	2.0
Harris Co. Jail - 1200 Baker Street Jail	5.1	2.6	9.8	2.5	1.2	5.2
Harris Co. Jail - 1307 Baker Street Jail	0.4	0.1	1.7	1.0	0.4	2.5
Harris Co. Jail - 701 North San Jacinto Street Jail[f]	0.3	0.1	1.5	2.9	1.5	5.6
Harris Co. Jail - 711 North San Jacinto Jail	1.5	0.4	4.9	0.0	0.0	5.7
Hays Co. Jail	0.8	0.2	3.3	3.1	1.1	8.7
Jefferson Co. Corr. Fac.	0.3	0.1	1.6	1.8	0.8	3.7
Johnson Co. Jail	2.4	1.2	4.5	2.8	1.6	5.0
Tarrant Co. Corr. Ctr.	0.9	0.3	3.1	1.9	0.7	5.2
Taylor Co. Jail	0.6	0.1	2.7	2.4	1.1	5.1
Titus Co. Jail	0.0	0.0	5.7	0.0	0.0	5.7
Travis Co. Corr. Fac.	2.7	0.9	7.6	0.0	0.0	3.5
Travis Co. Jail	0.0	0.0	13.3	0.0	0.0	13.3
Uvalde Co. Jail	0.0	0.0	18.4	3.6	0.9	14.1
Victoria Co. Jail	1.6	0.4	6.6	0.0	0.0	8.6
Washington Co. Jail	1.3	0.5	3.2	1.4	0.5	3.5
Webb Co. Jail	0.0	0.0	3.4	0.6	0.1	2.7

Percent of jail inmates reporting nonconsensual sexual acts and abusive sexual contacts, by facility, National Inmate Survey, 2011–12

Facility name	Nonconsensual sexual acts[a]			Abusive sexual contacts only[b]		
		95%-confidence interval[c]			95%-confidence interval[c]	
	Percent victimized[d]	Lower bound	Upper bound	Percent victimized[d]	Lower bound	Upper bound
Utah						
Box Elder Co. Jail	0.0%	0.0%	8.8%	0.0%	0.0%	8.8%
Davis Co. Jail	3.2	1.5	6.7	1.6	0.7	3.6
Weber Co. Corr. Fac.	1.2	0.5	3.1	2.5	1.1	5.5
Virginia						
Alexandria Det. Ctr.	0.0%	0.0%	3.1%	0.6%	0.1%	2.6%
Arlington Co. Det. Fac.	0.0	0.0	2.3	0.8	0.2	3.2
Bristol City Jail	0.0	0.0	3.7	0.8	0.3	2.3
Hampton Corr. Fac.	0.5	0.1	2.0	0.5	0.1	1.8
Henrico Co. Regional Jail West	1.8	0.8	3.9	0.9	0.3	2.8
Mecklenburg Co. Jail	0.0	0.0	5.4	0.0	0.0	5.4
Montgomery Co. Jail	0.0	0.0	6.0	0.0	0.0	6.0
Newport News City Jail	2.0	0.9	4.2	1.5	0.6	3.4
Piedmont Regional Jail	0.0	0.0	2.0	2.3	1.1	4.7
Rappahannock Regional Jail	2.4	1.2	4.8	2.1	1.0	4.2
Richmond City Jail	0.9	0.3	2.8	2.6	1.3	5.2
Riverside Regional Jail	1.8	0.8	4.3	3.1	1.7	5.6
Virginia Beach Municipal Corr. Ctr.	1.0	0.4	2.6	1.4	0.6	3.3
Washington						
Benton Co. Jail	0.1%	0.0%	0.4%	2.3%	0.8%	6.0%
Cowlitz Co. Jail	1.1	0.5	2.8	0.6	0.2	2.0
King Co. Regional Justice Ctr.	0.6	0.1	2.7	0.8	0.2	2.4
Snohomish Co. Jail	1.0	0.3	3.1	0.0	0.0	1.6
Sunnyside City Jail	0.0	0.0	18.4	0.0	0.0	18.4
Whatcom Co. Jail	0.5	0.1	1.8	2.5	1.2	5.1
Yakima City Jail	0.0	0.0	9.0	1.8	0.5	5.9
West Virginia						
Eastern Regional Jail	3.3%	1.4%	7.5%	3.2%	1.6%	6.6%
South Central Regional Jail	1.8	0.6	4.8	4.2	1.8	9.2
Western Regional Jail	2.9	1.6	5.3	1.9	0.9	4.2
Wisconsin						
Brown Co. Jail	1.2%	0.4%	3.9%	2.9%	1.4%	6.1%
Columbia Co. Jail	2.1	0.6	7.5	2.1	0.6	7.5
Milwaukee Co. Corr. Fac. South	1.0	0.3	3.2	3.2	1.6	6.3
Oconto Co. Jail	0.0	0.0	18.4	0.0	0.0	18.4
Rock Co. Jail	0.8	0.2	3.0	2.5	1.2	5.3
Walworth Co. Jail	0.0	0.0	3.7	2.5	1.3	5.0
Washington Co. Jail	0.0	0.0	5.4	4.5	2.4	8.6
Wood Co. Jail	0.0	0.0	12.9	0.0	0.0	12.9
Wyoming						
Lincoln Co. Jail	0.0%	0.0%	25.9%	0.0%	0.0%	25.9%

[a]Includes all inmates who reported unwanted contacts with another inmate or any contacts with staff that involved oral, anal, or vaginal penetration, hand jobs, and other sexual acts occurring in the past 12 months or since admission to the facility, if shorter.

[b]Includes all inmates who reported unwanted contacts with another inmate or any contacts with staff that involved touching of the inmate's buttocks, thigh, penis, breasts, or vagina in a sexual way occurring in the past 12 months or since admission to the facility, if shorter.

[c]Indicates that different samples in the same facility would yield prevalence rates falling between the lower and upper bound estimates 95 out of 100 times.

[d]Weights were applied so that inmates who responded accurately reflected the entire population of each facility on select characteristics, including age, sex, race, sentence length, and time served. (See *Methodology*.)

[e]Female facility.

[f]Facility housed both males and females; only males were sampled at this facility.

[g]Privately operated facility.

Source: Bureau of Justice Statistics, National Inmate Survey, 2011–12.

APPENDIX TABLE 9
Characteristics of special correctional facilities and prevalence of sexual victimization, by facility, National Inmate Survey, 2011–12

Special correctional facilities	Number of inmates in custody[c]	Respondents to sexual victimization survey[d]	Response rate[e]	Inmates reporting sexual victimization[a] Percent[f]	95%-confidence interval[b] Lower bound	95%-confidence interval[b] Upper bound
Immigration and Customs Enforcement facilities						
El Centro SPC (CA)	386	115	47.8%	0.8%	0.2%	3.4%
Jena/LaSalle Det. Fac. (LA)[g]	767	97	39.6	1.1	0.2	5.4
Krome North SPC (FL)	584	60	22.9	3.8	1.2	11.9
Otero Co. Processing Ctr. (NM)	618	140	59.0	1.7	0.6	4.4
Port Isabel Processing Ctr. (TX)	1173	161	39.3	2.3	1.0	5.6
Military facilities						
Midwest Joint Regional Corr. Fac., Fort Leavenworth (KS)	188	82	56.2%	3.9%	1.9%	7.9%
Naval Consolidated Brig, Charleston (SC)	138	94	80.7	4.4	2.6	7.4
Naval Consolidated Brig, Miramar (CA)[h]	312	121	64.1	6.6	3.8	11.2
Northwest Joint Regional Corr. Fac. (WA)	140	85	71.0	6.6	2.9	14.1
United States Disciplinary Barracks, Fort Leavenworth (KS)	464	157	69.5	2.6	1.2	5.6
Indian country jails						
Hualapai Adult Det. Ctr. (AZ)[g]	15	7	60.0%	:	:	:
Laguna Det. Ctr. (NM)[g]	38	26	73.7	0.0%	0.0%	12.9%
Oglala Sioux Tribal Offenders Fac. (SD)[g]	115	56	51.8	10.8	6.2	17.9
San Carlos Dept. of Corr. and Rehabilitation - Adult and Juvenile Det. (AZ)[g]	133	79	83.8	1.6	0.6	4.2
Standing Rock Law Enforcement and Adult Det. Ctr. (ND)[g]	35	7	72.7	:	:	:

: Not calculated.

[a]Includes all types of sexual victimization, including oral, anal, or vaginal penetration, hand jobs, touching of the inmate's butt, thighs, penis, breasts, or vagina in a sexual way, and other sexual acts occurring in the past 12 months or since admission to the facility, if shorter.

[b]Indicates that different samples in the same facility would yield prevalence rates falling between the lower and upper bound estimates 95 out of 100 times.

[c]Number of inmates in custody on day when the facility provided the sample roster.

[d]Number of respondents completing to the sexual victimization survey. (See *Methodology*.)

[e]Response rate is equal to the number of respondents divided by the number of eligible inmates sampled times 100 percent.

[f]Weights were applied so that inmates who responded accurately reflected the entire population of each facility on select characteristics, including age, sex, race, time served, and sentence length. (See *Methodology*.)

[g]Facility housed both males and females; both were sampled at this facility.

[h]Facility housed both males and females; only males were sampled at this facility.

Source: Bureau of Justice Statistics, National Inmate Survey, 2011–12.

APPENDIX TABLE 10
Standard errors for table 2: Prevalence of sexual victimization across inmate surveys, by type of incident, National Inmate Survey, 2007, 2008–09, and 2011–12

Type of incident[c]	Percent of prison inmates NIS-1 2007	Percent of prison inmates NIS-2 2008–09	Percent of prison inmates NIS-3 2011–12	Percent of jail inmates NIS-1 2007	Percent of jail inmates NIS-2 2008–09	Percent of jail inmates NIS-3 2011–12
Total	0.3%	0.3%	0.2%	0.1%	0.1%	0.2%
Inmate-on-inmate	0.1%	0.2%	0.1%	0.1%	0.1%	0.1%
Nonconsensual sexual acts	0.1	0.1	0.1	0.1	0.1	0.1
Abusive sexual contacts only	0.1	0.1	0.1	0.1	0.1	0.1
Staff sexual misconduct	0.2%	0.2%	0.2%	0.1%	0.1%	0.1%
Unwilling activity	0.1	0.2	0.1	0.1	0.1	0.1
Excluding touching	0.1	0.1	0.1	0.1	0.1	0.1
Touching only	0.1	0.1	0.1	--	--	--
Willing activity	0.1%	0.1%	0.1%	0.1%	0.1%	0.1%
Excluding touching	0.1	0.1	0.1	0.1	0.1	0.1
Touching only	--	--	--	--	--	--

--Less than 0.05%.

Source: Bureau of Justice Statistics, National Inmate Survey, 2007, 2008–09, and 2011–12.

Standard errors for table 7: Prevalence of sexual victimization, by type of incident and inmate characteristics, National Inmate Survey, 2011–12

Characteristic	Prison inmates reporting sexual victimization			Jail inmates reporting sexual victimization		
	Number of inmates	Inmate-on-inmate	Staff sexual misconduct	Number of inmates	Inmate-on-inmate	Staff sexual misconduct
Sex						
Male	85,500	0.1%	0.2%	31,500	0.1%	0.1%
Female	8,900	0.7	0.3	6,800	0.3	0.2
Race/Hispanic origin						
White	29,400	0.3%	0.2%	11,700	0.2%	0.1%
Black	38,500	0.1	0.2	16,400	0.1	0.2
Hispanic	30,900	0.2	0.4	13,500	0.3	0.1
Other	3,500	0.4	0.7	1,800	0.3	0.4
Two or more races	8,500	0.5	0.6	2,800	0.4	0.4
Age						
18–19	2,300	0.7%	0.6%	1,900	0.3%	0.4%
20–24	12,100	0.3	0.4	7,300	0.2	0.2
25–34	26,800	0.2	0.3	11,900	0.2	0.2
35–44	27,900	0.2	0.4	7,800	0.2	0.1
45–54	18,900	0.3	0.2	6,500	0.2	0.1
55 or older	9,900	0.2	0.2	2,000	0.4	0.1
Education						
Less than high school	48,900	0.2%	0.2%	17,900	0.2%	0.1%
High school graduate	19,700	0.3	0.4	8,600	0.1	0.2
Some college	15,900	0.3	0.2	7,100	0.2	0.2
College degree or more	6,000	0.4	0.4	3,200	0.4	0.4
Marital status						
Married	16,100	0.2%	0.3%	7,900	0.1%	0.2%
Widowed, divorced, or separated	23,700	0.2	0.2	8,600	0.3	0.2
Never married	47,400	0.2	0.2	19,500	0.2	0.1
Body Mass Index						
Underweight	1,200	1.1%	1.3%	600	0.9%	0.5%
Normal	21,600	0.2	0.2	12,400	0.1	0.1
Overweight	37,500	0.1	0.2	14,300	0.1	0.1
Obese	22,700	0.2	0.2	6,900	0.3	0.2
Morbidly Obese	2,700	0.6	0.9	900	0.6	0.7

--Less than 0.05%.

Source: Bureau of Justice Statistics, National Inmate Survey, 2011–12.

APPENDIX TABLE 12
Standard errors for table 8: Prevalence of sexual victimization, by type of incident and inmate sexual characteristics, National Inmate Survey, 2011–12

Sexual characteristic	Prison inmates reporting sexual victimization			Jail inmates reporting sexual victimization		
	Number of inmates	Inmate-on-inmate	Staff sexual misconduct	Number of inmates	Inmate-on-inmate	Staff sexual misconduct
Sexual orientation						
Heterosexual	78,900	0.1%	0.2%	31,700	0.1%	0.1%
Non-heterosexual	7,400	0.8	0.7	3,300	0.9	0.5
Number of sexual partners						
0–1	17,000	0.2%	0.2%	6,300	0.3%	0.2%
2–4	9,700	0.3	0.3	5,400	0.2	0.2
5–10	15,300	0.2	0.2	5,800	0.2	0.1
11–20	12,500	0.3	0.4	6,000	0.3	0.2
21 or more	29,600	0.2	0.3	12,100	0.2	0.2
Prior sexual victimization						
Yes	12,900	0.7%	0.5%	5,700	0.8%	0.4%
No	75,600	0.1	0.2	30,300	--	0.1

--Less than 0.05%.

Source: Bureau of Justice Statistics, National Inmate Survey, 2011–12.

APPENDIX TABLE 13
Standard errors for table 9: Prevalence of sexual victimization, by type of incident and inmate criminal justice status and history, National Inmate Survey, 2011–12

Criminal justice status and history	Prison inmates reporting sexual victimization			Jail inmates reporting sexual victimization		
	Number of prison inmates	Inmate-on-inmate	Staff sexual misconduct	Number of jail inmates	Inmate-on-inmate	Staff sexual misconduct
Most serious offense						
Violent sexual offense	25,500	0.4%	0.3%	1,900	0.6%	0.4%
Other violent	34,200	0.2	0.2	7,500	0.3	0.3
Property	16,000	0.3	0.3	8,300	0.2	0.2
Drug	22,000	0.1	0.2	7,400	0.1	0.1
Other	11,600	0.4	0.5	10,500	0.1	0.2
Sentence length						
Less than 1 year	6,100	0.4%	0.4%	:	:	:
1–4 years	23,400	0.2	0.1	:	:	:
5–9 years	16,500	0.2	0.3	:	:	:
10–19 years	23,700	0.2	0.2	:	:	:
20 years or more	30,000	0.4	0.4	:	:	:
Life/death	14,300	0.4	0.4	:	:	:
Time in a correctional facility prior to current facility						
Less than 1 month	17,300	0.2%	0.2%	10,500	0.2%	0.1%
1–5 months	9,700	0.3	0.4	6,300	0.2	0.1
6–11 months	6,900	0.2	0.3	3,400	0.2	0.3
1–4 years	22,700	0.2	0.2	7,800	0.1	0.2
5 years or more	30,100	0.2	0.2	8,300	0.3	0.3
Number of times arrested						
1 time	13,800	0.3%	0.2%	4,700	0.4%	0.2%
2–3 times	28,500	0.2	0.2	9,800	0.2	0.2
4–10 times	34,700	0.2	0.2	13,600	0.1	0.1
11 or more times	13,400	0.2	0.3	8,300	0.2	0.2
Time since admission						
Less than 1 month	6,500	0.4%	0.2%	12,300	0.1%	0.1%
1–5 months	22,100	0.2	0.2	16,100	0.1	0.1
6–11 months	21,100	0.2	0.3	5,300	0.5	0.3
1–4 years	35,300	0.2	0.2	4,800	0.3	0.4
5 years or more	24,400	0.5	0.4	200	1.3	1.6

: Not calculated.

Source: Bureau of Justice Statistics, National Inmate Survey, 2011–12.

APPENDIX TABLE 14
Standard errors for table 10: Juvenile inmates reporting sexual victimization, by type of incident, National Inmate Survey, 2011–12

Type of incident	Standard errors		
	All facilities	Prisons	Jails
Total	0.7%	1.2%	0.9%
Inmate-on-inmate	0.5%	0.8%	0.6%
Nonconsensual sexual acts	0.2	0.8	0.1
Abusive sexual contacts only	0.4	0.2	0.5
Staff sexual misconduct	0.6%	1.0%	0.7%
Unwilling activity	0.4	0.3	0.5
Excluding touching	0.4	0.3	0.5
Touching only	0.1	0.0	0.2
Willing activity	0.5	1.0	0.6
Excluding touching	0.5	1.0	0.6
Touching only	0.0	0.0	0.0
Number of inmates	:	:	:

: Not calculated.

Source: Bureau of Justice Statistics, National Inmate Survey, 2011–12.

APPENDIX TABLE 15
Standard errors for table 11: Prevalence of sexual victimization, by type of incident and age of inmate, National Inmate Survey, 2011–12

Age	Prison inmates			Jail inmates		
	Number	Inmate-on-inmate	Staff sexual misconduct	Number	Inmate-on-inmate	Staff sexual misconduct
16–17	360	0.8%	1.0%	950	0.6%	0.7%
18–19	2,280	0.7	0.6	6,080	0.3	0.4
20–24	12,070	0.3	0.4	22,240	0.2	0.2
25–34	26,820	0.2	0.3	38,050	0.2	0.2
35–44	27,890	0.2	0.4	23,090	0.2	0.1
45–54	18,890	0.3	0.2	16,170	0.2	0.1
55 or older	9,910	0.2	0.2	4,750	0.4	0.1

Source: Bureau of Justice Statistics, National Inmate Survey, 2011–12.

APPENDIX TABLE 16
Standard errors for table 12: Prevalence of sexual victimization among juveniles ages 16–17 and inmates ages 18–19 and 20–24, by type of incident and inmate characteristics, National Inmate Survey, 2011–12

| | Prison and jail inmates reporting sexual victimization | | | | | | | | |
| Characteristic | Number of inmates | | | Inmate-on-inmate | | | Staff sexual misconduct | | |
	Ages 16–17	18–19	20–24	Ages 16–17	18–19	20–24	Ages 16–17	18–19	20–24
All inmates	790	5,020	25,500	0.5%	0.3%	0.2%	0.6%	0.3%	0.2%
Sex									
Male	740	4,750	23,760	0.5%	0.3%	0.2%	0.6%	0.3%	0.3%
Female	110	510	2,790	1.7	1.5	0.8	0.6	0.5	0.4
Race/Hispanic origin									
White	150	1,210	6,410	3.2%	1.1%	0.4%	1.8%	0.7%	0.3%
Black	450	2,410	10,650	0.5	0.3	0.2	0.8	0.5	0.3
Hispanic	350	1,560	8,030	0.4	0.5	0.3	1.5	0.6	0.7
Other	20	230	1,120	0.0	1.5	0.5	0.0	1.3	1.9
Two or more races	110	610	2,650	0.8	0.8	0.9	0.8	1.1	0.8
Body Mass Index									
Underweight	80	190	470	5.7%	1.7%	1.1%	5.7%	1.0%	1.9%
Normal	470	3,070	11,840	0.3	0.4	0.2	0.7	0.5	0.2
Overweight	180	1,570	9,500	1.0	0.5	0.3	0.7	0.6	0.5
Obese	100	480	3,360	3.8	0.9	0.6	2.8	0.5	0.7
Morbidly obese	30	80	480	0.0	3.4	1.8	0.0	4.3	1.9
Sexual orientation									
Heterosexual	740	4,680	23,100	0.5%	0.2%	0.1%	0.6%	0.3%	0.2%
Non-heterosexual	50	410	2,300	3.1	4.1	1.4	0.8	1.5	2.0
Most serious offense									
Violent sexual	30	320	2,480	4.3%	5.0%	1.4%	4.7%	1.5%	0.6%
Other violent	360	1,790	8,710	0.5	0.4	0.3	1.2	0.7	0.5
Property	280	1,870	6,100	0.5	0.4	0.4	0.6	0.6	0.3
Drug	110	770	4,830	4.2	0.6	0.3	2.9	0.6	0.3
Other	120	820	4,410	2.2	0.7	0.2	1.0	0.5	0.4

Source: Bureau of Justice Statistics, National Inmate Survey, 2011–12.

APPENDIX TABLE 17
Standard errors for table 13: Circumstances surrounding incidents among juveniles ages 16–17 and inmates ages 18–19 and 20–24, by type of victimization, National Inmate Survey, 2011–12

| | Victims in prisons and jails | | | | | |
| Circumstance | Inmate-on-inmate | | | Staff sexual misconduct | | |
	Ages 16–17	18–19	20–24	Ages 16–17	18–19	20–24
Number of victims	40	190	710	50	220	1,110
Number of incidents						
1	17.6%	9.4%	5.4%	8.0%	4.4%	5.4%
2 or more	17.6	9.4	5.4	8.0	4.4	5.4
Type of coercion or force						
Without pressure or force	~	~	~	7.7%	5.9%	3.9%
Pressured	11.7%	7.8%	3.0%	9.8	6.4	4.9
Force/threat of force	9.4	9.1	3.7	9.9	5.5	4.0
Ever injured	12.8%	7.4%	2.2%	4.2%	3.8%	3.5%
Ever report an incident	6.8%	6.9%	2.5%	3.4%	3.6%	3.5%

~Not applicable.

Source: Bureau of Justice Statistics, National Inmate Survey, 2011–12.

APPENDIX TABLE 18

Standard errors for table 14: Prevalence of victimization by current mental health status and history of mental health problems among inmates, by type of facility, National Inmate Survey, 2011–12

	Adult prison inmates				Adult jail inmates			
	Number	Percent	Inmate-on-inmate	Staff sexual misconduct	Number	Percent	Inmate-on-inmate	Staff sexual misconduct
Current mental health status								
No mental illness	57,200	0.8%	0.1%	0.1%	17,000	0.6%	0.1%	0.1%
Anxiety-mood disorder	13,600	0.4	0.3	0.4	7,700	0.3	0.2	0.1
Serious psychological distress	12,400	0.5	0.6	0.4	10,400	0.5	0.3	0.2
History of mental health problems								
Ever told by mental health professional had disorder								
Yes	27,600	1.2%	0.3%	0.2%	16,300	0.8%	0.3%	0.2%
No	57,900	1.2	0.1	0.1	19,100	0.8	0.1	0.1
Had overnight stay in hospital in year before current admission								
Yes	8,000	0.4%	0.6%	0.6%	5,900	0.4%	0.5%	0.3%
No	74,100	0.4	0.1	0.1	28,700	0.4	0.1	0.1
Used prescription medications at time of current offense								
Yes	11,600	0.8%	0.4%	0.3%	8,600	0.6%	0.3%	0.2%
No	72,900	0.8	0.1	0.1	26,200	0.6	0.1	0.1
Ever received professional mental health therapy								
Yes	27,600	1.0%	0.3%	0.3%	14,100	0.6%	0.3%	0.2%
No	55,900	1.0	0.1	0.1	20,800	0.6	0.1	0.1

Source: Bureau of Justice Statistics, National Inmate Survey, 2011–12.

APPENDIX TABLE 19

Standard errors for table 15: Prevalence of serious psychological distress among adults in prisons, jails, and the U.S. civilian noninstitutional population, 2011–12

	Percent with serious psychological distress		
	U.S. noninstitutional adult population	Inmates age 18 or older	
Demographic characteristic		Prison	Jail
Total	0.2%	0.5%	0.5%
Sex			
Male	0.2%	0.5%	0.5%
Female	0.2	1.1	0.9
Race/Hispanic origin			
White	0.2%	0.6%	0.7%
Black	0.3	0.6	0.8
Hispanic	0.4	0.8	0.8
Age			
18–44	0.2%	0.6%	0.5%
45–64	0.3	0.8	0.8
65 or older	0.3	1.4	3.5

Source: Bureau of Justice Statistics, National Inmate Survey, 2011–12; and Centers for Disease Control and Prevention, National Health Interview Survey, 2012.

APPENDIX TABLE 20
Standard errors for table 16: Prevalence of inmate-on-inmate victimization, by current mental health status and inmate characteristics, National Inmate Survey, 2011–12

Characteristic	Prison inmates reporting sexual victimization			Jail inmates reporting sexual victimization		
	No mental illness	Anxiety-mood disorder	Serious psychological distress	No mental illness	Anxiety-mood disorder	Serious psychological distress
Sex						
Male	0.1%	0.3%	0.6%	0.1%	0.2%	0.4%
Female	0.4	1.1	1.3	0.4	0.4	0.7
Race/Hispanic origin						
White	0.2%	0.6%	0.8%	0.2%	0.3%	0.4%
Black	0.1	0.3	0.9	0.1	0.2	0.4
Hispanic	0.1	0.5	1.1	0.2	0.3	0.7
Age						
18–24	0.1%	0.8%	1.1%	0.1%	0.4%	0.4%
25–34	0.1	0.5	0.7	0.2	0.2	0.4
35–44	0.1	0.4	1.0	0.1	0.2	0.7
45 or older	0.2	0.5	0.9	0.2	0.3	0.8
Sexual orientation						
Heterosexual	--	0.2%	0.4%	0.1%	0.1%	0.2%
Non-heterosexual	0.8%	1.5	2.2	0.8	0.8	2.0
Most serious offense						
Violent sexual offense	0.3%	0.7%	1.4%	0.6%	1.5%	1.2%
Other violent	0.2	0.4	0.9	0.4	0.5	0.5
Property	0.1	0.6	1.1	0.1	0.3	0.6
Drug	0.1	0.4	0.7	0.1	0.2	0.4
Other	0.2	0.5	0.9	0.1	0.2	0.4

--Less than 0.05%.

Source: Bureau of Justice Statistics, National Inmate Survey, 2011–12.

APPENDIX TABLE 21
Standard errors for table 17: Prevalence of staff sexual misconduct, by current mental health status and inmate characteristics, National Inmate Survey, 2011–12

Characteristic	Prison inmates reporting sexual victimization			Jail inmates reporting sexual victimization		
	No mental illness	Anxiety-mood disorder	Serious psychological distress	No mental illness	Anxiety-mood disorder	Serious psychological distress
Sex						
Male	0.1%	0.5%	0.5%	0.1%	0.1%	0.3%
Female	0.2	0.4	0.7	0.2	0.3	0.3
Race/Hispanic origin						
White	0.1%	0.3%	0.6%	0.1%	0.1%	0.3%
Black	0.2	1.2	0.8	0.1	0.3	0.5
Hispanic	0.2	0.4	1.5	0.1	0.2	0.5
Age						
18–24	0.3%	0.7%	1.5%	0.1%	0.3%	0.5%
25–34	0.2	0.5	0.8	0.2	0.2	0.4
35–44	0.2	1.1	0.8	0.1	0.2	0.4
45 or older	0.1	0.4	0.7	0.1	0.3	0.3
Sexual orientation						
Heterosexual	0.1%	0.5%	0.4%	0.1%	0.1%	0.2%
Non-heterosexual	0.6	0.9	2.0	0.7	0.6	0.8
Most serious offense						
Violent sexual offense	0.3%	0.7%	0.8%	0.5%	0.4%	1.1%
Other violent	0.2	0.6	0.9	0.3	0.4	0.6
Property	0.2	0.6	1.2	0.1	0.3	0.4
Drug	0.1	1.3	0.6	0.1	0.2	0.4
Other	0.3	0.5	1.2	0.2	0.2	0.5

Source: Bureau of Justice Statistics, National Inmate Survey, 2011–12.

APPENDIX TABLE 22
Standard errors for table 18: Circumstances surrounding incidents among adult inmates, by current mental health status and type of victimization, National Inmate Survey, 2011–12

| | Victims in prisons and jails | | | | | |
| | Inmate-on-inmate | | | Staff sexual misconduct | | |
Circumstance	No mental illness	Anxiety-mood disorder	Serious psychological distress	No mental illness	Anxiety-mood disorder	Serious psychological distress
Number of victims	860	790	1,450	1,250	1,260	1,200
Number of incidents						
1	4.5%	6.0%	2.5%	2.6%	2.7%	2.3%
2 or more	4.5	6.0	2.5	2.6	2.7	2.3
Type of coercion or force						
Without pressure or force	~	~	~	3.2%	3.5%	2.9%
Pressured	3.4%	2.5%	2.5%	3.0	4.4	2.7
Force/threat of force	3.4	3.5	2.2	2.7	4.7	2.9
Ever injured	2.0%	2.3%	2.2%	1.4%	1.6%	2.4%
Ever report an incident	3.0%	2.4%	2.3%	2.2%	2.8%	2.6%

~Not applicable.

Source: Bureau of Justice Statistics, National Inmate Survey, 2011–12.

APPENDIX TABLE 23
Standard errors for table 19: Prevalence of sexual victimization, by type of incident and inmate sexual orientation, National Inmate Survey, 2011–12

| | Inmate-on-inmate | | Staff sexual misconduct | |
Characteristic	Heterosexual	Non-heterosexual	Heterosexual	Non-heterosexual
Sex				
Male	0.1%	0.9%	0.2%	0.7%
Female	0.3	0.7	0.2	0.4
Race/Hispanic origin				
White	0.1%	1.1%	0.1%	0.5%
Black	0.1	1.2	0.2	0.9
Hispanic	0.1	1.2	0.3	1.6
Age				
18–24	0.1%	1.5%	0.2%	1.8%
25–44	0.1	0.8	0.2	0.5
45 or older	0.1	1.1	0.1	0.7
Education				
Less than high school	0.1%	0.9%	0.2%	0.5%
High school graduate	0.2	1.4	0.3	1.5
Some college or more	0.1	1.0	0.2	0.6
Mental health problems				
None	--	0.6%	0.1%	0.5%
Anxiety-mood disorder	0.1%	1.1	0.3	0.6
Serious psychological distress	0.2	1.5	0.2	1.3

--Less than 0.05%.

Source: Bureau of Justice Statistics, National Inmate Survey, 2011–12.

APPENDIX TABLE 24
Standard errors for table 20: Circumstances surrounding incidents of sexual victimization among heterosexual and non-heterosexual inmates, National Inmate Survey, 2011–12

| | Victims in prisons and jails | | | |
| | Inmate-on-inmate | | Staff sexual misconduct | |
Circumstance	Heterosexual	Non-heterosexual	Heterosexual	Non-heterosexual
Number of victims	1,530	1,490	3,680	1,000
Number of incidents				
1	3.5%	3.2%	1.8%	2.5%
2 or more	3.5	3.2	1.8	2.5
Type of coercion or force				
Without pressure or force	~	~	1.9%	5.0%
Pressured	2.4%	1.9%	1.7	6.7
Force or threat of force	2.5	2.3	1.9	5.0
Ever injured	2.0%	2.2%	1.4%	3.3%
Ever report an incident	2.2%	2.2%	1.7%	4.3%

~Not applicable.

Source: Bureau of Justice Statistics, National Inmate Survey, 2011–12.

www.ingramcontent.com/pod-product-compliance
Lightning Source LLC
Chambersburg PA
CBHW080309290526
45790CB00005B/1978